Lecture Notes in Artificial Intelligence 10315

Subseries of Lecture Notes in Computer Science

LNAI Series Editors

Randy Goebel
University of Alberta, Edmonton, Canada
Yuzuru Tanaka
Hokkaido University, Sapporo, Japan
Wolfgang Wahlster
DFKI and Saarland University, Saarbrücken, Germany

LNAI Founding Series Editor

Joerg Siekmann
DFKI and Saarland University, Saarbrücken, Germany

More information about this series at http://www.springer.com/series/1244

Stephen Cranefield · Samhar Mahmoud
Julian Padget · Ana Paula Rocha (Eds.)

Coordination, Organizations, Institutions, and Norms in Agent Systems XII

COIN 2016 International Workshops
COIN@AAMAS, Singapore, Singapore, May 9, 2016
COIN@ECAI, The Hague, The Netherlands, August 30, 2016
Revised Selected Papers

 Springer

Editors
Stephen Cranefield 🆔
University of Otago
Dunedin
New Zealand

Julian Padget 🆔
University of Bath
Bath
UK

Samhar Mahmoud 🆔
King's College London
London
UK

Ana Paula Rocha 🆔
Universidade do Porto
Porto
Portugal

ISSN 0302-9743   ISSN 1611-3349   (electronic)
Lecture Notes in Artificial Intelligence
ISBN 978-3-319-66594-8   ISBN 978-3-319-66595-5   (eBook)
DOI 10.1007/978-3-319-66595-5

Library of Congress Control Number: 2017952380

LNCS Sublibrary: SL7 – Artificial Intelligence

Printed on acid-free paper

This Springer imprint is published by Springer Nature
The registered company is Springer International Publishing AG
The registered company address is: Gewerbestrasse 11, 6330 Cham, Switzerland

Preface

This volume contains the papers presented at the two 2016 editions of the Coordination, Organization, Institutions and Norms in Agent Systems workshop series. These are the revised, selected papers from COIN@AAMAS, held in Singapore in May 2016 and COIN@ECAI, held in The Hague, The Netherlands in August 2016.

From these workshops, nine papers were invited to be considered for the annual post-proceedings volume, of which this is the 12th edition. Each submission went through two rounds of reviews: the first for the workshop presentation and the second for the post-proceedings, with continuity of reviewers between workshop and proceedings to ensure that first-round revisions were appropriately implemented. Subsequently, all nine papers were accepted.

Three themes emerged from the papers this year, namely social issues, teams, and rights and values, which are the headings under which we introduce the contributions.

Social Issues

The four papers in this section focus on the security of personal data, support for self-care for individuals with chronic conditions, analysis of the risk of information leakage in social networks, and an analysis of issues arising in the design of on-line environments whose participants are human and software:

1. Towards a Distributed Data-Sharing Economy (Cauvin et al.) addresses the problem of how users can describe fine-grained data access policies in a distributed environment, with the help of a reference architecture and demonstration of how that protects against several standard attacks.
2. Modelling Patient-Centric Healthcare Using Socially Intelligent Systems: The AVICENA Experience (Gómez-Sebastià et al.) outlines how intelligent support systems can be conceived to assist individuals with cognitive impairments in following their daily medication regimes, by taking account not only of regulation but also the social circumstances of the human actors.
3. 'How Did They Know?' – Model-Checking for Analysis of Information Leakage in Social Networks (Dennis et al.) uses formal models of digital crowds to establish probabilistic models of the propagation of information across intersecting social networks, and hence the risk of such information reaching unintended recipients.
4. A Manifesto for Conscientious Design of Hybrid Online Social Systems (Noriega et al.) considers a broad range of issues that might impact upon the design and construction of effective systems for collective action, where the actors are a blend of humans and software, by emphasizing the need to underpin designs with the ethical and social values of the participants.

Teams

The two papers in this section consider different aspects of team work: which kinds of knowledge sharing best contribute to effective team performance and how to organize a team to function effectively in different kinds of scenarios.

1. Communication and Shared Mental Models for Teams Performing Interdependent Tasks (Singh et al.)[1] examines the effect of communicating intentions and beliefs on team performance, establishing that the former matter more the higher the level of interdependence, and the latter for the converse.
2. An Empirical Approach for Relating Environmental Patterns with Agent Team Compositions (Franco et al.) presents an experimental evaluation of team organizational structures in the context of an Agents on Mars scenario, showing how taking account of domain-specific and topological features leads to team performance improvements.

Rights and Values

The three papers in this section examine complementary issues that influence the effective design of normative systems, namely, how to detect opportunism so that it may be discouraged, how the values of individuals influence (collective) decision-making processes, and how rights and powers relate to value and conflict resolution in nested organizational structures.

1. Monitoring Opportunism in Multi-Agent Systems (Luo et al.) takes the view that opportunism is undesirable and should be punished through enforcement, leading to the problem of how to determine whether an action is opportunistic, and a logical framework that allows the specification of approaches to monitoring actions for this kind of violation.
2. The Role of Values (Pigmans et al.) suggests that improved understanding of stakeholder values, and through the conceptual model advanced here, of their relationship to norms and consequent actions, can offer benefits to the decision-making process.
3. On the Minimal Recognition of Rights in Holonic Institutions (Pitt et al.) begins an exploration of the problems arising from the embedding of one organization in another, using the principles from Ostrom's framework for common-pool resource institutions. The authors put forward an axiomatic specification of nested organizations as a basis for the computational investigation of rights and powers in such hierarchical structures.

---

[1] This paper has appeared previously in the volume of best workshop papers from AAMAS 2016 as: Singh R., Sonenberg L., Miller T. (2016) Communication and Shared Mental Models for Teams Performing Interdependent Tasks. In: Osman N., Sierra C. (eds) AAMAS 2016 Workshops. LNCS (LNAI), vol. 10002, pp. 163–179. Springer International Publishing AG (2016). doi 10.1007/978-3-319-46882-2_10

In conclusion, we gratefully acknowledge the Programme Committees for the workshops, who are listed after this preface, and likewise the COIN Steering Committee.

July 2017

Stephen Cranefield
Samhar Mahmoud
Julian Padget
Ana Paula Rocha

Organization

COIN@AAMAS 2016 Co-chairs

Stephen Cranefield   University of Otago, New Zealand
Samhar Mahmoud   King's College London, UK

COIN@AAMAS 2016 Programme Committee

Mohsen Afsharchi   University of Zanjan, Iran
Huib Aldewereld   Delft University of Technology, The Netherlands
Estefania Argente   Universidad Politécnica de Valencia, Spain
Alexander Artikis   National Centre for Scientific Research, Greece
Tina Balke   University of Surrey, UK
Guido Boella   University of Turin, Italy
Patrice Caire   University of Luxembourg, Luxembourg
Cristiano Castelfranchi   Institute of Cognitive Sciences and Technologies, Italy
Rob Christiaanse   Delft University of Technology, The Netherlands
Luciano Coutinho   Universidade Federal do Maranhao, Brazil
Natalia Criado   Liverpool John Moores University, UK
Mehdi Dastani   Utrecht University, The Netherlands
Geeth de Mel   IBM Research, UK
Frank Dignum   Utrecht University, The Netherlands
Virginia Dignum   Delft University of Technology, The Netherlands
Nicoletta Fornara   Università della Svizzera Italiana, Lugano, Switzerland
Amineh Ghorbani   Delft University of Technology, The Netherlands
Aditya Ghose   University of Wollongong, Australia
Chris Haynes   King's College London, UK
Özgür Kafalı   Royal Holloway, University of London, UK
Anup Kalia   North Carolina State University, USA
Martin Kollingbaum   University of Aberdeen, UK
Christian Lemaitre   Universidad Autónoma Metropolitana, Mexico
Henrique Lopes Cardoso   University of Porto, Portugal
Maite López Sánchez   University of Barcelona, Spain
Emiliano Lorini   IRIT-CNRS, France
Eric Matson   Purdue University, USA
Felipe Meneguzzi   Pontifical Catholic University of Rio Grande do Sul, Brazil
John-Jules Meyer   Utrecht University, The Netherlands
Daniel Moldt   University of Hamburg, Germany
Pablo Noriega   IIIA-CSIC, Spain
Andrea Omicini   Università di Bologna, Italy
Nir Oren   University of Aberdeen, UK

Sascha Ossowski	University Rey Juan Carlos, Spain
Julian Padget	University of Bath, UK
Simon Parsons	King's College London, UK
Alessandro Ricci	University of Bologna, Italy
Juan-Antonio Rodríguez-Aguilar	IIIA-CSIC, Spain
Bastin Tony Roy Savarimuthu	University of Otago, New Zealand
Murat Şensoy	Özyeğin University, Turkey
Christophe Sibertin-Blanc	University of Toulouse, France
Jaime Sichman	Universidade de Sao Paulo, Brazil
Viviane Silva	IBM Research, Brazil
Liz Sonenberg	University of Melbourne, Australia
Luca Tummolini	ISTC-CNR, Italy
Leendert van der Torre	University of Luxembourg, Luxembourg
Wamberto Vasconcelos	University of Aberdeen, UK
Harko Verhagen	Stockholm University, Sweden
George Vouros	University of Piraeus, Greece

COIN@ECAI 2016 Co-chairs

Julian Padget	University of Bath, UK
Ana Paula Rocha	University of Porto, Portugal

COIN@ECAI 2016 Programme Committee

Mohsen Afsharchi	University of Zanjan, Iran
Huib Aldewereld	Delft University of Technology, The Netherlands
Estefania Argente	Universidad Politécnica de Valencia, Spain
Alexander Artikis	National Centre for Scientific Research, Greece
Tina Balke	University of Surrey, UK
Patrice Caire	University of Luxembourg, Luxembourg
Javier Carbó	Charles III Univerity of Madrid, Spain
Cristiano Castelfranchi	Institute of Cognitive Sciences and Technologies, Italy
Daniel Castro Silva	University of Porto, Portugal
Rob Christiaanse	Delft University of Technology, The Netherlands
Luciano Coutinho	Universidade Federal do Maranhao, Brazil
Natalia Criado	Liverpool John Moores University, UK
Mehdi Dastani	Utrecht University, The Netherlands
Frank Dignum	Utrecht University, The Netherlands
Nicoletta Fornara	Università della Svizzera Italiana, Lugano, Switzerland
Amineh Ghorbani	Delft University of Technology, The Netherlands
Aditya Ghose	University of Wollongong, Australia
Chris Haynes	King's College London, UK
Jie Jiang	University of Surrey, UK
Anup Kalia	North Carolina State University, USA

JeeHang Lee	University of Bath, UK
Tingting Li	Imperial College, UK
Henrique Lopes Cardoso	University of Porto, Portugal
Maite López Sánchez	University of Barcelona, Spain
Emiliano Lorini	IRIT-CNRS, France
Samhar Mahmoud	King's College London, UK
Eric Matson	Purdue University, USA
Felipe Meneguzzi	Pontifical Catholic University of Rio Grande do Sul, Brazil
John-Jules Meyer	Utrecht University, The Netherlands
Daniel Moldt	University of Hamburg, Germany
Pablo Noriega	Artificial Intelligence Research Institute, Spain
Andrea Omicini	Universita di Bologna, Italy
Nir Oren	University of Aberdeen, UK
Sascha Ossowski	University Rey Juan Carlos, Spain
Alessandro Ricci	University of Bologna, Italy
Juan-Antonio Rodríguez-Aguilar	IIIA-CSIC, Spain
Bastin Tony Roy Savarimuthu	University of Otago, New Zealand
Murat Şensoy	Özyeğin University, Turkey
Christophe Sibertin-Blanc	University of Toulouse, France
Viviane Silva	IBM Research, Brazil
Liz Sonenberg	University of Melbourne, Australia
Luca Tummolini	ISTC-CNR, Italy
Leendert van der Torre	University of Luxembourg, Luxembourg
Wamberto Vasconcelos	University of Aberdeen, UK
Harko Verhagen	Stockholm University, Sweden
George Vouros	University of Piraeus, Greece

COIN Steering Committee

Huib Aldewereld	Hogeschool Utrecht, The Netherlands
Tina Balke-Visser	University of Surrey, UK
Olivier Boissier	Ecole Nationale Supérieure des Mines de Saint-Etienne, France
Stephen Cranefield	University of Otago, New Zealand
Marina De Vos	University of Bath, UK
Frank Dignum	Utrecht University, The Netherlands
Virginia Dignum	Delft University of Technology, The Netherlands
Nicoletta Fornara	Università della Svizzera Italiana, Lugano, Switzerland
Eric Matson	Purdue University, USA
Pablo Noriega	IIIA-CSIC, Spain
Julian Padget	University of Bath, UK
Jaime Sichman	Universidade de São Paulo, Brazil
Viviane Silva	IBM Research, Brazil

Contents

Social Issues

Towards a Distributed Data-Sharing Economy

Samuel R. Cauvin(✉), Martin J. Kollingbaum, Derek Sleeman,
and Wamberto W. Vasconcelos

Department of Computing Science, University of Aberdeen, Aberdeen, UK
{r01src15,m.j.kollingbaum,d.sleeman,w.w.vasconcelos}@abdn.ac.uk

Abstract. We propose that access to data and knowledge be controlled through fine-grained, user-specified explicitly represented policies. Fine-grained policies allow stakeholders to have a more precise level of control over who, when, and how their data is accessed. We propose a representation for policies and a mechanism to control data access within a fully distributed system, creating a secure environment for data sharing. Our proposal provides guarantees against standard attacks, and ensures data security across the network. We present and justify the goals, requirements, and a reference architecture for our proposal. We illustrate through an intuitive example how our proposal supports a typical data-sharing transaction. We also perform an analysis of the various potential attacks against this system, and how they are countered. Additionally, we provide details of a proof-of-concept prototype which we used to refine our mechanism.

Keywords: Peer-to-peer · Data sharing · Data access policies

1 Introduction

Large scale data sharing is important, especially now, with more open societies of components such as Smart Cities [4,37] and the Internet of Things [2,18] creating data sharing ecosystems. Currently, data access policies tend to be managed centrally, which comes with a number of problems such as information ownership and reliance on a centralised authority.

In [23] the author suggests taking a "data-oriented view" and developing methods for treating access policies and data items as a single unit. This allows data to prescribe their own policies, which can be checked when the data is shipped around between data management systems. Such a proposal of tying policies directly to data is described by, e.g., [35] as *policy-carrying data* that allows the specification of fine-grained policies for data items. In this paper, we present novel policy-based data sharing concepts for distributed peer-to-peer networks of data providers and consumers. Our working hypothesis is that it is possible to (a) create a fully distributed mechanism to facilitate data sharing with security guarantees, and (b) to implement a fine-grained control over how data may be exchanged between stakeholders.

© Springer International Publishing AG 2017
S. Cranefield et al. (Eds.): COIN 2016 Workshops, LNAI 10315, pp. 3–21, 2017.
DOI: 10.1007/978-3-319-66595-5_1

We propose access to data and knowledge to be controlled through fine-grained, user-specified explicitly represented policies. These policies regulate data exchange in a peer-to-peer environment in which some peers have data which they want to provide (called Providers) and some peers have data which they want to acquire (called Requestors). Providers set policies that establish how their data can be accessed and by whom. These policies can be defined with different levels of granularity, allowing peers precise control over their data.

Our policies may express general regulatory statements such as, for example, "no drug records and medical records can be obtained by the same party", or more specific, such as "I will only provide 10 records to each person". Fine-grained policies allow stakeholders to have a more precise level of control over who, when, and how their data is accessed. We propose a representation for policies and a mechanism to control data access within a fully distributed system, creating a secure environment for data sharing. We discuss data as if it were stored in a database, but this could be expanded to cover any form of structured information.

These policies will be enforced by a distributed infrastructure of "policy decision points" (taking inspiration from the traditionally centralized XACML PDP architecture [10]) throughout the network. We regard a data exchange or sharing activity between peers (provider and requestor) as a transaction. Transactions are recorded and are an important means for checking policy compliance. During a data request, transaction records are taken into account to test whether a requestor complies with the policies specific to such a request and the data involved. Due to the distributed nature of making policy decisions at peer-to-peer network nodes, a requirement for encrypting information components to be exchanged for this decision process arises. We take inspirations from encryption concepts in distributed applications, such as CryptDB [28], BlockChain [17, 29] and Bitcoin [26].

We provide a simple case example demonstrating the feasibility of this mechanism, including reasoning on encrypted data using the mechanism. Ours is a starting point from where more sophisticated policy representations and reasoning mechanisms can be developed. The work presented here is an initial investigation into this kind of reasoning process which can be made more sophisticated, to address arbitrary reasoning and more complex interactions.

This paper touches upon each of the following areas of research: *Coordination, Organisation, Institutions, and Norms.* We use a peer-to-peer mechanism as a simple form of coordination, which can in the future become more sophisticated [1, 3, 20]. Our policies make use of roles which are normally embedded in organisations [8, 21, 30]. We capture institutions not just in the enforcement of our policies but also through their policing, including sanctioning and rewarding behaviours [13, 14]. Norms and policies are similar concepts, and most components of our policies appear in norms [32, 33, 36].

Section 2 details a general example of a simple transaction between two parties and then discusses the key components and concepts within our solution. Section 3 provides an overview of the requirements and architecture of the system. Section 4 describes the detail of a transaction scenario, discussing how each part of the mechanism is involved in the process. Section 5 evaluates the mechanism's resistance to standard attacks. Section 6 discusses a proof-of-concept implementation of our solution. Section 7 provides an overview of related research. Section 8 discusses the limitations of our solution, provides overall conclusions, and outlines future work.

2 Policy Compliance

In our approach, so-called "transaction records" play an important role in whether any action related to sharing data is compliant with the policies relevant for this data. To illustrate how our mechanism performs a simple transaction, we consider a general case where two parties, a "requestor" and a "provider", want to exchange data. Such a transaction represents a secure, tamperproof interaction between requestor and provider. Following this example we discuss transaction records (Sect. 2.1), numerical encoding of data elements (Sect. 2.2), and policies (Sect. 2.3) in more detail.

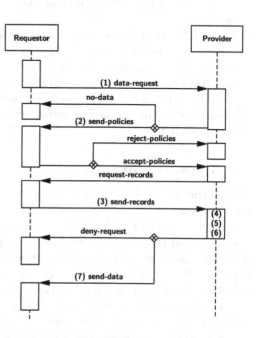

Fig. 1. AUML for a transaction

Let R be the requestor, P be the provider, and D be the data element. The transaction will proceed as follows, where each number corresponds to the numbers in Fig. 1:

1. Requestor R sends a data request for data D to provider P.
2. P processes this request, and if the provider possesses D, it will create a list of policies relevant to D or R. If any policy in this list prohibits sending D to R (regardless of transaction records), then the data request will be denied, a transaction record will be generated and sent to R, and the process will terminate here. If not, P will send a message to R containing the policies associated with D.
3. R will reason on these policies to determine which transaction records are "relevant" (see Sect. 2.4). To achieve this, the mechanism checks each policy and extracts a list of unique data elements referred to in the policy. At the end of this the list will contain each "relevant" data element (encoded as a number as discussed in Sect. 2.2).

4. The mechanism will then identify which of R's transaction records are relevant using Algorithm 1 (in Sect. 2.4).
5. P receives records from R and determines if any of the records prohibit the provision of D. For each of P's policies the mechanism processes all records to determine if the data element is subsumed by a data element of P, and thus if the conditions of P hold. While processing, a cumulative total for each type of record will be kept. This total can be calculated without decrypting, as it requires only basic arithmetic on numerical entries. After processing all records, this total will be checked against the policy to determine if it holds or not.
6. If this policy establishes a permission, then sending D (the requested data and a record of the transaction, encrypted in a single package) to R is approved, and D will be sent from P to R.
7. R will decrypt the package, adding the transaction record to its records, and store the data. This single encrypted package is received by the mechanism, ensuring that the transaction record will be stored as ignoring it will prevent receipt of data.

2.1 Transaction Records

Our policies relate data collections and events following the usual semantic of norms/policies (e.g., [27,30]), whereby events and their authors are explicitly represented (together with additional information such as time, location, duration, etc.) and used to check for (non-) compliance. In our proposal, events are named transaction records, and are stored encrypted within the information kept by each peer. Whenever a policy needs to be checked for its applicability, a subset of transaction records is retrieved from the encrypted storage, and used to compare the credentials/identification of the peer, assess the applicability to data elements currently available and verify if the conditions of our policies hold.

Transaction records are tuples of the form $\langle dataset, m \rangle$. The *dataset* component refers to an ontological term, which is defined in one of the ontologies held by peers. Policies and transaction records refer to descriptions of data elements – these are labels describing, for instance, fields of a database or names of predicates of an ontology [5]. We adopt a numeric representation for these labels, and rather than using, for instance, *nameOfClient* or *fatherOf* (to represent, respectively a field of a database or a predicate), we use a numeric encoding as explained below in Sect. 2.2.

2.2 Numerical Encoding of Data Elements

Policy checking is performed on encrypted transaction records without decrypting them, and performing operations on encrypted numerical data is far easier than on encrypted string data. To enable this, we introduce a numbering scheme that represents such a hierarchy of concepts and sub-concepts, including the encoding of concept properties. For this, we assign to each level in the subsumption hierarchy found in an ontology a code out of the range of $[0 \ldots 99]$: when we use the notation $[00\dots 99]_1$, $[00\dots 99]_2$, $[00\dots 99]_3$, then we are expressing that a concept hierarchy has three levels (where the subscripts indicate levels), and each concept can relate to a maximum of 100 (0 to 99) sub-concepts. By concatenating the level codes from a top-level concept to a particular sub-concept, we arrive at a unique code for each concept in a hierarchy. Consider the taxonomy in Fig. 2 (with the encoded number at the start of each line).

010000 Prescriptions
  010100 Name
  010200 Drugs
  010300 Patient Notes
    010301 Other Medications
    010302 Other Conditions
  010400 Renewal Date

020000 DrugX
  020100 Trial Number
  020200 Patient Notes
    020201 Other Medications
    020202 Other Conditions
  020300 Recorded Side-effects
  020400 Treatment Effectiveness

030000 Vehicles
  030100 Motorcycles
    030101 Owner
    030102 Brand
    030103 Horsepower
  030200 Cars
    030201 Owner
    030202 Brand
    030203 Horsepower

Fig. 2. Example taxonomy

In that taxonomy Vehicles is the third top level concept represented by $[03]_1[00]_2[00]_3$. A concept below that, Motorcycles, is $[03]_1[01]_2[00]_3$ which indicates it is the first sub-concept of Vehicles. The size of each level and total number of levels can be increased, but this will also increase the size of each encoded number. The subsumption relation between two encoded numbers allows us to capture "is-a" relationships among concepts of a taxonomy, as in $030100 \sqsubseteq 030000$, this is defined in Definition 1.

Definition 1 (Taxonomy). *A taxonomy $\mathbf{T} \subset \mathbb{N}$ is a subset of natural numbers. We define a reflexive and transitive subsumption relation $\sqsubseteq\; \subseteq \mathbf{T} \times \mathbf{T}$, over a taxonomy $\mathbf{T}$ to represent its structure.*

2.3   Policies

Policies enforce how data can be shared within the network. Some are network-wide (e.g., "no drug records and medical records can be obtained by the same party"), while others can be specified by an individual provider (e.g., "I will only provide 10 records to each person"). These policies are stored by each peer locally. We define our policies as follows:

Definition 2 (Policies). *A policy π is a tuple $\langle M, I, D, \varphi \rangle$ where*

- *$M \in \{\mathsf{O}, \mathsf{F}, \mathsf{P}\}$ is a deontic modality/operator, denoting an obligation (O), a prohibition (F) or a permission (P).*
- *$I \in \{id_1, \dots, id_n\}$ is a unique peer identifier*
- *$D \in \mathbf{T}$ is a descriptor of a data element (cf. Definition 1)*
- *$\varphi = L_1 \wedge \cdots \wedge L_m$ is a conjunction of possibly negated literals (cf. Definition 3)*

A sample policy is $\langle \mathsf{P}, id_1, 010000, noRec(010000) < 5 \rangle$ representing a permission to allow the peer with id 1 to access up to 5 records of 010000. Our policies above refer to descriptions of data elements – these are labels describing, for instance, fields of a data base or names of predicates of an ontology [5]. These labels are represented using the numerical encoding detailed in Sect. 2.2.

Our policies allow the representation of *conditions* under which the policy should hold – this is what the component φ of Definition 2 is meant for. We have designed a simple vocabulary of "built-in" tests which are relevant to our envisaged application scenarios, and these are defined below:

Definition 3 (Literals). *A literal L is one of the following, where $D \in \mathbf{T}$ (a descriptor of a data element), $\circ \in \{<, >, \leq, \geq, =\}$ is a comparison operator, and $n \in \mathbb{N}$ is a natural number:*

- *$noRec(D) \circ n$ holds if the number of retrieved instances of data element D satisfies the test "$\circ$ n".*
- *$lastReq(D) \circ n$ holds if the (time point of the) last retrieved instance of data element D satisfies the test "$\circ$ n".*
- *$lastAccess(D) \circ n$ holds if the (time point of the) last granted access to an instance of data element D satisfies the test "$\circ$ n".*
- *$\perp$ and $\top$ represent, respectively, the vacuously false and true values.*

In the remainder of our presentation, however, we make use of a "customised" version of policies, as these are more commonly used in our envisaged scenarios. We use the following shorthand:

$$\langle M, I, D, (noRec(D) < n \wedge noRec(D') < n') \rangle \equiv \langle M, I, D, n, D', n' \rangle$$

Some examples of policies are as follows:

- $\pi_1 = \langle \mathsf{P}, id_1, 010000, 5, 0, 1 \rangle$, that is, peer id_1 is permitted to access 5 items of data element 010000; the remainder of the policy condition is idle, that is, $noRec(0) < 1$ imposes no further restrictions.
- $\pi_2 = \langle \mathsf{P}, id_2, 020200, \infty, 0, 1 \rangle$, that is, peer id_2 is permitted to access unlimited (∞ stands for a very high natural number) items of data element 020200; the remainder of the policy condition is idle and imposes no further constraints.
- $\pi_3 = \langle \mathsf{P}, any, 010200, 5, 010000, 1 \rangle$ that is, any peer (denoted by the *any* identifier) is permitted to access 5 items of data element 010200; provided that they accessed less than 1 record of 010000.

This is a simple representation of policies which ignores time. The language of policies could be made more expressive for the mechanism we are proposing. A more expressive language would allow more complex interactions between policies, which would also require a more complex reasoning process (we sketch possible extensions in Sect. 8).

In Definition 2 we put forth the notion of obligations, which can be thought of as deferred policies: actions to be taken (or not taken) after data has been received from a provider for a pre-specified period of time (or possibly indefinitely). For instance, an obligation could be defined that requires the requestor to provide 5 records of data element 010000 to the provider in exchange for 10 records of data element 020000. The description in Sect. 2 of the interactions (encounter) between two parties could also cater for situations where obligations can be transferred between parties. For example, with three parties A, B, and C: A provides data to B, and B is then obliged to provide data to A. B then provides data to C, and transfers their obligation to C. Now C is obliged to provide data to A, and B has no obligation to A.

We define in Eq. 1 how to check if two data elements D and D' encoded in our numbering scheme of Sect. 2.2, are subsumed by one another. The definition makes use of two extra parameters, namely, BS which provides the size of each band (2, in the above example), and ZB which provides the number of zero-bands in D' (for instance, 020200 above has 1 zero-band [02][02][00]; calculating the number of zero bands is trivial for an unencrypted integer):

$$D \sqsubseteq_{ZB}^{BS} D' \text{ if, and only if, } \lfloor D/10^{BS \times ZB} \rfloor = \lfloor D'/10^{BS \times ZB} \rfloor \qquad (1)$$

Each peer is provided a copy of the encoded ontology upon joining the network. If the ontology is too large, a subset could be provided containing concepts that the peer deals with and each transaction would provide the "vocabulary" of the requestor. In this way only a small amount of data is transferred when a new peer joins the network, but peers will slowly converge towards holding a complete ontology as transactions occur. Alternatively, the peer could be provided only with a URI, allowing them to download the full encoded ontology as required.

Automatic encoding of the ontology is fairly trivial. The superclass-subclass relationships can be condensed into a simple tree structure; from this tree we can then count the maximum depth and maximum size at each depth to determine the number of bands, and size of banding, respectively. This may take some time to complete, but this operation only has to be performed once when the ontology is first introduced.

Alternative numerical encoding mechanisms have been suggested that used ring theory, prime numbers, or multiples; however none seemed to precisely suit our needs. Specifically, none could incorporate entailment information whilst retaining a mathematically simple comparison operation. Mechanisms of this type have been widely explored [9,19], and these mechanisms could replace the one currently proposed. For the purposes of our research we wanted to create a simple example encoding, however others could have been used.

2.4 Finding Relevant Transaction Records

The mechanism itself chooses relevant transaction records to send to a provider, the peer is unable to intervene. The challenge is ensuring that the records held by a given peer are tamper-proof; this is achieved by storing records in an encrypted format, using the numerical encoding in Sect. 2.2. Equation 1 allows identification of records that match a specific concept (or one of its parents). Using this information, and a reasoning process that references both policies and what is known about the requested data, a subset of relevant records can be identified and sent to a provider. On receipt of these records, the provider must also reason with them to determine if they violate any policies.

The mechanism identifies relevant records by processing each transaction record and performing a numerical comparison operation, without decrypting the data. Each transaction has an associated data element, which is compared to each data element in the policies for the current transaction using Eq. 1. If the test is successful, then the transaction will be retained as a relevant record. When all records have been processed, all relevant records will be sent to P. This process is detailed in Algorithm 1.

Algorithm 1. Finds Relevant Transaction Records

Require: Π (a set of policies), *Records* (a set of records)
Ensure: *RelevantRecords* (a set of relevant records)
   procedure FINDRELEVANTRECORDS()
      RelevantRecords ← ∅
      for all $R \in$ *Records* **do**
         for all $\pi \in \Pi$ **do**   ▷ Each data type referred to in policies
            if *encodedComparison*(π, R) **then**   ▷ *encodedComparison* refers to Eq. 1
               RelevantRecords ← *RelevantRecords* ∪ $\{R\}$
            end if
         end for
      end for
   end procedure

The mechanism must be able to detect potential violations and protect against them; either by updating policies, anonymising part of the data, or rejecting the request. When making this decision the mechanism will check if the user's identity allows them to access the data, if they have fulfilled all past obligations, and if the records provided prohibit them from receiving the requested data.

When deciding whether to share data, both ends of the transaction are black-boxed; this prevents both requestor and provider from tampering with records. The encrypted records and (unencrypted) policies are processed through a black-box mechanism, which returns a boolean value to indicate if the transaction can go ahead. If the transaction is denied, then an encrypted record will be returned to the requestor that contains a justification as to why it was denied. This can then "bootstrap" the reasoning process next time; as this record will be sent (by the requestor) as a relevant record. The provider can then examine the proof and decide if it still applies, reducing reasoning overheads.

The other challenge is designing the selection procedure in the mechanism so that just the right amount of information can be shared; since peer-to-peer connections are opportunistic, the less information sent the better – however enough has to be sent to allow the provider to make an informed decision about whether to share.

3   Requirements and Architecture

The hypotheses in Sect. 1 emphasise the aspects of the problem that we are concentrating on, and can be broken down further into the following requirements:

R1 To allow fine-grained (table and column level) control over data access policies.

R2 To ensure transaction records and data remain tamper-proof throughout the lifetime of a transaction.

R3 To allow operations to be performed on encrypted transaction records, without exposing those records to the user.

R4 To ensure that policies are enforced across the network and cannot be subverted to the advantage of an attacker.[1]

An architecture to meet these requirements is presented in Fig. 3. The architecture has two main components: the hostcache sub-architecture (A), and the peer sub-architecture (B).

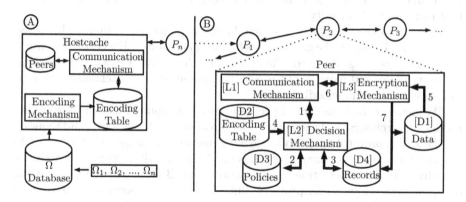

Fig. 3. Hostcache (A) and Peer (B) architecture

It should be noted that our approach refers to database concepts (tables, columns, and rows); however this is a specific case for our broader solution. While we assume that our mechanism will be used on data stored in a database, any data repository could be used instead.

The hostcache sub-architecture (A), which follows established peer-to-peer hostcache operations [3], has access to a collection of ontologies (obtained from many parties), which are input to the encoding mechanism. The encoding mechanism outputs the encoding table, which is a numerically encoded representation of the ontology (explained in Sect. 2.2). The hostcache also stores a collection of peer ids, each new peer that contacts the hostcache will have its peer id added

---

[1] An attacker is any party (requestor, provider, or third party) who attempts to subvert the system.

to the collection. The hostcache processes requests from peers by generating ids, providing copies of the encoding table to peers and providing information about potential neighbours to enquiring peers. The hostcache is a central element whose main functions are to generate ids for each peer, and to provide a list of potential neighbours on request.

The peer sub-architecture (B) is a collection of storage and functionalities. The encoding table (D2) on the peer is obtained directly from the hostcache, and is only referred to by the decision mechanism (L2). The decision mechanism is responsible for performing the decision operations discussed later in this document (whether to provide data, what records are "relevant"). The peer also holds data (D1 – the data which it provides), records (D4 – encrypted transaction records), and policies (D3 – policies detailing how data is shared, discussed in Sect. 2.3). There is also the communication mechanism (L1) which handles message processing (both receiving and sending), generating data requests, and invoking the decision mechanism. Lastly is the encryption mechanism (L3), which can encrypt and decrypt data and record packages (but not records themselves) received from the network (discussed further in Sect. 4). While not noted in the architecture, each peer also holds an encrypted id, issued by the hostcache, that confirms their identity.

Each component in the peer sub-architecture is needed to fulfil at least one requirement. **R1** needs the decision mechanism and policies. **R2** needs all components *except* policies. **R3** needs the decision mechanism, encryption mechanism, encoding table, and records. **R4** needs the communication mechanism, encryption mechanism, and encoding table.

We engineer the behaviour of peers so as to make contact with the hostcache, establish neighbours, and then enter a loop responding to messages and requesting data. The protocol adopts non-blocking message exchanges, that is, peers do not wait for replies (as communication is unreliable and these may never arrive or be delivered). The interactions in sub-architecture B are numbered to represent an approximate interaction protocol, but as interactions occur in a distributed environment they cannot be considered as sequential operations on a single peer. More accurately, there are four (main) paths through the architecture diagram for two interacting peers. Peer id_1, upon receiving a data request from Peer id_2, will follow steps 1, 2, 4, 1 (from the annotated arrows of Fig. 3). Peer id_2 will follow steps 1, 2, 3, 1. Peer id_1 will follow steps 1, 2, 4 and then 5, 6. Peer id_2 will then follow steps 6, 7.

4   Illustrative Scenario

We illustrate our solution with a scenario in which we consider two parties: P (the provider) and R (the requestor). The provider is a research lab that developed DrugX, and tracks prescriptions of DrugX. The requestor is a health authority who regulates all prescriptions for the region they operate in attempting to counteract the side effects of Drug X. This example uses a subset of the encoding table in Fig. 2.

The requestor wishes to get information on the trials carried out on DrugX by the provider, so sends a data request for ten 020000 (DrugX and subclasses) records. The provider checks its policies and finds nothing prohibiting the requestor's access to 020000, so the provider then sends the following (relevant) policies to the requestor:

- $\langle$P, any, 010300, ∞, 020200, 1$\rangle$ – Provide 010300 to anyone without 020200
- $\langle$P, any, 020200, ∞, 010300, 1$\rangle$ – Provide 020200 to anyone without 010300

These policies are defined using the shorthand from Sect. 2.3.

The requestor processes these policies and extracts the following data elements: 010300 and 020200. The requestor then has to check through their transaction records (the format is $\langle dataset, numberOfRecords\rangle$): $\langle$010100, 50$\rangle$, $\langle$010301, 50$\rangle$, $\langle$010302, 50$\rangle$, $\langle$010100, 10$\rangle$, $\langle$010200, 10$\rangle$, $\langle$010400, 10$\rangle$.

Each relevant data element is then compared with the records to determine its entailment, following Eq. 1, that is, 010301 $\sqsubseteq_{ZB}^{BS}$ 010300, and 010302 $\sqsubseteq_{ZB}^{BS}$ 010300 hold; none of the remaining cases hold.

For each pair (D, D') we must test both $D \sqsubseteq_{ZB}^{BS} D'$ and $D' \sqsubseteq_{ZB}^{BS} D$, as the test only checks if the first element is a subclass of the second. Applying both tests allows both relationships to be captured. Of the six records two of them are found to be relevant: $\langle$010301, 50$\rangle$ and $\langle$010302, 50$\rangle$. These records are now sent to the provider so that it can determine if they violate any policy. This process is similar that performed by the requestor, so we will not discuss it in as much detail. Performing the same basic process the mechanism determines that both records violate Policy 2 (Provide 020200 to anyone without 010300). At this point, the provider can do one of two things: the data request can be rejected (a justification will be sent to the requestor), or the prohibited part of the requested data can be omitted. The latter will be used in this situation, as the policy only prevents a specific part (020200) of the requested data (020000) from being sent.

The provider then generates records for the current transaction ($\langle$020100, 10$\rangle$, $\langle$020300, 10$\rangle$, $\langle$020400, 10$\rangle$), and assembles the result package (containing 10 records of 020100, 020300, and 020400). These are then encrypted together using the requestor's public key[2] and sent to the requestor. The requestor's mechanism receives this package and decrypts it using the requestor's private key. The "receipt" is added to the requestor's collection of transaction records and the mechanism returns the extracted data to the requestor, completing the transaction.

5 Analysis of Our Solution

We evaluated our proposal by exploring many cases and concluded that there was no incentive for any of the participants to subvert the system, as it provided

---

[2] This is an extra security precaution; assuming that all peers have public/private key pairs ensures that data can be sent across a peer-to-peer network securely.

no advantages. Below we provide an analysis of our approach against classic attacks.

- *Impersonation* – All peers, in order to join the network, must be given a unique encrypted id by the host cache. Ids cannot be falsified as only the hostcache has keys to generate these appropriately and the chances of falsifying ids coherently are very low.
- *Modification of policies* – Providers could modify policies during transactions, however doing so could cause them to receive irrelevant transaction records. These irrelevant records could cause them to make an incorrect decision to provide or withhold data (which they would have no incentive to do).
- *Modification of transaction records* – Transaction records cannot be tampered with as they are encrypted throughout exchanges; attempts to tamper with records would require the encryption mechanisms be broken.
- *Man in the Middle* – Transaction records and data both travel encrypted. Policies are transmitted unencrypted, but it would be trivial to create a RSA-like encryption to transmit them. Man-in-the-middle can not access the data as it travels encrypted.
- *Denial of Service (DOS)* – Requiring a hostcache creates a vulnerability to DOS attacks, however this DOS would only affect new peers joining the network. Existing peers in the network would be able to function as normal. A DOS could also target individual peers, but this will not have a major effect on the rest of the network.
- *Subvert timestamp in records (Provider)* – This timestamp is generated by the mechanism, so cannot be altered. The provider could potentially alter it by garbling the record, but this would only serve to disadvantage them in the future.
- *Provider sends malformed record* – A malformed record will never be considered a "relevant" record, as it cannot be processed properly by the mechanism, so if they are sent, they will be ignored. Hence, there is no incentive for a peer to send malformed records. To prevent this record from remaining indefinitely a record purging functionality periodically scans the set of records and discards those elements which cannot be processed/parsed.
- *Requestor does not record transaction* – The mechanism forces transaction records to be stored. Providing the data and updating the set of records are two stages of an atomic operation carried out within the black-box mechanism.
- *Code tampering* – Tampering with code is impossible, as it is provided as a blackbox.
- *Record fabrication* – Records could be fabricated, but the chances of producing anything meaningful are very low, since these have to be encrypted and the peers do not hold the keys or indeed have access to the encryption mechanism by itself.
- *Sybil Attack*[3]*/Fake peer generation* – The only purpose to generating extra peers would be to generate fake records for yourself, but there is no bene-

---

[3] A sybil attack [12] happens when one of the participants generates many fake ids to skew the balance of power in one's own favour, as in, for instance, voting.

fit from having extra records as these will not make approval more likely, moreover, it could cause data requests to be rejected.

- *Data Modification* – After a peer receives data from another peer, that data is no longer under the control of the data provider. We propose a way of mitigating this by adding the concept of data "ownership". All data within the network can be stored in "packages" encrypted with the id of the original owner. Anyone can decrypt these packages to get the data, but they are only able to encrypt data packages with their own id. This means that the original source of the data is in no way associated with the dSta after it has been modified by a third party.

Our solution incorporates a small amount of centralisation: a one-time check-in when connecting to the network, to aid with system functions. It may be possible to design a system where this is not the case, but we would have to make trade-offs (no verified identities, no shared encoding, cold-start issues, etc.) to achieve this. This minor centralisation ensures that no one "owns" all the data within the system, and also creates a robust network for data exchange; the only contact with a central authority (hostcache) is when a peer joins the network, after that no data is sent to the hostcache.

6 Proof of Concept Implementation

We investigated the design space by creating a proof-of-concept prototype[4] to perform the operations of a single peer with a set of simulated neighbours. Our prototype does not implement full message passing, but does demonstrate the mechanism which we have described. The prototype is implemented in Java, so some definitions have been adapted to fit with object-oriented programming concepts. The cryptography implemented in the prototype is not a full encryption mechanism, but simulates one through the use of numerical objects that can have simple mathematical operations performed on them without exposing their value. If we ignore these adaptations, our implementation follows the peer architecture (part B of Fig. 3).

To reflect the modularity of our architecture we have introduced features to customise the simulation using a number of parameters, currently specified as variables within the code. These parameters supply the (ontology) encoding table, data, records, and policies of each neighbouring peer. The simulation itself tracks a number of metrics to provide an analysis of performance. The policies implemented within our prototype follow our policy language provided in Definition 2, specifically they make use of the shorthand we describe in Sect. 2.3.

We have also performed a feasibility analysis by using this prototype to simulate an extended version of the scenario from Sect. 4. The scenario considers a single peer attempting to get data from four neighbours that each have data and policies. This simulation completes in a single cycle (each neighbour is queried

---

[4] The source code for our implementation is https://github.com/Glenugie/REND-Peer.

for each desired data item once) with all of the requested data being received. The prototype tracks which peers provided the data, allowing this to be compared to their policies; through this we observed that policies were not violated at any point.

Using our prototype we tracked the total number of messages sent between peers, total simulation time, and the minimum, average, and maximum size of messages. Message sizes are given in quantity of numbers transferred, with encrypted numbers taking twice the space, and each array adding an extra number as overhead. 40 messages were exchanged, with a minimum size of 1 (initial data request), an average size of 4.5, and a maximum size of 17. The simulation took a total of 10 ms to complete, 2 ms of which was the single cycle; the other 8 were network initialisation. This time could be considered inaccurate as we envisage our mechanism running on a large number of devices with little computing power; rather than the one powerful device that our simulation was run on.

Implementing this prototype allowed us to locate and correct a number of inconsistencies in our mechanism. One such correction was to apply the encoded number comparison from Eq. 1 in pairs to capture entailment in both directions, as mentioned in Sect. 4.

7 Related Work

Our investigation draws upon many disparate areas such as Smart Cities [4,37], Internet of Things [2,18], BlockChain [17,29], Bitcoin [26], and encryption [16, 28]. Below we review the work from each of these areas that we consider most relevant.

Within our peer-to-peer system it is important for peers to have control over who, when, and how their data is shared. This can be achieved through the use of policies/norms [32,33,36]. Norms are a formal representation of expected behaviours of software agents, such as prohibitions, and duties. An integral part of norms concerns deontic logic [25,34], considering permissions, prohibitions, and obligations. Norms and agents are often paired together, as norms provide means to control behaviour in societies of self-interested components [11].

Our research will develop alternative policy languages to be combined with data as a single component with benefits such as increased control over how data is exchanged. This combination of policies and data draws upon the techniques and methods reported in [27], but it has a significantly different focus, and most importantly, provides a distributed solution which can scale up and is resilient to many kinds of attacks. There have been other research threads which also use the term "Policy Carrying Data" [31,35], which suggests similar concepts but without the focus on a distributed environment. They instead focus on a centralised scenario which creates a single-point of failure, a lack of scalability, and data ownership issues.

Berners-Lee makes a case for an online Magna Carta [22] to protect the openness and neutrality of the internet. The work being proposed here attempts to develop a mechanism to support the normative principles promoted in Berners-Lee's design [24].

Role Based Access Control (RBAC) could be seen as a similar approach, though with a stronger focus on a controlled environment. While work has been pursued to address RBAC in a distributed environment [8,21,30], many issues, such as a reliance on the ability to observe and control principals, have not yet been satisfactorily resolved. [8] uses user-to-user relationships to form a "path" of authorisation, but does not consider user-to-resource relationships which limits its usefulness. [21] focuses on transactions passing between two secure environments, rather than between two (potentially) insecure parties. [30] discusses automating compliance within a single secure environment, but does not discuss implementing this in a fully distributed environment.

We detect and overlap between our approach and Risk-Aware Access Control [6,7,15]. This refers to the automatic assessment of risk involved in allowing access to data, which could help peers to formulate their policies for data access.

One candidate for operations on encrypted data is homomorphic encryption schemes [16] which are applicable to our proposal. This method of encryption allows operations to be applied to encrypted data without decrypting. One limitation of this approach is that a data request must specify the amount of data to be retrieved, and the result will either be truncated or padded out. This method is semantically secure, i.e. given a cipher c that encrypts either m_0 or m_1, adversary α (when given the two choices) has probability of $\frac{1}{2} + \epsilon$ of guessing correctly. ϵ, called α's advantages should be negligible, else (informally) α has "broken" the semantic security.

Another candidate is CryptDB [28], though this is less suited to the required context. CryptDB relies on a trusted proxy to process a user's query and send it to the database management system (DBMS), which then returns the decrypted result. This seems problematic, as the proxy returns the result in a decrypted format (so, while the DBMS has not seen anything decrypted, the decrypted result could be intercepted between proxy and user).

We note a substantial overlap between our proposal and initiatives such as BlockChain[5] and Bitcoin[6]. BlockChain is a permissionless distributed database [17,29] based on the Bitcoin protocol [26] that achieves tamper resistance by timestamping a hash of "batches" of recent valid transactions into "blocks". Each block references the prior timestamp, creating a cryptographically enforced chain. Blockchain requires either a group of always-on data-store nodes, or for every individual "peer" to store a copy of the full chain. There are important similarities between BlockChain and our proposal, but BlockChain is centralised in nature and has high storage requirements on data store nodes.

---

[5] https://blockchain.info/.

[6] https://bitcoin.org/en/.

8 Conclusions, Discussions, and Future Work

We proposed a solution to enable the control of data through fine-grained, user-specified access policies. This solution was designed to operate in a peer-to-peer environment in which some peers have data which they want to provide (called Providers) and some peers have data which they want to acquire (called Requestors). Providers can set "policies", i.e. rules which govern how their data can be accessed and also by whom. These policies will be enforced by mechanisms throughout the network.

For simplicity we assume that a fixed ontology is provided on network initialisation, and that this is then encoded by the hostcache. In the future, it would be possible for this to be extended to a dynamic ontology where each peer reports their sub-ontology on joining the network, which is then added to the master encoding table. This fixed ontology allows for the correct banding size and depth to be determined for the encoding. If the encoding is dynamic, one shortcoming is that it is then possible to run out of encoding space; this can be offset by choosing a high starting size but this will increase message size.

The mechanism and example that we have presented in this paper consider a simple case with a number of limitations which can be improved upon through a number of extensions, some of which we sketch below.

Our mechanism currently only allows a requestor to (implicitly) accept or reject policies within a transaction; if they reject the policies specified by the provider they simply do not send relevant records to the provider. In the future we could implement a "policy negotiation" phase, in which requestor and provider can propose and counter-propose policies to attempt to reach an agreement. For instance, the provider could propose an obligation which requires the requestor to provider 10 temperature readings. The requestor could counter-propose that they only provide 5 temperature readings. This process can continue until an agreement is reached, or either party withdraws.

We have considered the notion of obligations, which can be thought of as deferred policies: they are actions to be taken (or not taken) after data has been received from a provider for a pre-specified period of time (or possibly indefinitely). Obligations could also be set to expire when certain conditions are satisfied (not just time-related), for instance once an obligation has been triggered a certain number of times. We could consider a more sophisticated solution where multiple obligations can be attached to a single piece of data, and each obligation can be individually negotiated. Another possibility would be to allow obligations to be assigned to the provider (and not just the requestor). This would allow obligations such as "If I send data to you, then I am obliged to keep you updated if that data changes." This could either be proposed by the provider or requestor during negotiations.

Another extension is automated record purging and clean-up. Peers want to hold a minimal set of records (as they take up storage space), so there needs to be an operation to purge records that are no longer useful. Each peer would purge its own records periodically. Records with unfulfilled obligations will always be kept (another incentive to fulfil obligations, as otherwise your storage space will get filled quickly). Peers could also perform record compaction, merging equivalent records (for example, $\langle 010200, 20 \rangle$ and $\langle 010200, 30 \rangle$ become $\langle 010200, 50 \rangle$).

Our implementation currently only includes one peer, but we have already started looking into ways of simulating realistic P2P networks, using scalable technologies such as PeerSim[7], which allows hundreds of thousands of peers to be simulated efficiently.

Our policy language is a starting point, and there are many possible extensions we would like to explore to provide finer-grained control but with adequate computational (performance) features. We have considered extensions that allow policies to have a time component. We also plan to provide reasoning mechanisms that allow users to see what the consequences of accessing a given piece of data are. Subsequently, we would need to make the reasoning process more sophisticated, allowing it to deal with complex interactions between policies. The mechanism could also be extended to allow policies to target groups of users; the present formalisation considers each peer to be an independent agent.

By making our policy language more sophisticated, we may cause difficulties for non-experts, as an expressive policy language is more complex for them to work with. It would be far too complex to provide support at design time as we must consider actions that are not known beforehand. There are, however, potential mitigations to this problem. For instance we could allow organisations or other peers to share their policies, with limited aspects of customisation, similar to rules of "IF-This-Then-That" (IFTTT[8]) to handle events of the Internet of Things. Additionally, we could provide alternative dialects of policies which provide limited functionality. These would be less expressive, but hopefully easier to understand for non-technical users.

References

1. Androutsellis-Theotokis, S., Spinellis, D.: A survey of peer-to-peer content distribution technologies. ACM Comput. Surv. (CSUR) **36**(4), 335–371 (2004)
2. Atzori, L., Iera, A., Morabito, G.: The internet of things: a survey. Comput. Netw. **54**(15), 2787–2805 (2010)
3. Buford, J., Yu, H., Lua, E.K.: P2P Networking and Applications. Morgan Kaufmann, San Francisco (2009)
4. Caragliu, A., Bo, C., Nijkamp, P.: Smart cities in Europe. J. Urban Technol. **18**(2), 6582 (2011)
5. Chandrasekaran, B., Josephson, J.R., Benjamins, V.R.: What are ontologies, and why do we need them? IEEE Intell. Syst. **1**, 20–26 (1999)
6. Chen, L., Crampton, J., Kollingbaum, M.J., Norman, T.J.: Obligations in risk-aware access control. In: Tenth Annual International Conference on Privacy, Security and Trust (PST), pp. 145–152. IEEE (2012)
7. Chen, L., Gasparini, L., Norman, T.J.: XACML and risk-aware access control. Resource **2**(10), 3–5 (2013)

---

[7] http://peersim.sourceforge.net/.
[8] https://ifttt.com/.

8. Cheng, Y., Park, J., Sandhu, R.: A user-to-user relationship-based access control model for online social networks. In: Cuppens-Boulahia, N., Cuppens, F., Garcia-Alfaro, J. (eds.) DBSec 2012. LNCS, vol. 7371, pp. 8–24. Springer, Heidelberg (2012). doi:10.1007/978-3-642-31540-4_2

9. Curé, O., Naacke, H., Randriamalala, T., Amann, B.: LiteMat: a scalable, cost-efficient inference encoding scheme for large RDF graphs. In: 2015 IEEE International Conference on Big Data (Big Data), pp. 1823–1830. IEEE (2015)

10. Dhankhar, V., Kaushik, S., Wijesekera, D.: Securing workflows with XACML, RDF and BPEL. In: Atluri, V. (ed.) DBSec 2008. LNCS, vol. 5094, pp. 330–345. Springer, Heidelberg (2008). doi:10.1007/978-3-540-70567-3_25

11. Dignum, F.: Autonomous agents with norms. Artif. Intell. Law **7**(1), 69–79 (1999)

12. Douceur, J.R.: The sybil attack. In: Druschel, P., Kaashoek, F., Rowstron, A. (eds.) IPTPS 2002. LNCS, vol. 2429, pp. 251–260. Springer, Heidelberg (2002). doi:10.1007/3-540-45748-8_24

13. Esteva, M., Rodríguez-Aguilar, J.-A., Sierra, C., Garcia, P., Arcos, J.L.: On the formal specification of electronic institutions. In: Dignum, F., Sierra, C. (eds.) Agent Mediated Electronic Commerce. LNCS, vol. 1991, pp. 126–147. Springer, Heidelberg (2001). doi:10.1007/3-540-44682-6_8

14. Garca-Camino, A., Noriega, P., Rodrguez-Aguilar, J.A.: Implementing norms in electronic institutions. In: Proceedings of the Fourth International Joint Conference on Autonomous Agents and Multiagent Systems, pp. 667–673. ACM (2005)

15. Gasparini, L.: Risk-aware access control and XACML. Ph.D. thesis, University of Padua (2013)

16. Gentry, C.: Computing arbitrary functions of encrypted data. Commun. ACM **53**(3), 97–105 (2010)

17. Grigorik, I.: Minimum viable block chain. https://www.igvita.com/2014/05/05/minimum-viable-block-chain/. Accessed 2014

18. Gubbi, J., Buyya, R., Marusic, S., Palaniswami, M.: Internet of things (IoT): a vision, architectural elements, and future directions. Future Gener. Comput. Syst. **29**(7), 1645–1660 (2013)

19. Harrison, J.: Theorem Proving with the Real Numbers. Springer, London (1996). doi:10.1007/978-1-4471-1591-5

20. Hayes, C.C.: Agents in a nutshell-a very brief introduction. IEEE Trans. Knowl. Data Eng. **11**(1), 127–132 (1999)

21. Karjoth, G., Schunter, M., Waidner, M.: Platform for enterprise privacy practices: privacy-enabled management of customer data. In: Dingledine, R., Syverson, P. (eds.) PET 2002. LNCS, vol. 2482, pp. 69–84. Springer, Heidelberg (2003). doi:10.1007/3-540-36467-6_6

22. Kiss, J.: An online Magna Carta: Berners-Lee calls for bill of rights for web. The Guardian, 12 March 2014

23. Landwehr, C.: Privacy research directions. Commun. ACM **59**(2), 29–31 (2016)

24. Lee, B.T., Fischetti, M.: Weaving the Web: The Original Design and Ultimate Destiny of the World Wide Web by Its Inventor. Harper, San Francisco (1999)

25. Meyer, J.J.C., Wieringa, R.J.: Deontic logic in computer science normative system specification. In: International Workshop on Deontic Logic in Computer Science (1993)

26. Nakamoto, S.: Bitcoin: a peer-to-peer electronic cash system (2008). www.cryptovest.co.uk. Accessed June 2016

27. Padget, J., Vasconcelos, W.W.: Policy-carrying data: a step towards transparent data sharing. Procedia Comput. Sci. **52**, 59–66 (2015)

28. Popa, R.A., Redfield, C., Zeldovich, N., Balakrishnan, H.: CryptDB: processing queries on an encrypted database. Commun. ACM **55**(9), 103–111 (2012)
29. Postscapes: Blockchains and the internet of things. http://postscapes.com/blockchains-and-the-internet-of-things. Accessed Mar 2016
30. Sackmann, S., Kahmer, M.: ExPDT: a policy-based approach for automating compliance. Wirtschaftsinformatik **50**(5), 366 (2008)
31. Saroiu, S., Wolman, A., Agarwal, S.: Policy-carrying data: a privacy abstraction for attaching terms of service to mobile data. In: Proceedings of the 16th International Workshop on Mobile Computing Systems and Applications, pp. 129–134. ACM (2015)
32. Sergot, M.: A computational theory of normative positions. ACM Trans. Comput. Logic (TOCL) **2**(4), 581–622 (2001)
33. Shoham, Y., Tennenholtz, M.: On social laws for artificial agent societies: off-line design. Artif. Intell. **73**(1), 231–252 (1995)
34. Von Wright, G.H.: Deontic logic. Mind **60**(237), 1–15 (1951)
35. Wang, X., Yong, Q., Dai, Y., Ren, J., Hang, Z.: Protecting outsourced data privacy with lifelong policy carrying. In: 10th IEEE International Conference on High Performance Computing and Communications and 2013 IEEE International Conference on Embedded and Ubiquitous Computing, HPCC/EUC 2013, Zhangjiajie, China, pp. 896–905, 13–15 November 2013. http://dx.doi.org/10.1109/HPCC.and.EUC.2013.128
36. von Wright, G.H.: Norm and Action: A Logical Enquiry. Routledge and Kegan Paul, London (1963)
37. Zheng, Y., Capra, L., Wolfson, O., Yang, H.: Urban computing: concepts, methodologies, and applications. ACM Trans. Intell. Syst. Technol. **5**(3), 38:1–38:55 (2014). http://dl.acm.org/citation.cfm?id=2629592

Modelling Patient-Centric Healthcare Using Socially Intelligent Systems: The AVICENA Experience

Ignasi Gómez-Sebastià[1,3]([✉]), Frank Dignum[2], Javier Vázquez-Salceda[1], and Ulises Cortés[1]

[1] Department of Computer Science, Universitat Politècnica de Catalunya
(BarcelonaTech), Barcelona, Spain
{igomez,jvazquez,ia}@cs.upc.edu
[2] Department of Information and Computing Science,
Universiteit Utrecht, Utrecht, The Netherlands
F.P.M.Dignum@uu.nl
[3] Department of Computer Sciences and Statistics,
Intelligent Pharma, Barcelona, Spain
igomez@intelligentpharma.com

Abstract. One of the effects of population ageing is the increase in the proportion of long-term chronic diseases, which require new therapeutical models that mostly take place at the patients' home rather than inside a health care institution. This requires that patients autonomously follow their prescribed treatment, which can be especially difficult for patients suffering some kind of cognitive impairment. Information technologies show potential for supporting medication adherence but the main challenge is the distributed and highly regulated nature of this scenario, where there are several tasks involving the coordinated action of a range of actors. In this paper we propose to use socially intelligent systems to tackle this challenge. These systems exhibit, understand, and reason about social behaviour, in order to support people in their daily lives. Such systems present an opportunity when applied to information technologies for supporting treatment adherence. We explore how concepts of socially intelligent systems, including social practices and social identities, can be applied to AVICENA, an ongoing project to create a platform for assisting patients in several daily tasks related to their healthcare. We first introduce AVICENA, briefly describe our previous attempts to model the system from an organizational perspective and an institutional one and discuss some of the limitations found in those models. Then the core concepts of socially intelligent systems are introduced and we show how they can be applied to create a socially aware framework for supporting medication adherence.

Keywords: Multi agent systems · Social intelligence · Assisted Living

© Springer International Publishing AG 2017
S. Cranefield et al. (Eds.): COIN 2016 Workshops, LNAI 10315, pp. 22–41, 2017.
DOI: 10.1007/978-3-319-66595-5_2

1   Introduction

One of the main challenges that national healthcare programs will face in the near future is population ageing (i.e., the increase of the proportion of old people within the total population). In the European Union the size of the population aged between 65 and 80+ years at this moment is 80 million, but studies indicate that this number may double by 2050 [30]. In the United States of America the group of older people (aged 60+ years) is estimated to grow from the current 11% to a 22% by 2050 [26]. Moreover this is not just a problem in developed countries, as population ageing is also present in developing countries and might have an even bigger impact in those countries.

One of the impacts of population ageing is the epidemiological shift in disease burden, from acute (short-term, episodic) to chronic (long-term) diseases. From the patients' perspective, chronic diseases imply lengthy treatments often involving the combination of various medications to be taken at different times. It is undeniable that many patients experience difficulties in following treatment recommendations, and poor adherence to these long-term therapies compromises their effectiveness and may even become a cause of death. Adherence to long-term therapy for chronic illnesses in developed nations averages 50%. In developing countries, the rates are even lower [32]. Adherence rates are typically higher in patients with acute conditions, as compared to those with chronic conditions, with adherence dropping most dramatically after the first six months of therapy and in prophylaxis [24]. Patients' non-adherence to a therapeutic regimen may result in negative outcomes for them and may be compounded in populations with multiple morbidities that require multiple drug therapy. The elderly exemplifies such population. Adherence may also be affected by access to medications, which may be restricted by the use of formularies or insurance programmes. However, non-adherence may represent a greater risk in older people resulting in poor disease control that may be compounded with multiple morbidity and poly-pharmacy. There are many reasons why patients do not follow their therapy as prescribed. One of the reasons is that they cannot tolerate the (long-term) side effects such as loss of hair or constant feeling of tiredness. It may also be that the high cost of some medicines prohibits acquisition of their medication. Where a condition is asymptomatic (such as hypertension), the patient may be lulled into thinking that their treatment has worked and that they no longer require to take their medication or follow their diet; distracted by the hectic pace of everyday life, perhaps they simply forget to take their pills.

From the national healthcare programs' perspective, the epidemiological increase of chronic diseases implies the need of a major shift of the programs, from the current one centered on rapid response to episodic, acute illnesses where most of therapies and treatments are managed and delivered inside the official institutional care setting, into one where most of the medical therapies for managing chronic diseases (*e.g.*, hypertension, diabetes, depression, Parkinson's disease, *etc.*) are performed away from the institutional care setting, typically at home. This distributed approach to daily care requires patients, especially elderly, to be capable and committed to autonomously taking various medications at different time intervals over extended periods of time. This can easily lead to forgetfulness or confusion when following the prescribed treatment, especially when the patient is suffering multiple pathologies that require a treatment with a cocktail of drugs. This gets worse when elderly suffer a cognitive impairment. Medication compliance is a critical component in the success of any medical treatment and can become a cause of death. Both concordance and adherence management are of high priority, having a significant effect on the cost effectiveness of therapy. This is especially important where there are disorders with high healthcare costs, such as oncological diseases, psychiatric disorders, HIV, geriatric disorders or dementia. Initiatives attempting to address medicine non-adherence promote patient involvement in treatment decisions but remain ineffective with older patients or with patients with cognitive disorders. Interventions using applied high-technology show potential for supporting medication adherence in patients with diseases that require poly-pharmacological treatment, as they could help to reach optimal cooperation between patients and the healthcare professionals.

In previous work, we presented the COAALAS project (COmpanion for Ambient Assisted Living on ALIVE SHARE-*it* platforms) [16], a framework for multi-agent systems that combines organisational and normative theories with Ambient Assisted Living (AAL) technologies. The project aims to create a society of organizational aware devices (typically sensors and actuators) that are able to adapt to a wide range of AAL situations. COAALAS models the device network around the user as a society, including the set of behavioural patterns the devices are expected to follow. COAALAS effectively supports smart assistive tools that integrate human actors with the surrounding devices, contributing to the state-of-the-art in semi-autonomous and intelligent devices for the elderly people by allowing the devices to be both social- and norm-aware.

The mid-term objective of COAALAS was to integrate a wide range of sensors and actuators in a domotic setting, in order to transparently assist the user in their daily activities, while keeping all the participants of the healthcare workflow involved. The first design and implementation of such a sensor/actuator is the social electronic reminder for pills [15], which tackles the supply of the required stock of medicines to a user with difficulties to leave their house, while supervising that he follows the medical treatment prescribed by his doctor, not missing any dose due to forgetfulness or taking it at the wrong time due to confusion.

In this context, Assistive Technologies (AT) have been able to provide successful solutions on the support of daily healthcare for elderly people, mainly focused on the interaction between the patient and the electronic devices. However, the distributed approach that such kind of healthcare has to follow in the current socio-economical setting requires more complex AT designs that go further than the interaction with a tool and are able to focus on the relationship between the patient and his social environment, mainly: caregivers, relatives and health professionals. In this paper we describe how AVICENA, a patient-centric AT system to support patients in their daily healthcare, may be enhanced into a socially aware system that promotes treatment adherence by keeping track of the patient's motivations. Next section describes AVICENA. Then in Sect. 3 we introduce the core concepts of socially intelligent systems that we will use for our solution. Section 4 shows how these concepts are used to convert AVICENA into a socially-aware system to support medication adherence. In Sect. 5 we discuss some related work and we end with some final conclusions and future work.

2 AVICENA

AVICENA is an ongoing project that proposes the development of an innovative m-Health [19] platform and well-tailored personalized services to substantially improve chronic patients' medication and treatment adherence. *AVICENA* offers the opportunity to solve the patient's non-adherence to treatments by encouraging self-management of the treatment and promoting the continuity of therapeutic regimen, reducing costs to the patient, the caregivers and the health system. *AVICENA* focuses on developing innovative control mechanisms for collaborative, adaptive, dynamic and user centred medical concordance assessment and management systems at preferred environments and highly cooperative, intuitive patient/machine/pharmacist/doctor interfaces over a network. The *AVICENA* platform (depicted in Fig. 1) includes:

- a **Smart pill dispenser** that provides the medication at the prescribed times. It controls missed doses via integrated sensors, controls the drug stock and contains a reasoning engine offering Smart services,
- ***AVICENA* mobile app**, empowering users with the ability to self manage their treatment, obtaining tailored information and feedback depending on their medical treatment adherence,
- a **new care model** involving all the stakeholders in the chronic treatment process and in the assessment and management of the treatment adherence,
- ***AVICENA* social network** connects all the stakeholders in the care process (i.e., patients, clinicians, caregivers and pharmacists).

The main goal of *AVICENA* [15] is to improve individuals' adherence to medical treatments. A major application of the system will be the assistance of elderly individuals with chronic systemic diseases for which complex drug therapies are prescribed. In fact, several factors may affect adherence to medical treatments of this individuals, among which memory failures and psychological frailty play a relevant role. Indeed, cognitive disorders and psychopathological alterations such as mood fluctuations, anxiety and reduced efficiency of control mechanisms, are relatively frequent in this clinical population. *AVICENA* should directly influence the caregiver-patient efficiency to follow medical prescriptions by improving both the communication with the other agents of drug therapy assistance (e.g., physician, pharmacist) and the capacity of the caregiver-patient system to recognize and cope with factors likely related to reduced compliance.

In previous work [15] we presented an early version of AVICENA's model based on the ALIVE [3] framework. In that first stage of the work we focused

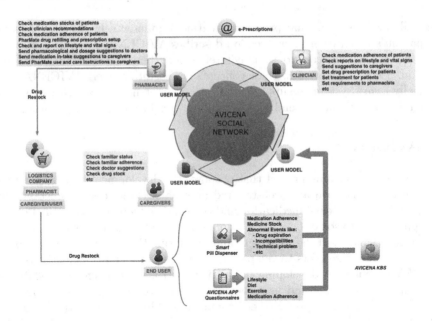

Fig. 1. *AVICENA* architecture

on the organizational model, and the ALIVE framework eased the design of the social network built around the patient (i.e., patient, doctor, health insurance company, pharmaceutic, delivery person, domotic house, intelligent medical dispenser and medical monitor) through a rich organisational, role-based model based on OperA [11]. The roles in all the scenarios were clearly defined, including their responsibilities and dependencies. But the normative model was still a simple one, and it was properly extended in [14]. Figure 2 shows some sample norms. The expected behavioural patterns to be abided by the actors in the scenario (including both human actors and computational agents) were properly connected to both constitutive and regulative norms, and an institutional monitor was set up to be able to infer the institutional state of an AVICENA setup. As a result we had a rich model which described the system from both a functional, organizationally-oriented perspective, an institutional perspective. Expected behaviour for all actors was clearly stated, and for those cases of non-compliance, violation-handling norms were added. But the patient being obliged to follow her treatment does not lead to its compliance, and there is no effective sanction mechanism that can be placed in this scenario that can handle forgetful patients or unmotivated ones. Furthermore, in the case of informal caregivers there is no contract establishing their precise roles and responsibilities, and very often they play a key role in the daily treatment process, exceeding their responsibilities as relatives by partially or completely taking a caregiver role. Modelling these informal interactions is the main motivation of the rest of this paper.

Property	Value
Activation Condition	$\wedge$ isPatient(p) $\wedge$ isTime(t) $\wedge$ isQuestionnarie(q) $\wedge$ Presented(q, p, t)
Deadline	Answered(q, p)
Expiration Condition	$\wedge$ isTime(tt) $\wedge$ hasTimeDifference(t, tt, OneDay)
Maintenance Condition	true
Norm ID	n1

Property	Value
Activation Condition	$\wedge$ isDoctor(d) $\wedge$ isTime(t) $\wedge$ isPatientReport(r) $\wedge$ sentReport(r, d, t)
Deadline	reviewReport(r, d)
Expiration Condition	$\wedge$ isTime(tt) $\wedge$ hasTimeDifference(t, tt, ThreeDays)
Maintenance Condition	true
Norm ID	n2

Property	Value
Activation Condition	$\wedge$ isMedicationDose(m) $\wedge$ isPatient(p) $\wedge$ isTime(t) $\wedge$ hasDose(m, p, t)
Deadline	takeDose(m, p)
Expiration Condition	$\wedge$ isTime(tt) $\wedge$ hasTimeDifference(t, tt, halfHour)
Maintenance Condition	true
Norm ID	n3

Property	Value
Activation Condition	violated(n1)
Deadline	lowerReputation(p)
Expiration Condition	false
Maintenance Condition	true
Norm ID	s1

Property	Value
Activation Condition	violated(n2)
Deadline	$\wedge$ isCompetentAuthorityOf(p, d, dd) $\wedge$ notified(dd)
Expiration Condition	false
Maintenance Condition	true
Norm ID	s2

Property	Value
Activation Condition	violated(n3)
Deadline	$\wedge$ isSPD(spd) $\wedge$ isPatient(p) $\wedge$ isMedicationDose(m) $\wedge$ (isCaregiver(c, p) $\vee$ isRelative(c, p)) $\wedge$ removeDose(spd, d) $\wedge$ log(m) $\wedge$ postNotify(c, p, m)
Expiration Condition	false
Maintenance Condition	true
Norm ID	s3

Fig. 2. Example of norms in *AVICENA* (source: [14]).

3   Socially Intelligent Systems

The goal of the actors in the AVICENA [15] scenario is for the patient to follow the treatment as accurately as possible while maintaining as much autonomy as possible. The second part of the goal is more interesting, because it leads to important social requirements. If the patient should be as autonomous as possible then the course of action should be driven mainly by internal motivations and not by contracts, obligations and prohibitions. Motivations differ from norms in the sense they are not enforced by external factors, but internalized by the agent, typically via social influences. Therefore, the agent (e.g., patient) will pursue his goals (e.g., follow the treatment) not because he has the obligation to follow, but because he is motivated to do it. Ideally, we would like the patient to have an internal motivation and capabilities to follow the necessary treatment with the support of caregivers whenever needed. In order to get to this situation we need models that go beyond the functional goals of following the treatment and that also take into account social aspects of the actors. In particular we need the *motives* (achievement, affiliation, power and avoidance), *values* (leading to preferences for types of situations), *social relations* (power, trust, status, responsibility, etc.), *social identity* (image that one wants to give, leading to coherent behavior around values and practices, norms and roles) and *social practices* (indicating standard packages of social and functional behavior combinations and interpretations of interactions that lead to both functional as well as social goals). These social aspects are introduced in [10]. In this document we will motivate the use of all these aspects in the AVICENA inspired scenario, discuss some of their background and their use in the scenario.

3.1 Motives

As we already indicated above the goal of AVICENA is not just that the patient gets her treatment, which could be achieved by having a person or system take care of reminding the patient or even forcing the patient to follow the treatment. However, the autonomy of the patient requires the careful consideration of social aspects that surround the treatment. In [9] we argued that agents can only become truly social when we take into consideration all basic types of motives as defined by McLelland [23]. Besides the *achievement motive*, which can be thought to drive the traditional functional goals achievement (i.e. trying to achieve a state of the world) he distinguished the affiliation, power and avoidance motives.

The *affiliation motive* underlies the need of people for (positive) social contact. This motive can be used (or abused) when a patient is not very mobile and is dependent on other people to come by for most social contacts. In that case a professional caregiver or family member that comes by to ensure that the patient follows the treatment (takes a pill or performs an exercise) also can fulfil the affiliation need of the patient as long as the person shows enough personal interest in the patient.

The *power motive* is NOT about gaining social power over other people. It is actually meant to designate the drive people have to master capabilities and thus processes. E.g. sportsmen practising skills and enjoying doing so comes from this motive. This motive can lead to the will to autonomously perform some actions related to a treatment. E.g. performing exercises that need physical or mental skills.

The *avoidance motive* drives people to avoid unwanted situations. This plays a role in treatments when medicines might have negative side-effects or it is unknown how they will affect a patient. This uncertainty might lead a patient to avoid taking the medicines.

3.2 Social Identity

The second important aspect that needs to be taken into account is the social identity of a person. In short, the social identity of a person determines what other people expect from someone in certain contexts. The social identity consists of three elements: the *perceived physical appearance*, the *identification with a stereotype* and *membership of social groups*.

The first element relates to what a person believes are his capabilities and thus what he believes other people expect him to do. I.e. if you are old you don't have to stand up for other people in public transport; if you consider yourself athletic you will take initiative when physical tasks have to be done for a group; if you consider yourself to be handicapped or ill (e.g. with heart failure) you might avoid going up stairs or taking a walk.

The second element of a social identity indicates an ideal image (or prototype) that one strives to mirror. Thus one compares himself with the expected behaviour of the ideal identity and also uses the expected behaviour to guide one's own behaviour. Thus if one believes that an ideal husband takes care of all broken appliances in the family home then the man will try to fix all of them or try to learn how to do this. He will consider himself bad if he fails in such tasks (even if they are not realistic). So, if a patient sees himself as a basically healthy person and healthy persons do not need assistance with any daily activity, the patient might refuse the support (even though he "knows" that he needs the support for the activity). This second element can be modelled with two parts; the first is the set of values that a person attaches to the ideal and that he therefore tries to uphold and the second is a set of social practices that he considers to be appropriate given this ideal. The social practices come again with their own set of norms and default behaviours and roles. In the next section we discuss the social practices in more detail.

The third element of the social identity of a person is his group membership. If a person is part of a social group he will adopt the social practices of this group and uphold its values. In how far he does this depends on his role in this group. The captain of a basketball team is more likely to follow the social practices of the team than a substitute. Membership and status of a group can in themselves also be goals of a person. Thus being a good family member can entice a patient to accept advice of another family member.

3.3   Social Practices

The final aspect of social agents that we will include in our models is that of social practices. In our every-day life most of our behaviour is governed by social practices. They are a kind of standardized way in which we conduct all kinds of interactions. They combine standard physical behaviours with standard social interpretations of this behaviour. E.g. greeting a person in The Netherlands at work with a handshake shows respect and an understanding that the meeting is formal. Someone that you see every day or who you consider to be a peer/friend you will greet by just saying "Hi". Thus there is both a *standard physical action* as well as *standard social meaning* attached to a social practice. The fact that these are combined makes them convenient in a complex world as it avoids to have to reason about both physical and social aspects separately. The reason that they work is exactly because they are standard. Thus their usefulness derives from their use rather than some intrinsic value of the actions themselves.

The existing theory on social practices is rather sparse (but see [27, 31] for some background) and not geared towards the use of them in operational contexts. However we use this social science theory as starting point. They have proposed a representation of social practices based on three broad categories [18]: materials, meanings and competences.

- Material: covers all physical aspects of the performance of a practice, including the human body (relates to physical aspects of a situation).
- Meaning: refers to the issues which are considered to be relevant with respect to that material, i.e. understandings, beliefs and emotions (relates to social aspects of a situation).
- Competence: refers to skills and knowledge which are required to perform the practice (relates to the notion of deliberation about a situation).

Based on these ideas, we developed a model to represent social practices that can be used in social deliberation by intelligent systems. Obviously, as is the case with e.g. the representation and use of norms, other representations of social practices are possible, given the many dimensions of the use of social practices. Our proposal, depicted in Fig. 3, is especially suitable for use in agent reasoning. The components of this representation model are as follows:

Abstract Social Practice - Visiting a relative	
Physical Context	
Resources	Drinks, chairs, tables
Places	Geometric position of all objects
Actors	a1, a2
Social Context	
Social interpretation	family loved, father respected
Roles	Father(a1), Daughter(a2)
Norms	Father should be autonomous Father should respect Daughter and Daughter respect Father One should tell family about problems
Activities	give advice, give news, chit chat, drink,...
Plan patterns	Inform about news **before** drink If problem **then** give advice **before** leaving Drink **before** leaving
Meaning	Show love and respect
Competences	• Domain knowledge and skills: know preferences family • Coordination skills : know when to drink **Choice/deliberation skills:** • When problems give advice • ...

Abstract Social Practice - Visit of caregiver	
Physical Context	
Resources	medicines, AVICENA tools,
Places	Geometric position of all objects
Actors	a1, a2
Social Context	
Social interpretation	Patient in bad health, caregiver trusted,
Roles	Patient (a1), Non-professionalCaregiver(a2)
Norms	Patient should comply to treatment Caregiver must support patient and respect autonomy of patient Doctor is obliged to try to keep patient alive
Activities	Take medicine, give advice, comfort patient,...
Plan patterns	Comfort patient **before** give medicine Give medicine **before** leaving
Meaning	Show care
Competences	• Domain knowledge and skills: know medicines • Coordination skills : know when to consult **Choice/deliberation skills:** • When patient health is bad consult doctor • When patient refuses medicine start enquiring why • When doctor advices caregiver needs to be able to explain advice • ...

Fig. 3. Abstract social practices

- *Physical Context* describes elements from the physical environment that can be sensed:
  - *Resources* are objects that play a role in the practice such as medicines, wheel chair, water, table and bed in the scenario.
  - *Places* indicates where all objects and actors are located relatively to each other, in space or time.
  - *Actors* are all people and autonomous systems involved, that have capability to reason and (inter)act.
- *Social Context* contains:
  - *Social Interpretation* determines the social context in which the practice is used.
  - *Roles* describe the competencies and expectations about a certain type of actors.
  - *Norms* describe the rules of (expected) behaviour within the practice.
- *Activities* indicate the normal activities that are expected within the practice. Not all activities need to be performed. They are meant as potential courses of action.
- *Plan Patterns* describe usual patterns of actions defined by the landmarks that are expected to occur.
- *Meaning* refers to the social meaning of the activities that are (or can be) performed in the practice. Thus they indicate social effects of actions
- *Competences* indicate the type of capabilities the agent should have to perform the activities within this practice.

Looking at the characteristics of social practices as given in Fig. 3 one can notice some resemblance to the aspects that also play a role in agent organization models (see e.g. [11]). This list can be seen as an analogue of the connection between imposed and emerging norms. Both organizations and social practices give a kind of structure to the interactions between agents. However, organizations provide an imposed (top-down) structure, while the social practices form a structure that arises from the bottom up. Thus where organizational interaction patterns indicate minimal patterns that agents should comply with, the patterns in a social practice indicate minimal patterns that can and are usually used by the agents.

3.4 Social Intelligent Systems

As we argued above socially intelligent agents should use motives, social identity and social practices. Although we will not develop a complete agent architecture for socially intelligent agents in this paper, we sketched some preliminary ideas in [12] where we combine the different aspects. What is important to mention here is that social practices provide a number of triggers that can be checked in the environment such as the time of day, the location, people and available objects. Those physical elements determine whether a social practice is relevant. If so, it can be started and used as a template context in which the agent finds the possible actions, roles, norms and expectations to follow. If any of the parts is not filled in or gives rise to choices the agent will get into its deliberation cycle in order to fill in the choices.

The social identity of an agent plays a major role in two ways. The different parts of the social identity of an agent all correspond to a set of social practices that are normally shared within a group or are seen as ideal behaviour according to a stereotype identity. Thus when a person is in a context where a social identity part is prominent (e.g. family membership when being at home with all family) he will check the social practices pertaining to this social identity.

The second way the social identity plays a role is that when a person identifies a certain social practice to be relevant he will choose his own role in that practice depending on what he expects his social identity will dictate. Thus a family member of the patient with no medical expertise might prefer to play the family role in the practice rather than the caregiver role, because he is not sure whether he will have all competences that would be needed for that role.

Where social practices tie into the reactive side of the agent, being triggered by some elements of the environment, the motives can drive the agent to seek out particular situations that would possibly fulfil that motive. Thus if the need of affiliation is high the agent can try to connect to his friends or family and this move might then lead him to a situation in which he can apply a social practice. In our scenario this can be seen when a family member goes visit a patient and when arriving at the patient noticing that he needs to take his medicine. This situation causes a conflict between family member and caregiver social identities. Whether the family member then takes up the role of caregiver or as family member depends on the experiences in this situation. If the patient gets very irritated and does not take the medicine when advised, the family member might try more subtle ways to attract the attention of the patient to the medicine and act more as family than caregiver.

4   SAwICENA

To motivate how concepts of socially intelligent systems can be applied to *AVICENA* we introduce a representative scenario. Jordi is a 75 year old widower from Barcelona who has three children. The younger one (Barbara) lives in Barcelona, the middle one (Ana) in Amsterdam and the older one (Patricia) in Paris. Jordi is enrolled in the *AVICENA* platform, so he has an electronic pill dispenser for supporting his treatment adherence. Jordi's daughters are responsible for re-filling the pill dispenser when new medication doses are required and taking the patient to the doctor for regular health checks and treatment updates. Jordi spends time with his three daughters visiting them for fourth months each in their respective cities *BCN*, *AMS* and *PAR* where he has a doctor assigned. The patient travels with an electronic health record so the different doctors can update it, keeping track of his state. E-prescription systems are available in *BCN* and *AMS* but not in *PAR*. Therefore legal situations must be considered to allow a smooth transition between the health-care system of the different cities, accounting both legal and technological issues.

The above scenario requires a complex institutional or organizational implementation. This can be modelled in *AVICENA*, but we only refer to this in as far as it pertains to the social aspects of the scenario. First of all, it is clear that Jordi wants to be with all his daughters regularly. Thus his affiliation motive seems to be an important driver for his behaviour. The daughters have two social identities (related to the scenario), they are both daughters and caregivers. With respect to the first identity there is a strong norm that one has to respect and obey one's parents. As a parent, Jordi does not want to be dependent on his children, because as a parent one has to provide for one's children, take care of them, etc., but his medical condition is weakening his abilities to fulfill his father role, and this is creating some internal struggle. The social identity of the daughters as being a caregiver does give them the responsibility to take care of their father's health. This might lead to a situation where they have to give him orders with respect to taking his medication. Thus we see a tension between the two identities. The tension can be resolved in an organisational way by appointing professional caregivers only for the caregiver role. However, this is not very cost efficient and even sometimes impossible due to the fact that Jordi moves around every four months.

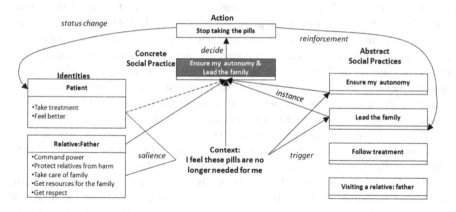

Fig. 4. Social deliberation for father/patient

We use the social practices to analyse the whole scenario. Figure 4 depicts the abstract social practices and identities associated to the patient Jordi and Fig. 5 the ones associated to his daughter Barbara. Those figures show snapshots of the social deliberation process during one of Jordi's visits to Barbara. The routine Jordi has to visit each of his daughters in turn every four months can be seen as a social practice. This social practice (*Visiting a relative*, shown in Fig. 3) stretches over the different locations in Barcelona, Paris and Amsterdam, and the actors involved are Jordi and his daughters. The social interpretation of the social practice is that the father loves his daughters and shows his devotion by visiting them in turn for equal length. The daughters show their love for their

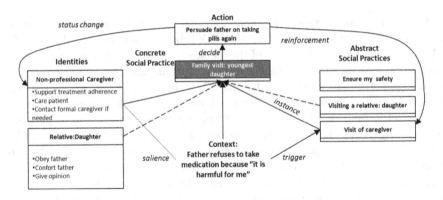

Fig. 5. Social deliberation for daughter/caregiver

father by hosting him for those four months. Thus the social meaning of the practice is to express the status of each in the family that is spread out over Europe. The roles are the father and the daughter role. The norms are that the father will provide for himself as much as possible, that the daughters involve their father in their family life, that the father commits to follow the round robin visits. The activities can be given as very general visiting and interacting of Jordi with his daughters. The plan pattern is just the round robin nature of the visits. The meaning of the whole social practice is to show the family ties and strengthen them. The competences expected are minimal. Jordi should have some financial means to travel and maybe contribute to the staying costs. The daughters should have the competence to cope with their father.

During their social deliberation process, actors' actions are guided by the set of abstract social practices that are triggered by the context. By default, in our scenario the *Visiting a relative* abstract social practice is associated to Jordi's and Barbara's father and daughter identities (*Relative:Father* and *Relative:Daughter* respectively) and instantiated into a concrete social practice (unifying actor variables to Jordi and Barbara). This concrete social practice will guide most of the social behaviour of Jordi and Barbara during his visit. In the same scenario there are other abstract social practices that may apply when medical issues are involved which are associated to Jordi's and Barbara's patient and caregiver social identities (*Follow treatment* and *Visit of caregiver* respectively).

Social practices start conflicting when Jordi's medication makes him feel weak due to some side effects (*e.g.* it causes nausea and dizziness symptoms). In this situation Jordi fears a loss of autonomy (i.e. a loss of power to decide over his own actions). Jordi thinks a father should be strong and provide for his family, so he does not want to be weak in front of his daughters. This situation creates a new context: *Medication makes me feel weak*, which strongly triggers the *ensure my autonomy* behavior. This leads to the familiar concrete social practice (see Fig. 4) where Jordi leads the family and *stops taking the pills*. Due to the electronic AVICENA system, Barbara will notice that her father

Concrete Social Practice - Family visit: youngest daughter	
Physical Context	
Resources	medicines, AVICENA tools,
Places	Geometric position of all objects
Actors	Jordi, Barbara
Social Context	
Social interpretation	Patient in bad health, care giver trusted, family loved
Roles	Patient(Jordi), Father(Jordi), Non-professionalCaregiver(Barbara), Daughter(Barbara)
Norms	Patient should comply to treatment Caregiver must support patient and respect autonomy of Patient Father should respect Daughter and Daughter respect Father Doctor is obliged to try to keep patient alive
Activities	Take medicine, give advice, comfort patient,...
Plan patterns	Comfort patient **before** give medicine Give advice **before** leaving
Meaning	Show love and respect
Competences	• Domain knowledge and skills: know medicines • Coordination skills : know when to consult **Choice/deliberation skills:** • When health bad consult doctor • When patient refuses medicine start enquiring why • When doctor advices caregiver needs to be able to explain advice • ...

Fig. 6. Concrete social practice for daughter/caregiver

is deviating from the prescribed treatment. The social practices of daughter-father interactions do not allow for her to order he father to take the medicine. She will first try to find out why her father did not take the medicine as it might be that he just forgot them. In that case the enquiry could be construed as an interest in her father's health and fit the social practice. However, when she realizes her father has strong arguments against taking the medicines the context changes from one where her father might have been forgetfull to one where he opposes to take the medicine any longer. In the context of (*Father refuses to take medication* as seen in Fig. 5), Barbara extends her identity from the *Relative:Daughter* identity to the *Non-Professional Caregiver* one, so the concrete social practice she was following (which was an instance of *Visiting a relative*) is extended with an instance of the *Visit of caregiver* social practice. The result is a new concrete social practice (shown in Fig. 6) which merges parts from the *Visiting a relative* and *Visit of caregiver* (shown in Fig. 3). By adopting the extended social practice Barbara will then take the action *Persuade father on taking pills again,* making Jordi understand that pills are not harmful. Note that this change cannot be established unilateral. Jordi should also accept that they enter a social practice in which his daughter takes the caregiver role. If he does not accept that role of his daughter they can break up at that point (get into a fight or end the visit). Otherwise, Jordi accepts that his daughter might also be capable as caregiver and accepts his role of patient in the social practice. The ensuing dialogue might cause Jordi to calm his concerns, change priorities among his motives and switch his main social identity from *Relative:Father* to *Patient* where following the treatment is his main concern. In case Barbara had not enough arguments to convince her father, she may contact the doctor to better understand the side effects of those pills or even ask for some advice on how to convince patients like her father.

The next step is to tie all these elements into the scenario where the daughters are somehow co-responsible for the treatment of their father and check whether he takes his medicines. We have established that the father has an intrinsic motive to visit his daughters. The social practice establishes a practical way of realizing this. If we want the *AVICENA* system to support the family such that Jordi will take his medicines at the right time it should connect with this social practice. A simple way to force this is to connect the medicine dispenser to the electronic patient file. While the medicines are dispensed in the correct dose on the right days and times nothing is reported in the electronic patient file. However, whenever there is a deviation this can be marked in the file. If the electronic patient file has several of these marks it might signal this fact and forbid the patient to travel due to health risks. Thus this event will disrupt the social practice. Following the treatment correctly now becomes tied to showing his love to his daughters and is motivated by his affiliation motive. Thus Jordi gets an internal motivation that is in line with his behaviour and makes him aware of the medicines not only from a health perspective, but also from a family perspective.

The above shows already the use of the social aspects in designing the support system. We could also go one step further and include the social aspects in the agents that are part of the *AVICENA* platform. Given that these agents would have an understanding of their role and the role of all the humans in this scenario they can support the patient by aligning their actions with the social practices of the patient. In the above we used the very large social practice of visiting the daughters for a few months. However, their are also daily practices that can be used to combine with dispensing medicines. E.g. with dinner or when the daughter checks in with her father. In that way the visit of the daughter every day becomes combined with taking medicines. This in itself will make it easier for the daughter to remind her father to take the medicines, because it has become part of the visit to take the medicines.

We have given some very preliminary sketches to show the added value of incorporating social aspects in these complex socio-technical systems, but it already indicates its potential at different levels.

5   Related Work

Assistive Technologies (AT) can be effectively used for guiding elderly with their prescribed treatments, avoiding major problems such as non-compliance with the treatment and adverse drug reaction. There exists a range of different technological approaches, from the use of smart devices by patients (such as smart pill dispensers [13]) to Ambient Intelligence [1, 28] (AmI) environments supporting independent living. The specific area of health monitoring devices is currently characterised by application-specific and hardware-specific solutions that are mutually non-interoperable and are made up of diverse architectures. Furthermore, systems mainly focused on activity monitoring and reminders tend to be rejected by end users, who may end up feeling that the system becomes too intrusive on their privacy [25]. Research on smart home environments and Ambient Assisted Living is moving towards a more holistic view, trying to create not only patient-centric AmI solutions, but also connecting the patient with other relevant actors in their medical treatments or event connecting patients to avoid isolation and depressive attitudes. In the rest of the section we will focus on some agent-oriented AmI solutions that are close to the work presented in the paper.

The GerAmi project [8] creates a networked AmI solution where agents are used to enhance communication and work scheduling, effectively making profesional caregivers' working hours more productive. Based in the THOMAS organizational architecture [4], roles, organizational units and norms have been modelled. However, none of the articles explaining the THOMAS architecture analysed so far includes a clear example of such organizational definition, or how norms are operationalised. Furthermore, social concepts such as social identity, social relations, values or social practices are not present in the framework.

$COMMODITY_{12}$ [20] focuses on providing advice, recommendations and alerts to diabetic patients based on their data, and at the same time assist medical personnel, who is in charge of these patients, facilitating informed and timely decisions. The system consists in two main components: first, a set of devices that collect health-related data (e.g., activity and body signals). Second, a set of personal agents with expert biomedical knowledge that interpret the data via a reasoning process to generate a high level representation of patient's health status. These interpretations are then provided to relevant actors in the scenario (e.g., patients and health care professionals) in the form of feedback reports. The main idea is integrating sensors, intelligent agents, knowledge bases and users within a single system. The work introduces the $\mathcal{LAMA}$ architecture for developing software agents that can reason about a medical domain. Agents are deployed using the GOLEM agent platform [5]. Unlike other approaches analysed (e.g., GerAmi and $AVICENA$) $COMMODITY_{12}$ does not explicitly define the social structure where agents and devices operate. In $COMMODITY_{12}$ norms are reflected implicitly in the behaviours of the agents. Furthermore, the representation of the social context in $COMMODITY_{12}$ is not explicit but recent research [21,22] demonstrates it can be acquired through lifestyle activity recognition of patient's interaction with the system.

In [2] a system for automated real-time monitoring of medical protocols is proposed. The system consists on two main components. First, a domain-independent language for protocol specification, accompanied by a user-friendly specification tool that allows health care experts to model a medical protocol and translate into the systems protocol specification language. Second, a semi-autonomous system that understands the protocols and supervises their application. Medical services are modelled as agents, and a medical protocol is interpreted as a negotiation process between agents. The system is able to observe the negotiation, effectively warning about forbidden actions and decisions. The system is applied to health care environments where every staff person plays one or more roles. A role specifies a particular service (e.g., infirmary, surgery, *etc.*) and a medical protocol specifies possible interactions between the different services in front of a particular pathology. The protocol can suggest or forbid medical decisions depending on the medical history and evolution of the patient. Agent interactions are performed as message exchanges through a communication layer. *Supervisor agents* track such interactions and validate them. Suggested actions correspond to medical guidelines and forbidden actions to medical protocols. However, the social model is too protocol-driven, and there is no way to model important issues such as, e.g., the patients' motives.

Robot ecologies [29] are a growing paradigm in agent-based AmI in which several robotic systems are integrated into a smart environment. Such systems hold great promises for elderly assistance. Robocare [6] is a project deployed on a domestic test-bed environment that combines a tracking component for people and robots and a task execution-supervision-monitoring component. The system is composed of several software and hardware agents, each providing a set of services, and an event manager that processes requests to the different services and directs them to the appropriate agents. The system also includes a monitoring agent, with knowledge of the assisted person's usual schedule. However, agent coordination and monitoring are heavy computational processes, limiting the tested scenarios to only 2–3 persons and only a small portion of the domestic environment. The ILSA (Independent LifeStyle Assistant) project [17] passively monitors the behaviours of the inhabitants of the residential laboratory, alerting relatives in case of potentially dangerous situations (*e.g.*, the user falls). ILSA presents two main innovations with regards to the Robocare project: (1) agents autonomously interact within them in order to achieve their goals, without the need of an event manager agent that coordinates them (but a centralized coordination agent is used to transform context-free perceptions provided by the agents into context-aware perceptions); and (2) agents are able to learn schedules based on the daily tasks performed by the inhabitants. However, once a schedule has been learned, the user is not able to deviate from it without raising an alarm. Focus in both systems is on activity monitoring and the coordination between the human and the artificial devices, and thus other social aspects such as the patients' relationship with caregivers are not part of the model.

An interestingly rich model is the AOE^2 framework presented in [7]. AOE^2 integrates (in a model that is both general and coherent) the main concepts to be considered in order to build an agent-based simulator for the particular domain of health care. It is able to reproduce the behaviour of the social system by presenting the decision making entities of the studied system as agents. The main idea behind the AOE^2 framework is focusing in high level conceptual issues regarding the health care model development process, while offering a guideline for carrying out this process independently of technical choices. The idea of applying a framework to agent-based simulations in the healthcare domain is appealing. The complexity and dynamics of the domain (e.g., the high degree of uncertainty inherent to clinical processes, the involvement of multiple distributed service providers and decision makers, *etc.*) make it useful for applying agent-based simulations. Furthermore, the approach is also valid for providing a tool able to asses the possible outcomes of the different actions that can be taken in order to improve the system, making it more efficient or sustainable from an economic point of view. However the model does not include mental models of the individuals' motives, values and social identities, thus being unable to tackle the informal relations that we are trying to model in our work.

6 Conclusion and Future Work

In this paper we have shown the potential of extending the *AVICENA* system with social intelligence. We have outlined which social aspects seem of particular importance. I.e. *social motives*, *social identity* and *social practice*. We have sketched their role in the agent deliberation and have shown their use both in the design of a socially intelligent system as well as how individual agents could profit from these social enhancements.

From the *AVICENA* perspective, we have moved from previous models, based on a full normative description of the expected (goal-driven) behaviour by all actors fully enacting roles into a new, richer model where motive-driven actors may (partially) enact one or several social identities at the same time, guiding their behaviour by a composition of the social practices that are applicable to the social context they perceive.

This paper only describes some preliminary steps of or work. One of the next steps we plan to take is to give a more formal representation of the social aspects such that we can give a more precise and formal account of their influence on the agent deliberation. We hope to do some of this work while actually starting on an implementation of the scenario in *AVICENA*.

A second important step is to describe the relations between all these different aspects in an agent deliberation not just for particular scenarios but also in a more generic way. I.e. do agents always start with social practices and then decide on actions based on their motives or decide upon their roles in the social practice based on their identity? Or do they start with their identity and find social practices fitting with that identity? Or even better, is there no fixed order but is that determined by the situation?

As can be seen there are many interesting issues that should be looked into, but this paper shows at least that these are issues worth investigating.

Acknowledgments. Ignasi Gómez-Sebastia's work has been partially funded by the Torres Quevedo program of the Spanish Ministry of economy and competitiveness.

References

1. Acampora, G., Cook, D.J., Rashidi, P., Vasilakos, A.V.: A survey on ambient intelligence in healthcare. Proc. IEEE **101**(12), 2470–2494 (2013)
2. Alsinet, T., Ansótegui, C., Béjar, R., Fernández, C., Manyà, F.: Automated monitoring of medical protocols: a secure and distributed architecture. Artif. Intell. Med. **27**(3), 367–392 (2003)

3. Álvarez-Napago, S., Cliffe, O., Padget, J.A., Vázquez-Salceda, J.: Norms, organisations and semantic web services: the ALIVE approach. In: Workshop on Coordination, Organization, Institutions and Norms at MALLOW 2009 (2009)
4. Bajo, J., Fraile, J.A., Pérez-Lancho, B., Corchado, J.M.: The THOMAS architecture in home care scenarios: a case study. Expert Syst. Appl. **37**(5), 3986–3999 (2010)
5. Bromuri, S., Stathis, K.: Situating cognitive agents in GOLEM. In: Weyns, D., Brueckner, S.A., Demazeau, Y. (eds.) EEMMAS 2007. LNCS, vol. 5049, pp. 115–134. Springer, Heidelberg (2008). doi:10.1007/978-3-540-85029-8_9
6. Cesta, A., Oddi, A., Smith, S.F.: A constraint-based method for project scheduling with time windows. J. Heuristics **8**, 109–136 (2002). http://dx.doi.org/10.1023/A:1013617802515
7. Charfeddine, M., Montreuil, B.: Toward a conceptual agent-based framework for modelling and simulation of distributed healthcare delivery systems. CIRRELT (2008)
8. Corchado, J.M., Bajo, J., Abraham, A.: GerAmi: improving healthcare delivery in geriatric residences. IEEE Intell. Syst. **23**(2), 19–25 (2008)
9. Dignum, F., Prada, R., Hofstede, G.: From autistic to social agents. In: AAMAS 2014, pp. 1161–1164, May 2014
10. Dignum, F., Dignum, V., Prada, R., Jonker, C.M.: A conceptual architecture for social deliberation in multi-agent organizations. Multiagent Grid Syst. **11**(3), 147–166 (2015)
11. Dignum, V.: A Model for organizational interaction: based on agents, founded in logic. SIKS Dissertation Series 2004-1, Ph.D. thesis, Utrecht University (2004)
12. Dignum, V., Dignum, F.: Contextualized planning using social practices. In: Ghose, A., Oren, N., Telang, P., Thangarajah, J. (eds.) COIN 2014. LNCS, vol. 9372, pp. 36–52. Springer, Cham (2015). doi:10.1007/978-3-319-25420-3_3
13. Georgia Institute of Technology: Aware Home Research initiative. Technical report, Georgia Institute of Technology (2012). http://www.cc.gatech.edu/fce/ahri/projects/index.html
14. Gómez-Sebastià, I.: NoMoDei: a framework for norm monitoring on dynamic electronic institutions. Ph.D. thesis, Universitat Politecnica de Catalunya (2016)
15. Gómez-Sebastià, I., Garcia-Gasulla, D., Álvarez-Napagao, S., Vázquez-Salceda, J., Cortés, U.: Towards an implementation of a social electronic reminder for pills. In: VII Workshop on Agents Applied in Health Care (2012)
16. Gómez-Sebastià, I., Garcia-Gasulla, D., Álvarez-Napago, S.: Society of situated agents for adaptable eldercare. ERCIM News **87**, 23–24 (2011)
17. Haigh, K.Z., Kiff, L.M., Myers, J., Guralnik, V., Geib, C.W., Phelps, J., Wagner, T.: The independent lifestyle assistant (I.L.S.A.): AI lessons learned. In. The Sixteenth Innovative Applications of Artificial Intelligence Conference (IAAI-04), pp. 25–29 (2004)
18. Holtz, G.: Generating social practices. JASSS **17**(1), 17 (2014). http://jasss.soc.surrey.ac.uk/17/1/17.html
19. Istepanian, R., Laxminarayan, S., Pattichis, C.S.: M-Health. Springer, New York (2006)
20. Kafalı, Ö., Bromuri, S., Sindlar, M., van der Weide, T., Aguilar Pelaez, E., Schaechtle, U., Alves, B., Zufferey, D., Rodriguez-Villegas, E., Schumacher, M.I., et al.: Commodity 12: a smart e-health environment for diabetes management. J. Ambient Intell. Smart Environ. **5**(5), 479–502 (2013)

21. Kafalı, Ö., Romero, A.E., Stathis, K.: Activity recognition for an agent-oriented personal health system. In: Dam, H.K., Pitt, J., Xu, Y., Governatori, G., Ito, T. (eds.) PRIMA 2014. LNCS (LNAI), vol. 8861, pp. 254–269. Springer, Cham (2014). doi:10.1007/978-3-319-13191-7_21
22. Luštrek, M., Cvetkovic, B., Mirchevska, V., Kafalı, Ö., Romero, A.E., Stathis, K.: Recognising lifestyle activities of diabetic patients with a smartphone. In: Proceedings of Pervasive Health 2015: Workshop on Personal Health Systems for Chronic Diseases (to be puslished)
23. McClelland, D.: Human Motivation. Cambridge University Press, Cambridge (1987)
24. National Council on Patient Information and Education: Enhancing prescription medicine adherence: a national action plan. Technical report, National Council on Patient Information and Education (2007)
25. Niemelä, M., Gonzalez Fuentetaja, R., Kaasinen, E., Lorenzo Gallardo, J.: Supporting independent living of the elderly with mobile-centric ambient intelligence: user evaluation of three scenarios. In: Schiele, B., Dey, A.K., Gellersen, H., Ruyter, B., Tscheligi, M., Wichert, R., Aarts, E., Buchmann, A. (eds.) AmI 2007. LNCS, vol. 4794, pp. 91–107. Springer, Heidelberg (2007). doi:10.1007/978-3-540-76652-0_6
26. Population Division UN Department of Economic Social Affairs: Population ageing and development: ten years after Madrid. Technical report. 2012/4, Population Division UN Department of Economic Social Affairs, December 2012
27. Reckwitz, A.: Toward a theory of social practices. Eur. J. Soc. Theor. 5(2), 243–263 (2002)
28. Sadri, F.: Ambient intelligence: a survey. ACM Comput. Surv. (CSUR) 43(4), 36 (2011)
29. Saffiotti, A., Broxvall, M., Gritti, M., LeBlanc, K., Lundh, R., Rashid, J., Seo, B., Cho, Y.J.: The PEIS-ecology project: vision and results. In: IEEE/RSJ International Conference on Intelligent Robots and Systems, IROS 2008, pp. 2329–2335. IEEE (2008)
30. Schäfer, G.: Europe in Figures. Eurostat Statistical Yearbook (2008)
31. Shove, E., Pantzar, M., Watson, M.: The Dynamics of Social Practice. Sage, Thousand Oaks (2012)
32. World Health Organization: Adherence to long-term therapies. Evidence for action. Technical report, World Health Organization (2003)

"How Did They Know?"—Model-Checking for Analysis of Information Leakage in Social Networks

Louise A. Dennis[1]($\boxtimes$), Marija Slavkovik[2], and Michael Fisher[1]

[1] Department of Computer Science, University of Liverpool, Liverpool, UK
L.A.Dennis@liverpool.ac.uk
[2] Department of Information Science and Media Studies,
University of Bergen, Bergen, Norway

Abstract. We examine the use of model-checking in the analysis of information leakage in social networks. We take previous work on the formal analysis of digital crowds and show how a variation on the formalism can naturally model the interaction of people and groups of followers in intersecting social networks. We then show how probabilistic models of the forwarding and reposting behaviour of individuals can be used to analyse the risk that information will leak to unwanted parties. We illustrate our approach by analysing several simple examples.

1 Introduction

Can we use formal verification to check whether the privacy settings for accessing posted content in social media are effective? In this work we make the first steps towards answering this question in the positive.

The proliferation of social network services has made it possible for vast amounts of contributed content to be shared online by users who simultaneously are members of more than one social network service (SNS). Consider, for simplicity, one SNS user; let us call him Bob. Most social network services allow for various privacy settings to be specified, which should allow Bob to control who can access or further propagate the content he contributes. We say "should allow control" instead of "does allow control" because, in reality, it is not Bob's privacy settings that ultimately determine accessibility to his shared content, but the combination of the privacy settings of Bob and the privacy settings of all of the users to whom Bob has allowed access to his shared content, *i.e.*, Bob's *followers*. In the same vein let us call Bob's *followees* all the users who have allowed access to their shared content to Bob. What is worse with respect to Bob's control over the privacy of his shared content, is that many of his followers may be users of more than one SNS, with automated interfacing set to synchronise their activities among all the mediums either because one social network allows direct linkage with the API of another (e.g., Livejournal[1] allows posts to be automatically reposted as a link to Facebook[2]) or via third party synchronisation services

---

[1] livejournal.com.
[2] facebook.com.

© Springer International Publishing AG 2017
S. Cranefield et al. (Eds.): COIN 2016 Workshops, LNAI 10315, pp. 42–59, 2017.
DOI: 10.1007/978-3-319-66595-5_3

such as IFTTT[3] and Zapier[4] which allow users to create customised rules to link their SNS accounts to each other (and often to additional services and devices such as home automation tools, calendars, alerts and emails). It is thus very difficult for Bob to track *information leakage* – information that Bob shares with his followers, but reach other agents who are not directly authorised to share it. We give a very simple example of information leakage.

Let Bob and his friend Cathy both be members of social network service SN1. Cathy and Bob are within each others' networks on SN1, meaning they are both each other's followers and followees. In turn Bob's boss, Jim, is neither a follower nor a followee of Bob. Bob regularly posts content on SN1 and has chosen to make his content visible only to his followers, believing that his boss cannot access them. Bob makes really sure of this, he checks Cathy's followers and makes sure Jim is not among them. However Cathy and Jim are within each others networks on SN2 and Cathy automatically synchronises her posts between these two SNSs. Bob, having a hard day, complains about his boss on SN1. Cathy, sympathising with Bob acknowledges Bob's message thus making it visible to her followers on SN1, but due to her content synchronisation with SN2, Bob's message also becomes visible to Cathy's followers on SN2. As a result Jim finds out what Bob really thinks of him and rescinds his planned promotion.

It is not simple for one user such as Bob to keep track of all possible combinations of privacy settings within his network and their ultimate effect on content accessibility. Therefore we propose that this task of checking the effective content visibility, *i.e.*, the risk of information leakage occurring, should be automated. As a possible means to accomplish such automation, we propose formal verification. Our aim is to make it feasible for social network services to regularly model-check [4] user settings to ensure that the content privacy settings are effective and efficient, although we are aware that this is a very hard theoretical and engineering problem.

Formal verification is the process of establishing, typically via techniques based on formal logic, that a designed system has its intended properties. Such approaches have become widespread, enabling deep and (semi) automated formal analysis of both software and hardware systems so providing greater clarity concerning reliability and correctness. While logical proof techniques can be used, it is exhaustive state-space exploration, in the form of *model-checking* [4], that is the predominant approach. As we wish to formally model SNSs, our aim here is to utilise formal verification tools to automatically verify their behaviour. In particular, we wish to establish formal properties concerning information leakage using automatic *model-checking* systems.

Consequently we begin, in Sects. 2 and 3 by considering the general class of systems and a specific formal model for these based on similar work for namely digital crowds [25] Indeed, the formal model here provides a simplification of that in [25] in that agents have much more limited capabilities. We then consider how model-checking can be used to analyse information leakage properties within

---

[3] ifttt.com.

[4] zapier.com.

this framework. This we do in Sect. 4, utilising the PRISM probabilistic model-checker [12]. Finally, in Sect. 5, we provide concluding remarks, incorporating both related and future work.

2   System Representation

A *rational* agent is an agent that is capable of obtaining information about her environment, including other agents, and using this information to select actions in order to achieve her goals [27]. A multi-agent system (MAS) is a system of agents that share the same environment and can cooperate or compete within it, as well coordinate their actions. A system of social network services (SNSs) and their users is not a "traditional" MAS, foremost because the networks are not considered to be agents. We propose that since the SNS does obtain information about the users it hosts, and adapts its services and information to the particular needs of specific users, it can be modelled as a rational agent. We use the catch-all phrase "social agent" to refer to both SNSs and their users. We now discuss how to represent a social agent, so that we can formally analyse her properties.

A rational agent can be represented by representing her mental attitudes, in particular her dynamic, informational and motivation aspects. This is exemplified by the popular BDI paradigm for representing agents via mental attitudes [20,21]. "BDI" denotes *Beliefs, Desires,* and *Intentions*. In terms of the analysis of information leakage we are primarily interested in the informational aspects of rational agency and so in what follows we will ignore the issue of an agent's desires and intentions[5].

As flexible and powerful as the BDI paradigm is, it is not completely suited for representing social agents since the mental attitudes of these agents, particularly if they are a SNS, are not available or they may not be visible. *E.g.*, a SNS may not have access to what Bob truly believes about his boss, only to what Bob has posted about his boss. Bob can know who Cathy's followers are on the SNS they share, but not on the SNSs they do not have in common. For reasons such as these, work in [25] introduces a new mental state, the communicational attitudes to describe the information about herself an agent shares with the world; $M^{\uparrow i}\varphi$ is used[6] to describe that the modelled agent has communicated φ to i, while $M^{\downarrow i}\varphi$ is used to describe that the modelled agent has received communication φ from agent i.

An agent can be modelled by only using communicational attitudes, when nothing of the private beliefs or goals of the agent is known. The agent representation in [25] builds upon formal agent organisational structures introduced in [8] and further studied in [7,10]. An extended agent, as given in [8], is one for which in addition to the agent's mental attitudes, two further sets of agents (or agent identifiers) are added, *content* and *context*, allowing for both simple

---

[5] Though note that these could be included.

[6] In [25], the formulas $M^{\uparrow i}\varphi$ and $M^{\downarrow i}\varphi$ have also subscripts that denote the nature of the communication, *i.e.*, whether it expresses a question, a statement, or an order, but we here only use statements and thus omit subscripts.

agents and a system of agents to be represented using the same model. Content and context sets of agents are related, specifically if agent A_1 is in the content set of agent A_2 then A_2 is in the context set of A_1.

An extended agent, as defined in [7,10], can further include an agent's specification that is visible, or accessible, to the agent's content or context respectively. This paradigm of extended agents is particularly suitable for modelling the visibility of posted content. We thus arrive at our model of social agents. Social agents model the individuals who use social networks and the avatars they maintain on each network. An individual has all the avatars of their followees in their context set and their own avatars in their content set. Each avatar's content contains the agent's followers on that social network while its context contains the individual who owns the avatar and any other agents or services to whom they have given posting access.

The model of a social agents and avators is given in Fig. 1. The mental attitudes of the social agent are private and it is not necessary to include any information in this agent part in order to specify a social agent. The information the agent shares to the avatar is made accessible by the avatar to the agents that are her followers.

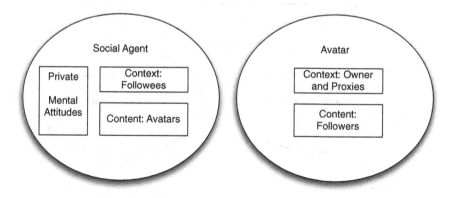

Fig. 1. Basic structure of socal agents and avatars.

Using this social agent structure, we can construct a model for the simple information leakage example outlined in Sect. 1. This model is given on Fig. 2.

3   Formal System Specification

The systems we need to specify are the SNS and their users. We represent both networks and users as extended agents using a simplification of the extended agent representation given in [25]. In [25], additional modalities were used to express language abilities as well as the type of the message that the agent sends or receives, linguistic structures that we do not have need for here.

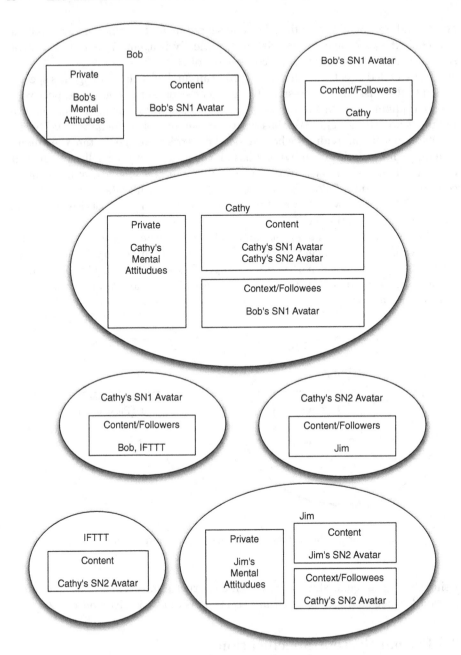

Fig. 2. The system of social agents from Sect. 1

Let Agt be a set of unique agent identifiers, let $Prop$ be a set of atomic propositions and constants, and $Pred$ be a set of a first-order predicates of arbitrary arity. We begin by defining a language $\mathcal{L}_p$ to be a set of grounded first order logic formulas without function symbols, namely the set of all φ_p such that

$$\varphi_p ::= p \mid \neg\varphi_p \mid \varphi_p \wedge \varphi_p \mid P(x_1, \ldots, x_m)$$

where $p \in Prop$, $P \in Pred$ and $x_1, \ldots, x_m \in Agt$.

Depending on the specific needs for a specification, different BDI operators can be used but, for demonstrating our specification approach, we use only the modal operator B which denotes the agent's informational attitudes. $\mathcal{L}_{BDI}$ is then the set of all formulas φ such that

$$\varphi ::= \varphi_p \mid B\varphi_p \mid \neg\varphi \mid \varphi \wedge \varphi$$

where $\varphi_p \in \mathcal{L}_p$.

Finally, we define the language for specifying communication among agents, $\mathcal{L}_M$. For this language we add operators to indicate the sending and receiving of messages. The language $\mathcal{L}_M$ is the set of all formulas θ such that

$$\theta ::= M^{\downarrow j}\varphi_p \mid M^{\uparrow j}\varphi_p \mid \neg\theta \mid \theta \wedge \theta$$

where $i, j \in Agt$ and $\varphi \in \mathcal{L}_{BDI}$. In [25], temporal information can be included in message formulas but we ignore that possibility here.

The messages are sent to an agent j, however either the *context* set CX or the *content* set CN as a whole can be the target of message broadcast (in the general model, both are agents). We use the shorthand[7]

$$M^{\uparrow CN}\varphi_p \equiv \bigwedge_{j \in CN} M^{\uparrow j}\varphi_p, \qquad M^{\uparrow CX}\varphi_p \equiv \bigwedge_{j \in CX} M^{\uparrow j}\varphi_p.$$

We interpret $M^{\downarrow j}\varphi_p$ as "Agent j told me that φ_p holds", while $M^{\uparrow j}\varphi_p$ we read as "I told agent j that φ_p holds". The formulas in the scope of a message operator are propositional logic formulas. The language $\mathcal{L}_{BDI}$ restricts the nesting of modal operators, while $\mathcal{L}_M$ forbids the use of BDI operators inside of the scope of a message operator and does not allow nesting of M operators. Nested messages express meta communication, allowing agents to communicate about what was communicated to them or by them. However, such nesting is not meaningful in our work here.

We can now give the following definition of an agent.

Definition 1. *Let Agt be a set of unique agent identifiers. An agent is a tuple $\langle ID, Bel, Com, CN, CX \rangle$, where $ID \in Agt$ is a unique agent identifier, $Bel \subset \mathcal{L}_p$*

---

[7] **Note:** We define the messages with individual agents, not sets as in [7,8,10], because a message can be broadcast to many agents, but it can be sent from one agent only, otherwise the sender is unknown, which cannot happen here — if your contexts sends you a message it is from exactly one context.

is the set of beliefs the agent holds about the world, $Com \subset \mathcal{L}_M$ is the set of messages the agent has received and sent, $CN \in \mathcal{P}(Agt \setminus \{ID\})$ is the set of agents contained and lastly $CX \in \mathcal{P}(Agt \setminus \{ID\})$ is the set of agents in which the agent is contained, i.e., its set of contexts, where $\mathcal{P}(S)$ is the power set of S. The set Bel is consistent and simplified.

In order to specify agents we have a language $\mathcal{L}_S$ of formulas φ_S

$$\varphi_s ::= \varphi_{BDI} \mid \varphi_M \mid CN(i) \mid CX(i)$$

where $i \in Agt$, $\varphi_{BDI} \in \mathcal{L}_{BDI}$ and $\varphi_M \in \mathcal{L}_M$.

Definition 2. *Given an agent* $i \in Agt$, *an agent specification describes the agent's state as some point in time. An agent specification is a set* $SPEC(i) \subset \mathcal{L}_S$, *where* $B\varphi$ *is true iff* $\varphi \in Bel$, $CN(j)$ *is true iff* $j \in CN$, $CX(j)$ *is true iff* $j \in CX$ *and* $M^{\downarrow i}\varphi_p$ *is true if* $M^{\downarrow i}\varphi_p \in Com$ *and* $M^{\uparrow i}\varphi_p$ *is true if* $M^{\uparrow i}\varphi_p \in Com$.

Note that we do not develop an axiomatisation for $\mathcal{L}_S$ and do not intend to prove soundness for this language, because we aim ultimately to use it to create specifications for model checking, where soundness is not necessary. The above, together with standard modal and temporal logic semantic structures [26], provides a formal basis for describing agents and SNSs, communication and, hence, behaviour.

In order to specify the behaviour of a system for model-checking we combine probabilistic and temporal operators.

$$\alpha ::= \mathtt{true} \mid \varphi_s \in SPEC(i) \mid \alpha \wedge \alpha \mid \neg\alpha \mid \mathrm{P}^{=n}\psi$$

$$\psi := \alpha \mathbf{U} \alpha \mid \bigcirc \alpha$$

where $i \in Agt$ $\varphi_s \in \mathcal{L}_S$, $0 \leq n \leq 1$. This is a simplication of the fragment of PCTL used in the PRISM model checker [9] but which uses statements about the inclusion of formulae in an agent specification instead of atomic propositions. The intuitive interpretation of our probabilistic operator: $P^{=n}\psi$ means that there is a probability of n that ψ is true. For our temporal logic operators $p\mathbf{U}q$ means that p is continuously true up until the point when q becomes true; $\bigcirc r$ means that r is true in the next moment in time. We will use the syntax $\Diamond\phi$ for $\mathtt{true}\mathbf{U}\phi$ which means that ϕ will be true at some moment in the future.

Finally, we assume, via (1), that if a message is sent then it will eventually be received. This is a property of communication among agents that should hold in the environment, for communication to be meaningful.

$$\forall i, j \in \mathrm{Agt}, M^{\uparrow j}\varphi_p \in SPEC(i) \Rightarrow \mathrm{P}^{=1}\Diamond M^{\downarrow i}\varphi_p \in SPEC(j) \qquad (1)$$

Here and in Definition 3 that follows, we use quantifiers. Note that this is only a slight abuse of notation to improve readability. The quantification is over the subset of agents which is finite, thus the quantified formulas stand as a shorthand for a set of formulas grounded for each $i \in \mathrm{Agt}$.

In order to consider communication among social networks, let us define the concept of *reachability* between two agents i and j. The agent i can reach agent j if, and only if, a message sent from i is eventually forwarded to j, under the assumption that avatar agents relay messages from one of their context agents to their followers. To help analyse this in social networks we define an *avatar context*. This is one which broadcasts to all its content agents the messages received from its context agents (*i.e.*, the agent for which it is an avatar or proxies or services authorised by that agent).

Definition 3. *Let i be an agent s.t. $CX(i) \neq \varnothing$. Agent i is an* avatar context *when all the messages sent to i by an agent in its context are sent on to all of its content agents:*

$$\forall j \in CX(i).(M^{\downarrow j}\varphi_p \to M^{\uparrow CN}\varphi_p) \in SPEC(i)$$

To show that information leakage to agent j does not happen to content posted by agent i we need to show that $SPEC(i_{av})$ (the specification for i's avatar) satisfies property (2):

$$(M^{\downarrow i}\varphi_p \wedge \neg CN(j)) \in SPEC(i_{av}) \to \neg \exists k.P^{=0} \Diamond M^{\downarrow k}\varphi_p \in SPEC(j) \qquad (2)$$

Recall that if i_{av} is an avatar of i then CN are her followees on that network. The property (2) states that it is not possible that what is posted to followers of i on any network where she has an avatar can be received by j who is not among i's followers.

Upon this basic framework we will now consider formal verification of key properties. To explain this, we will work through a relatively simple series of examples, showing the properties that can be formally established via model-checking.

4 Model Checking Information Leakage

PRISM [12] is a probabilistic symbolic model-checker in continuous development since 1999, primarily at the Universities of Birmingham and Oxford. Typically a model of a program (or in our case a network of agents) is supplied to PRISM in the form of a probabilistic automaton. This can then be exhaustively checked against a property written in PRISM's own probabilistic property specification language, which subsumes several well-known probabilistic logics including PCTL, probabilistic LTL, CTL, and PCTL*. PRISM has been used to formally verify a variety of systems in which reliability and uncertainty play a role, including communication protocols, cryptographic protocols and biological systems [19]. In this paper we use PRISM version 4.1.beta2.

PRISM is an attractive option for modelling agents and social networks in our formalism since its probabilistic aspects allow us to reason not only about which messages are definitely sent and received, but also about the chance, or risk, that information leakage may occur.

We use a simple set of examples in order to illustrate our approach.

4.1 Basic Scenario

Alice, Bob, and Charlie share two social networks, SN1 and SN2. Alice is a follower of Bob on SN1 but Charlie is not. Charlie is a follower of Bob on SN2 but Alice is not. We treat all three agents, Alice, Bob and Charlie as *modules* in PRISM. Following our formalism we also treat the avatars Bob on the two networks as agents and so also as PRISM modules. The avatars of Bob on SN1 and SN2 are both 'avatar' contexts as defined in Definition 3 – i.e. all information from Bob is automatically transmitted to all content members.

The syntax of prism commands is [?label] guard -> prob_1:update_1 + ...+ prob_n:update_n where label is an optional keyword used for synchronisation, guard is a logical formula over the values of global and local variables, prob_1 to prob_n are probabilities which sum to 1 and update_1 to update_n specify changes to the global and local variables.

We modelled our scenario as a *Discrete Time Markov Chain* in PRISM[8]. Therefore '->' indicates a transition from one discrete time step to another. Synchronisation labels force commands in several modules to make a transitions at the same time.

```
module SN1Bob
sn1bob_relays_message: bool init false;

[bobmessagetosn1] bob_sent_message_to_sn1 = true ->
                    1.0:(sn1bob_relays_message' = true);
[sn1bobmessage] sn1bob_relays_message = true ->
                    1.0:(sn1bob_relays_message' = false);


endmodule
```

Fig. 3. A PRISM model of Bob's followees on SN1.

We show the model for Bob's avatar on SN1, SN1Bob, in Fig. 3. In this model bob_sent_message_to_sn1 is a variable in the Bob module that is true if Bob has sent a message to SN1. sn1bob_relays_message is a variable in SN1Bob that is true if SN1 relays a message from bob to all his followees on SN1. SN1Bob contains two PRISM commands, both with synchronisation labels. The first specifies that if Bob has sent a message to SN1 then, with a probability of 1.0, sn1 will relay

---

[8] PRISM allows models to be created as Discrete Time Markov Chains (DTMCs), Continuous Time Markov Chains (CTMCs) and Markov Decisions Procedures (MDPs). Since our models had no continuous or non-deterministic aspects that would have required more complex models we opted to use the simplest of these (DTMCs) in modelling. We opted for a representation based on Markov Chains since they capture stochastic processes well and it seemed plausible that models of information leakage in social networks might need to be cyclic. If the possibility of cyclic models could be ruled out then Bayesian Networks would also be a plausible candidate formalism.

the message. This transition is synchronised with commands in other modules labelled `bobmessagetosn1` (specifically it synchronises with a command in the Bob module that sends the message). The second specifies that if sn1 relays a message then a synchronised transition will take place after which this variable is set to false (pending receipt of a new message from Bob).

To represent the receipt of messages by Bob's followers we use the synchronisation label `sn1bobmessage`. All the commands with this label in all modules make transitions together. In practice this means all Bob's followers receive a message in the same time step. So, for instance, in the representation of Alice in the model, when SN1 relays Bob's message she, with probability 1.0, has a message.

```
[sn1bobmessage] sn1bob_relays_message = true &
                         1.0:(alice_has_message' = true);
```

If there were a second agent, Debbie say, among Bob's SN1 followers then Debbie would contain a similar command.

```
[sn1bobmessage] sn1bob_relays_message = true &
                         1.0:(debbie_has_message' = true);
```

Taken together the synchronised commands in the content agents and the relaying command in `SN1Bob` ensure that `SN1Bob` meets the specification of an avatar context.

4.2   Example 1

In our first, and simplest, example Alice, Bob and Charlie are the only relevant actors on each network. Bob posts a message to SN1. With the simple model and probabilities PRISM tells us that there is a probability of 1 that eventually Alice will receive the message[9]:

$$P^{=1}\Diamond M^{\downarrow sn1bob} \; message \in SPEC(alice) \qquad (3)$$

This is expressed as `P>=1 [F(alice_has_message = true)]` in PRISM's property specification language.

We can also prove that there is probability of zero that Charlie will eventually know the message, since the message was relayed only to Bob's followers on SN1 and not to those on SN2.

$$P^{=0}\Diamond M^{\downarrow sn1bob} \; message \in SPEC(charlie) \qquad (4)$$

---

[9] We use the notation $P^{=n}$ to indicate that there is a probability of n that something will occur.

4.3 Example 2

We now expand our example to consider the addition of a synchronisation agent, SYNC. Bob has set SYNC up so that when he posts a message to SN1 it is forwarded to the SN2 *as if it was Bob doing so* – i.e., he has placed SYNC in the context of his avatar agent on SN2. We use a *global variable* sync_sends_as_bob to represent that sync can send a message as if it were Bob. When this variable is true then the Bob module sends the message to SN2 using the command

```
[] sync_sends_as_bob = true ->
        1.0: (bob_sent_message_to_sn2' = true) &
             (sync_sends_as_bob' = false);
```

The synchronisation agent is shown in Fig. 4.

```
module SYNC
sync_has_message: bool init false;

[sn1bobmessage] sn1bob_relays_message = true &
                            sync_has_message = false ->
                1.0:(sync_has_message' = true);

[] sync_has_message = true ->
                1.0: (sync_has_message' = false) &
                     (sync_sends_as_bob' = true);
endmodule
```

Fig. 4. PRISM model of a simple synchronisation service

So, on receipt of a message from Bob's avatar on the first network, the SYNC agent forwards it to SN2 *as if it was Bob doing so*. Under these circumstances we can use PRISM to show that the probability that eventually Charlie receives the message is 1.

4.4 Example 3

Let us now remove the synchronisation agent and consider the possibility that Bob's followers on SN1 may forward the message to their avatars. Assume both Alice and Debbie follow Bob and that Charlie follows both Alice and Debbie. With both Alice and Debbie there is a possibility of 0.1 that they may forward a message to their avatars.

$$\forall i.M^{\downarrow i}\varphi_p \in SPEC(alice) \Rightarrow P^{=0.1}\lozenge M^{\uparrow sn1alice}\varphi_p \in SPEC(alice) \tag{5}$$

$$\forall i.M^{\downarrow i}\varphi_p \in SPEC(debbie) \Rightarrow P^{=0.1}\lozenge M^{\uparrow sn1debbie}\varphi_p \in SPEC(debbie) \tag{6}$$

The PRISM model for Debbie's behaviour is shown in Fig. 5 (Alice's module is identical except for variable names and labels). We also add new synchronisation

```
module Debbie
debbie_has_message: bool init false;
debbie_sent_message_to_sn1: bool init false;

[] debbie_has_message = true ->
                  0.9:(debbie_has_message' = false)
                + 0.1:(debbie_has_message' = false) &
                      (debbie_sent_message_to_sn1' = true);

[sn1bobmessage] sn1bob_relays_message = true ->
                  1.0:(debbie_has_message' = true);
[debbiemessagetosn1] debbie_sent_message_to_sn1 = true ->
                  1.0:(debbie_sent_message_to_sn1' = false);

endmodule
```

Fig. 5. PRISM model for Debbie

commands to Charlie's model to indicate a receipt of messages from Alice or Debbie's SN1.

In this network PRISM tells us there is a probability of 0.19 that Charlie will eventually receive the message having had it forwarded to him by either Alice or Debbie (or by both of them).

4.5   Example 4

Suppose at the same time that Bob sends his message he requests that it not be reposted. We view this request as the establishment of a norm and assume this further modifies the chance that Alice or Debbie will forward the message to 0.01. We represent this by modifying the behaviour of agents when they have a message as show in Fig. 6:

```
[] debbie_has_message = true & do_not_repost_norm = false ->
                  0.9:(debbie_has_message' = false)
                + 0.1:(debbie_has_message' = false) &
                      (debbie_sent_message_to_sn1' = true);
[] debbie_has_message = true & do_not_repost_norm = true ->
                  0.99:(debbie_has_message' = false)
                + 0.01:(debbie_has_message' = false) &
                      (debbie_sent_message_to_sn1' = true);
```

Fig. 6. PRISM command showing Debbie's behaviour when a norm is in place

Under these circumstances, PRISM tells us that the probability of Charlie receiving drops to 0.0199.

4.6   Example 5

Lastly we combine our various scenarios as follows: Bob is followed by Alice and Debbie on SN1 and by Charlie on SN2. Debbie and Alice are followed by Charlie on SN1. Debbie has a synchronisation agent set up on SN2 to forward her message automatically to SN1. Debbie is not followed by Charlie on SN2. This set up is shown in Fig. 7.

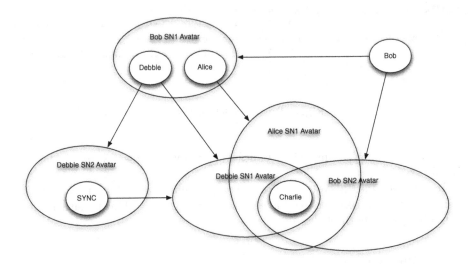

Fig. 7. Social Network for Example 5. Arrows indicate content/context relationships between social agents and their avatars (*i.e.*, "posting privileges"). Content/Context relationships between avatars and followers are shown by inclusion; a social agent appears within the avatars it follows.

If Bob asks that his message *not* be forwarded to Charlie then both Alice and Debbie have a 0.01 probability of reposting the message to SN1. However there is a 0.09 probability that Debbie will forward the message to SN2 since Charlie does not follow her there, forgetting that she has a synchronisation agent set up. In these circumstance the probability that Charlie receives the message is 0.109, either because Alice or Debbie has forwarded it directly to SN1, or because Debbie forwarded it to SN2 and then SYNC reposted it to SN1.

4.7   Results Summary

We summarise the results of our examples in the table below, in each case showing the probability, $P^{=?}$ that Alice, Charlie, Debbie or sync eventually receive Bob's message.

	Example				
	1	2	3	4	5
$P^{=?}\Diamond M^{\downarrow}\varphi \in SPEC(alice)$	1	1	1	1	1
$P^{=?}\Diamond M^{\downarrow}\varphi \in SPEC(charlie)$	0	1	0.19	0.0199	0.109
$P^{=?}\Diamond M^{\downarrow}\varphi \in SPEC(debbie)$	n/a	n/a	1	1	1
$P^{=?}\Diamond M^{\downarrow}\varphi \in SPEC(sync)$	n/a	1	n/a	n/a	0.09

5 Discussion

The analyses of information leakage that we have presented assume that it is possible to gain some information about the composition of interlinked social networks in order to construct a model for analysis. In particular we assume that we can model the probability with which a user will forward messages; that we can gather information about the followers of users on different social networks (and identify users across social networks); and that we can tell when a user is using a synchronisation agent. We will briefly discuss each of these assumptions.

How likely is a user to forward a message? A decision made by an individual user over whether or not to repost a message to their own followers on a Social Network is obviously highly dependent upon the user, the content of the message, and external factors such as the time of day. However some work already exists in modelling the chances that a message becomes disseminated within a social networks [15] so it is reasonable to assume that realistic probabilities could be generated to assess both the risk of messages in general, and of some specific message being forwarded within a network. Adding in assumptions about normative behaviour clearly makes such modelling harder however work also exists in modelling the norms of behaviour on social networking sites [3].

Can we gather information about a user's followers on different social networks and identify users across social networks. While some social networks make the list of a user's followers public, many do not and this obviously presents considerable difficulty in modelling the intersection of these networks. Moreover, for practical reasons the depth of exploration — i.e. the number of forwards — will need to be limited. However, it would not be unreasonable to assume a model in which once a message has been forwarded n times it can count as having "gone viral" and the information therein has irrevocably leaked. We have not considered this possibility here. Typically forwarding of messages happens primarily within the network where the message was generated. In this instance the network itself could choose to offer information leakage analysis from its vantage point of access to all follower groups.

How can we tell if a user is using a synchronisation agent? The main danger of information leakage between networks arises when a user is employing a synchronisation agent. While it is generally easy to tell if a person you follow on a social network is using an agent to repost to that network from some other network, it is considerably harder to tell if they have a synchronisation agent that posts from the network you share to one that you don't. It may be that the existence of such agents for other users will need to be modelled as part of user behaviour. However it is easy to obtain information about synchronisation agents owned by the user wishing to perform a risk analysis. Since users can easily forget that they have set up synchronisations and the synchronisation rules they have may interact in unexpected ways, explicit analysis of these agents remains valuable.

Nevertheless, *in spite of* the difficulty in gaining accurate probabilistic data for the behaviour of humans in the social networks we believe that model-checking does provide a tool which would allow some understanding of the risks of privacy violations and information leaks in social networks. Services which allowed networks to be evaluated on a regular basis in order to asses general risk could be of significant value. While only applied here to very simple examples, we believe the approach described could form the basis for exactly these services.

5.1 Related Work

Padget et al. have considered a formalisation of intersecting networks that has many similar features to ours [16,17]. They use Answer Set programming to identify vulnerabilities and to experiment with normative rules that modify the behaviour of agents within these networks in order to reduce risk. Their analysis is not probabilistic but it is the first example of which we are aware, in which someone applies techniques from formal methods and verification to the analysis of privacy on social networks.

There is a large literature on security models which is obviously of relevance. Most of this literature is focused on access permissions within a single enterprise sytems (e.g., [11]) but [18] introduces socio-technical aspects into the models via the use of obligations and prohibitions and analyses the models for attacks using answer set programming and graph-based models.

"Information leakage" is a term typically used in the context of software engineering, to denote the event when a software system designed to be closed for unauthorised parties reveals some information to them nonetheless. In [14] the use of an agent-based approach to facilitate software information leakage is proposed.

Involuntary information leakage within the context of social network services has been considered for sensitive information, such as personal data and location. A study showed that even if people do not directly reveal their personal information in a social networking service, this may happen indirectly with personal information becoming either directly accessible or inferable from accessible information [13]. Multi-agent system (MAS) technology use is proposed in [1] to assess the vulnerability of particular user profiles on a social network service. Specifically, a software agent is associated with each user profile to extract the user's updates and send them to a controller agent which saves the history of each user and analyses it for possible vulnerabilities.

The DEPNET and DEPINT systems [23, 24] reason about social dependency in multi-agent systems. They allow agents to reason about the goals, actions, resources and plans of other agents in order to decide questions such as coalition formation, or where to send requests. This framework doesn't explicitly model information flow among the agents but represents early work reasoning about social structures in mult-agent systems.

Logic-based representation of social network service users and their interactions is an increasing area of research, although work is mainly aimed at studying the information diffusion in a social network. In particular, [22] proposes a two-dimensional modal logic for reasoning about the changing patterns of knowledge and social relationships in networks. Model-checking as a method for verifying properties of information diffusion in open networks has been studied in [2]. The authors, however, focus on modelling the entire (open dynamic agent) network whereas we are modelling a software agent in a social network service system.

5.2 Further Work

As this paper simply sets out a broad direction, and gives quite simple examples, there is much further work to be done.

Although we define the $\mathcal{L}_{BDI}$ language and we make it part of the agent specification, we do not actually use these kind of formulas in our examples. The language $\mathcal{L}_{BDI}$ specifies the internal, or *private* reasoning of the agent that are not accessible to either his avatars or to other agents. In the future we would like to use this part of the specification to express how an agent reasons with respect to sending and receiving messages. For example, including $M^{\downarrow bob}\varphi \wedge M^{\downarrow debbie}\varphi \rightarrow B\varphi \in SPEC(alice)$ represents that Alice believes some information holds, if she sees it shared by both Bob and Debbie.

In the context of overlapping social network services, it may be more natural to have multiple avatars representing the (real) user in each of the services with the relationships between the avatars included in the specification of the user. This new model would require further analysis of the relationships between an agent's Content/Context on one hand, and her internal specification involving $\mathcal{L}_{BDI}$ formulas and publicly accessible states involving only $\mathcal{L}_{M}$ formulas.

We would also be interested in extending our system to look at, for instance, how information through different routes (e.g. location information sent to one social network service and information about companions sent to another) can be combined to leak key information in unanticipated ways (*e.g.*, someone can now know the location of your companion). Formal verification would surely be more complex but still viable.

The examples we have provided have been built "by hand" and so it would be advantageous to provide a route whereby (some at least) social networks could be automatically extracted into our formalism.

Finally, we here use a relatively standard model-checker, namely PRISM, as we are not primarily concerned with anything more than the beliefs of our agents. As we move to more complex systems it would be ideal to verify complex BDI behaviours. An agent model-checker capable of this exists [6], and indeed this can also be configured to export models to PRISM [5] if probabilistic results are desired. However, it would be ideal to enhance the agent model-checker with explicit content/context constructs in order to facilitate a more direct relationship between our formalism and the model analysed by the tool than we could achieve via a direct translation into PRISM. This would also allow for the practical verification of higher-level properties.

Acknowledgments. This work was partially funded through EPSRC Grants EP/L024845 ("Verifiable Autonomy") and EP/N007565 ("Science of Sensor System Software"). The authors would also like to thank Dagstuhl for their facilities and hospitality, something that provided the impetus for this work.

Access to Data. The PRISM models used in this work will are available in the University of Liverpool's Data Catalogue at DOI:10.17638/datacat.liverpool.ac.uk/163.

References

1. Abdulrahman, R., Alim, S., Neagu, D., Holton, D.R.W., Ridley, M.: Multi agent system approach for vulnerability analysis of online social network profiles over time. Int. J. Knowl. Web Intell. **3**(3), 256–286 (2012). http://dx.doi.org/10.1504/IJKWI.2012.050854
2. Belardinelli, F., Grossi, D.: On the formal verification of diffusion phenomena in open dynamic agent networks. In: Proceedings of International Conference on Autonomous Agents and Multiagent Systems (AAMAS), pp. 237–245 (2015). http://dl.acm.org/citation.cfm?id=2772912
3. Bryant, E.M., Marmo, J.: The rules of facebook friendship: a two-stage examination of interaction rules in close, casual, and acquaintance friendships. J. Soc. Pers. Relat. **29**(8), 1013–1035 (2012). http://spr.sagepub.com/content/29/8/1013. abstract
4. Clarke, E., Grumberg, O., Peled, D.: Model Checking. MIT Press, Cambridge (1999)
5. Dennis, L.A., Fisher, M., Webster, M.: Two-stage agent program verification. J. Logic Comput. (2016). http://logcom.oxfordjournals.org/content/early/2015/02/16/logcom.exv002.abstract
6. Dennis, L.A., Fisher, M., Webster, M., Bordini, R.H.: Model checking agent programming languages. Autom. Softw. Eng. **19**(1), 5–63 (2012)
7. Fisher, M., Dennis, L., Hepple, A.: Modular Multi-Agent Design. Technical report ULCS-09-002, Department of Computer Science, University of Liverpool (2009). http://www.csc.liv.ac.uk/research
8. Fisher, M., Kakoudakis, T.: Flexible agent grouping in executable temporal logic. In: Proceedings of the 12th International Symposium on Languages for Intensional Programming (ISLIP). World Scientific Press (1999)
9. Hansson, H., Jonsson, B.: A logic for reasoning about time and reliability. Formal Aspects Comput. **6**, 102–111 (1994)
10. Hepple, A., Dennis, L., Fisher, M.: A common basis for agent organisation in BDI languages. In: Dastani, M., Fallah Seghrouchni, A., Leite, J., Torroni, P. (eds.) LADS 2007. LNCS (LNAI), vol. 5118, pp. 71–88. Springer, Heidelberg (2008). doi:10.1007/978-3-540-85058-8_5

11. Holm, H., Sommestad, T., Ekstedt, M., Nordström, L.: CySeMol: a tool for cyber security analysis of enterpises. In: 22nd International Conference and Exhibition Electricity Distribution (CIRED 2013), pp. 1–4. IET (2013)
12. Kwiatkowska, M., Norman, G., Parker, D.: PRISM 4.0: verification of probabilistic real-time systems. In: Gopalakrishnan, G., Qadeer, S. (eds.) CAV 2011. LNCS, vol. 6806, pp. 585–591. Springer, Heidelberg (2011). doi:10.1007/978-3-642-22110-1_47
13. Lam, I.-F., Chen, K.-T., Chen, L.-J.: Involuntary information leakage in social network services. In: Matsuura, K., Fujisaki, E. (eds.) IWSEC 2008. LNCS, vol. 5312, pp. 167–183. Springer, Heidelberg (2008). doi:10.1007/978-3-540-89598-5_11
14. Lee, Y.C., Bishop, S., Okhravi, H., Rahimi, S.: Information leakage detection in distributed systems using software agents. In: Proceedings of the IEEE Symposium on Intelligent Agents, pp. 128–135 (2009)
15. Lu, X., Yu, Z., Guo, B., Zhou, X.: Predicting the content dissemination trends by repost behavior modeling in mobile social networks. J. Netw. Comput. Appl. 42, 197–207 (2014). http://www.sciencedirect.com/science/article/pii/S1084804514000599
16. Padget, J., Elakehal, E.E., Satoh, K., Ishikawa, F.: On requirements representation and reasoning using answer set programming. In: 1st International Workshop on Artificial Intelligence for Requirements Engineering (AIRE 2014), Karlskrona, Sweden, pp. 35–42 (2014)
17. Padget, J.A., Satoh, K., Ishikawa, F.: A normative approach to exploring multi-agency privacy and transparency. In: Proceedings of the 7th International Workshop on Juris-informatics (JURISIN 2013), Yokohama, Japan, pp. 9–22 (2013)
18. Pieters, W., Padget, J., Dechesne, F., Dignum, V., Aldewereld, H.: Effectiveness of qualitative and quantitative security obligations. J. Inf. Secur. Appl. 22, 3–16 (2015). http://www.sciencedirect.com/science/article/pii/S2214212614000805. Special Issue on Security of Information and Networks
19. PRISM: Probabilistic Symbolic Model Checker. http://www.prismmodelchecker.org. Accessed 31 May 2013
20. Rao, A.S., Georgeff, M.P.: Modelling agents within a BDI-architecture. In: Proceedings of the International Conference on Principles of Knowledge Representation and Reasoning (KR). Morgan Kaufmann (1991)
21. Rao, A.S., Georgeff, M.P.: BDI agents: from theory to practice. In: Proceedings of the 1st International Conference on Multi-Agent Systems (ICMAS), pp. 312–319 (1995)
22. Seligman, J., Liu, F., Girard, P.: Facebook and the epistemic logic of friendship. In: Proceedings of the 14th Conference on Theoretical Aspects of Rationality and Knowledge (TARK) (2013). http://www.tark.org/proceedings/tark_jan7_13/p.229-seligman.pdf
23. Sichman, J.S.: DEPINT: dependence-based coalition formation in an open multi-agent scenarios. J. Artif. Soc. Social Sim. 1(2) (1998)
24. Sichman, J.S., Conte, R., Demazeau, Y., Castelfranchi, C.: A Social Reasoning Mechanism Based on Dependence Networks, pp. 188–192. John Wiley and Sons (1994)
25. Slavkovik, M., Dennis, L., Fisher, M.: An abstract formal basis for digital crowds. Distrib. Parallel Databases 33(1), 3–31 (2015). http://dx.doi.org/10.1007/s10619-014-7161-y
26. Stirling, C.: Modal and temporal logics. In: Handbook of Logic in Computer Science. Oxford University Press (1992)
27. Wooldridge, M., Jennings, N.R.: Intelligent agents: theory and practice. Knowl. Eng. Rev. 10(2), 115–152 (1995)

A Manifesto for Conscientious Design of Hybrid Online Social Systems

Pablo Noriega[1]([✉]), Harko Verhagen[2], Mark d'Inverno[3], and Julian Padget[4]

[1] IIIA-CSIC, Barcelona, Spain
`pablo@iiia.csic.es`
[2] Stockholm University, Stockholm, Sweden
`verhagen@dsv.su.se`
[3] Goldsmiths, University of London, London, UK
`dinverno@gold.ac.uk`
[4] Department of Computer Science, University of Bath, Bath, UK
`j.a.padget@bath.ac.uk`

Abstract. Online Social Systems such as community forums, social media, e-commerce and gaming are having an increasingly significant impact on our lives. They affect the way we accomplish all sorts of collective activities, the way we relate to others, and the way we construct are own self-image. These systems often have both human and artificial agency creating what we call online hybrid social systems. However, when systems are designed and constructed, the psychological and sociological impact of such systems on individuals and communities is not always worked out in advance. We see this as a significant challenge for which coordination, organisations, institutions and norms are core resources and we would like to make a call to arms researchers in these topics to subscribe a conscientious approach to that challenge.

In this paper we identify a class of design issues that need attention when designing hybrid online social systems and propose to address those problems using *conscientious design* which is underpinned by ethical and social values. We present an austere framework to articulate those notions and illustrate these ideas with an example. We outline five lines of research that we see worth pursuing.

1 Introduction

We are witnessing major social changes caused by the massive adoption of online social systems that involve human users alongside artificial software entities. These hybrid online social systems promise to satisfy and augment our social needs and the rise of such systems and their use are nothing short of spectacular. Because of the speed of their uptake their has been limited research that looks at the relationship between system design and potential long-term psychological, sociological, cultural or political effects.

Examples of the undesirable consequences of such systems (with varying degrees of autonomous agency participation) include:

© Springer International Publishing AG 2017
S. Cranefield et al. (Eds.): COIN 2016 Workshops, LNAI 10315, pp. 60–78, 2017.
DOI: 10.1007/978-3-319-66595-5_4

- the increasing importance of social media expressions and reactions in building and maintaining identity,
- the possibility of determining personal data from facial recognition applications such as *FindFace*,
- the possibility of determining personal information via automatic scrubbing of online dating services such as *OKCupid*,
- the everchanging algorithm for presenting messages on *Facebook*, outside of the control of the user.

The social impact of these applications is magnified by the accessibility of mobile devices, ubiquitous computing and powerful software paradigms that enable innovations in AI to be readily integrated. Despite this, design takes place in an *ad-hoc* and opaque way so that the social consequences of online actions are unknown. The effect of online actions in the real social world is often not understood, we often do not know whether actions are private or public, we cannot be sure of the way in which the actions of others is presented to us, and nor do we know how information about our activity is being used.

As the AI community plays a key role as inventors and builders of the scientific and technological enablers of this phenomenon, we have a moral responsibility to address these issues that requires a sustained, long term commitment from our community. We believe that what is needed is a collective interdisciplinary endeavour across design, sociology, formal methods, interface design, psychology, cultural theory, ethics, and politics to develop a clearer understanding of how we approach and design online social systems. Together we can play an active role in the design of systems where users' understanding of actions, relationships and data is fair and clear. The challenge is great, but then so is the responsibility. Those of us working in the theory, design and implementation of agent-based systems now have a fantastic opportunity to apply our methods and tools in ways which could have impact far beyond that we might have imagined even a few years ago.

This paper then is *a call to arms* for such an initiative, specifically to the COIN community, in the spirit of the "Research Priorities for Robust and Beneficial Artificial Intelligence: an Open Letter". We articulate our proposal around the notion of *conscientious design* as a threefold commitment to a design that is *responsible, thorough* and *mindful*.[1]

Conscientious design starts by developing an awareness of the concerns manifest in the current landscape, and understanding how multi-agent techniques can be applied as an effective means to operationalise systems to ameliorate such concerns, and bring it to bear upon our everyday scientific and technological activity. For this we need to (further) develop theories and models of norms, roles, relationships, languages, architectures, governance and institutions for such systems, and do so in a way that naturally lends itself to interdisciplinary research. We need to be *empiricists* (in applying our techniques to modelling current systems), *theorists* (in building implementable models of hybrid social systems), and *designers* (in designing systems); open to working in a strong *interdisciplinary* way across arts, humanities and social sciences. We may also need to break

---

[1] http://futureoflife.org/static/data/documents/research_priorities.pdf.

away from our natural comfort zones describing idealised scenarios for agents but we can do so when we recognise just how potentially significant the impact of our research can be.

In this paper we postulate the need to address this challenge, propose a focus of attention —Hybrid Online Social Systems (HOSS)— and give a rough outline of what we see as the main research questions. The paper is structured as follows: In Sect. 2 we point to some background references so as to motivate our election of problematic aspects of HOSS and our proposal of conscientious design, addressed in Sect. 3. In Sect. 4 we propose the core ideas —based on the WIT framework [14]— to make conscientious design operational and in Sect. 5 we illustrate these ideas with an example. All these elements are then put together as a research programme towards conscientious design and implementation of HOSS.

2 Background

2.1 The Problem

The range of behaviours that we can carry out online may support all kinds of activity that was not possible even a few years ago. It can affect how we see ourselves, how we choose to communicate, how we value notions of privacy and intimacy, and how we see our value in the world. We are building new metaphors of ourselves while we are in contact with everyone and everybody [7]. The issue that is overlooked by many users is that almost anything that can happen in the real social world —i.e. the one which existed before online systems— can potentially happen in any online one, and worse. We are facing a "Collingridge dilemma" since we do not yet know how to take advantage of the opportunities of this technology and avoid its unwanted consequences but we are justifiably concerned that by the time we understand its side-effects it may be too late to control them [5].

2.2 An Approach to the Solution

We concern ourselves with those systems where there is artificial agency; either because there are software socio-cognitive agents that have some autonomy or because the system infrastructure incorporates agency (such as by actively producing outcomes that are not the ones users expect, or because third parties may interact with that system without the system or its users being aware or intending it to happen). For these "hybrid online social systems", or HOSS, we identify the generic type of features we find problematic and propose a "conscientious" design approach in response.

Our proposal is in tune with the *Onlife Manifesto* [7] and thus aims to respond to the sensitivities and challenges captured in that document. For instance, a *new understanding* of values, new uses of norms and the new guises that their enforcement should take; attention to how values like trust, fairness, solidarity are understood; give users control over the way their own values may become incorporated in the tools they create or adopt. Our proposal can be framed as a part of the "value alignment problem".[2]

Our proposal is akin to the Value-sensitive design (VSD) research framework [8] and similar approaches like *Values in Design* [11] and *disclosive computer ethics* [2]. The main concern in VSD is how values are embedded (mostly unconsciously) in technological artefacts, and postulate that what is usually missing during the design and development phases is a critical reflection upon this unconscious inscription of values. We advocate a *conscientious* approach to put in practice that critical reflection.

VSD offers three "investigation" schemata for inscribing values into the design of systems (i) *conceptual-philosophical* whose aim is to identify relevant values, and relevant direct and indirect stakeholders (not only users), (ii) *empirical* the use of qualitative and quantitative research methods from the humanities and social sciences, to study how people understand and apply values, and (iii) *technical* to determine the role that values play in technologies and how to implement those values identified in the two previous schemata into the systems that are being designed.

We propose a narrower but complementary strategy. We propose to focus attention in those values that are associated with three broad areas of concern that we believe are encompassed by conscientiousness: *thoroughness* (the sound implementation of what the system is intended to do), *mindfulness* (those aspects that affect the individual users, and stakeholders) and *responsibility* (the values that affect others). We postulate an approach to software engineering that is directed towards a particular class of systems (HOSS). It is an approach close to VSD because it rests on a particular categorisation of values but we go further because we understand that those values are instrumented by means of institutional (normative) prescriptions that have an empirical and conceptual grounding, and then implemented through technological artefacts that have a formal grounding. Consequently, while from a teleological point of view we see our approach closer to the ideas of value-sensitive-design, from a technological and methodological point of view, the domain and the proposal are clearly within the COIN agenda.

2.3   The Role of COIN

We believe there is a critical need for a science and discipline of conscientious design for online hybrid social systems that contain human and computational entities. Some of the questions that present themselves to our community are given below.

– How can the agent/AI community collectively recognise this opportunity and spring into action to take part in the development of a science of hybrid online social systems (HOSS) that can lead to their principled design?

---

[2] Stuart Russell: "... *The right response [to AI's threat] seems to be to change the goals of the field itself; instead of pure intelligence,* we need to build intelligence that is provably aligned with human values...". https://www.fhi.ox.ac.uk/edge-article/.

- How can we build models, tools, methods and abstractions that come from our own specialities across agent design, interaction protocols, organisations, norms, institutions and governance to underpin the principled design of software incorporating human and artificial agents?
- How can we encourage and support a greater degree of responsibility in the design of online environments in exactly the same way as an urban planner would feel when designing a new locale?

This is not an easy task as the domain is such a diverse and complex one. This is necessarily an early foray into setting up the challenges of charting this space and defining some of the challenges we face in order to do so and doing so in way in which we can build bridges to other communities. Naturally, we want any undertaking to be wide ranging, to be inclusive so that people from all fields of the agent and AI communities can take part, and where groups from other parties can join with a clear sense of what we mean by a science of online social systems. Studies from other disciplines often lead to important critiques of technological development, what *our community can uniquely provide is a scientific framework* for system design that can both critique current systems but also enable a collective design of future conscientious systems. We will all lose out if there cannot be a collective and interdisciplinary approach to understanding how to design such systems. We need a common technological and scientific framework and language to argue for how we should design the next generation of such systems.

3   Choice of Problems and Approach: Conscientious Design of HOSS

The first challenge we propose to address is to develop a precise characterisation of HOSS. As suggested in [4], this can be approached in two directions.

First a bottom-up task that consists of studying existing HOSS to identify their essential features and typologies. For each typology we suspect there will be particular ways in which desired properties may be achieved. The task would be to elucidate how values like transparency, accountability, neutrality, and properties like hidden agency and such are achieved in the actual systems and look for those design and implementation resources that tell the degree to which those properties exist.

Secondly, a top-down approach would aim to approximate agent-based abstract definitions of ideal classes of HOSS and gradually make them precise in order to *analytically* characterise the features and properties of the HOSS we design and build. Far the moment we will speak of HOSS in not-formal terms from the top-down perspective.

3.1   A Top-Down Characterisation of HOSS

Loosely speaking, HOSS—or perhaps more appropriately *socio-cognitive technical systems*—are IT enabled systems that support collective activities which involve individuals—human or artificial—that reason about social aspects and act within a stable shared social space.

A tentative "analytic" definition of HOSS (from [14]) is:

Notion 1. *A* Hybrid online social sytem (HOSS) *is a multiagent system that satisfies the following assumptions:*

A.1 System. *A socio-cognitive technical system is composed by two ("first class") entities: a social space and the agents that act within that space. The system exists in the real world and there is a boundary that determines what is inside the system and what is out.*

A.2 Agents. *Agents are entities who are capable of acting within the social space. They exhibit the following characteristics:*

    A.2.1 Socio-cognitive. *Agents are presumed to base their actions on some internal decision model. The decision-making behaviour of agents, in principle, takes into account social aspects because the actions of agents may be affected by the social space or other agents and may affect other agents and the space itself [3].*

    A.2.2 Opaque. *The system, in principle, has no access to the decision-making models, or internal states of participating agents.*

    A.2.3 Hybrid. *Agents may be human or software entities (when there is no need to differentiate, we shall call them simply "agents" or "participants").*

    A.2.4 Heterogeneous. *Agents may have different decision models, different motivations and respond to different principals.*

    A.2.5 Autonomous. *Agents are not necessarily competent or benevolent, hence they may fail to act as expected or demanded of them.*

A.3 Persistence. *The social space may change either as effect of the actions of the participants, or as effect of events that are caused (or admitted) by the system.*

A.4 Perceivable. *All interactions within the shared social space are mediated by technological artefacts—that is, as far as the system is concerned only those actions that are mediated by a technological artefact that is part of the system may have a direct effect in the system.*[3]

---

[3] Take for example "correspondence chess" where players use some form of long distance asynchronous communication —post, email, pigeons—to exchange properly written messages that indicate which piece is moved where. In this case, the rules of the game state that no other action, no other way of expressing a move may have an effect on the board. The fact that one of the players is advised by the best experts before each move will help this player make better moves—and probably make this player win—but *the state of the board* changes only when the instruction is properly sent and received. As H. Simon would say about the market [19], a HOSS is an "interface" between the *opaque* (**A.2.2**) decision-making models of individual agents and their collective goal, in this case, of playing a game of chess. This point is clarified in Sec 4 when we propose that the tripartite view of a socio-cognitive technical systems demands that if any action in $\mathcal{W}$ is to be recognised as a valid institutional action in $\mathcal{I}$, it has to be an input that is duly processed in $\mathcal{T}$.

Note that although such actions might be described in terms of the five senses, they can collectively be considered percepts.

A.5 Openness. *Agents may enter and leave the social space and a priori, it is not known (by the system or other agents) which agents may be active at a given time, nor whether new agents will join at some point or not.*

A.6 Constrained. *In order to coordinate actions, the space includes (and governs) regulations, obligations, norms or conventions that agents are in principle supposed to follow.*

Such systems have been labelled "socio-technical" [21] because of the use of an IT system to support some human interaction. We move away from that label because we want to stress their *hybrid* (**A.2.3**) quality involving human and artificial agents, and for this reason they would be "socio-technical" more in the line of [20]).

Jones et al. [10] differentiate a subclass very similar to ours with the word "intelligent" to reveal an assumption of rationality in the system participants (without necessarily assuming hybrid systems), although they put forward the characteristic feature that these "intelligent socio-technical systems" involve entities that *"interact with each other against a social, organisational or legal background"* (as in **A.1** and **A.2** above).

Castelfranchi calls them *socio-cognitive technical systems* in order to stress— as we do with **A.2.1** above—the need to *"'understand' and reproduce features of the human social mind like commitments, norms, mind reading, power, trust, 'institutional effects' and social macro-phenomena"* [3]. We adhered to that label in [14], although there we occasionally referred to them as *artificial socio-cognitive systems* to underline that the motivation of that paper was to talk about the design and construction of such systems.

Why use the new label *Hybrid on-line social systems* for *socio-cognitive technical systems*, then? Simply because these common-use, self-explanatory, terms grab essentially the same class of systems.

3.2   Our Focus of Attention: Hidden Agency

The main problems with HOSS are what for a lack of a better term we'll call "unawareness problems" such as *hidden agency, insufficient stakeholder empowerment,* and *lack of social empathy.*

Perhaps more than anything, we need to draw out the extent to which these systems have or may acquire *hidden agency.* We mean, those side-effects or functionalities of the system that are exploitable by its owner or others without the user being fully aware of them, even if they were unintended by the designer of the system. In the language of multi-agent systems from 25 years ago, there is an assumption that the agency of online systems is benevolent [9] but if the hidden agency was revealed to users it would often be entirely unwelcome and unwanted. And in the same language, we may see hidden agency as hidden limits to the autonomy of the user.

An example of hidden agency is the recent case of mining on *OKCupid* where a group of researchers not only mined the data of the online dating service but even put the data collection of 70,000 users online on the Open Science Framework for anyone to use. Although real names were not included, the data of personal and intimate character could easily be linked to find the real identity behind the user names. Even more so, if it would be connected via the profile pictures (which the researchers left out of the database due to space reasons, not ethical considerations) to other social media when using software such as *Facefind* (http://www.findbyface.com/) and *Findface* (http://www.findface.ru). Although *OKCupid* managed to have the data removed on copyright violations, in what way the users had an opinion on or say in this is very unclear (a case of insufficient stakeholder empowerment).

A case of lack of social empathy is how the use of *Facebook* for memorial pages may have distressing effects [16]. Large turn-ups at funerals offer comfort and support to those who have lost a loved one. The same effect also applies to online shows of mourning such as the deluge of messages posted when a famous person dies. They show up in the trending topics bar on *Facebook*, spreading the news fast. Even for less famous persons, *Facebook* is playing a role in the mourning process. *Facebook* pages are kept alive, messages are sent to the deceased and memorial pages are put online. But not all is good. Just as a low turn-up at a funeral will cast doubt on the legitimacy of ones own sorrow so is the failure of attention in *Facebook* creating doubts. Moreover, the turn-up at a funeral is a private observation limited in time and space whereas *Facebook* measures and shows it all. The number of visitors can be compared to the number of likes or other *emojis* and the number of comments, for all to see.

3.3   What We Mean by Conscientious Design

We will go beyond value-sensitive design towards conscientious design and development. As we mentioned in Sect. 2, we propose to look into a particular set of values—involving technical, individual and social domains—that are linked to the description, specification, implementation and evolution of HOSS. Thus conscientious design and development of HOSS responds to three properties:

1. *Thoroughness.* This is achieved when the system is technically correct, requirements have been properly identified and faithfully implemented. This entails the use of appropriate formalisms, accurate modelling and proper use of tools.
2. *Mindfulness.* This describes supra-functional features that provide the users with awareness of the characteristics of the system and the possibility of selecting a satisfactory tailoring to individual needs or preferences. Thus, features that should be accounted for should include ergonomics, governance, coherence of purpose and means, identification of side-effects, no hidden agency, and the avoidance of unnecessary *affordances*.
3. *Responsibility.* This is true both towards users and to society in general. It requires a proper empowerment of the principals to honour commitments

and responsiveness to stakeholders legitimate interests. Hence, features like its scrutability, transparency and accountability alongside a proper support of privacy, a "right to forget"; proper handling of identity and ownership, attention to liabilities and proper risk allocation, and support of values like justice, fairness and trustworthiness.

This is the place where the agent metaphor for systems design provides a clear opportunity for providing models that can be understood by academics, users and designers of HOSS. For the commercial-driven applications we might think of designing conscientiousness sensors, small apps that show warning flags when the online application in use collides with the values of the user. But in the remainder of the paper we will look at applications developed in a conscientious way and illustrate the points we wish to make by revisiting applications developed by or close to us.

4   An Abstract Understanding of HOSS

In order to design HOSS using a conscientious approach we need to come up with a clear characterisation of these systems. Eventually, we should be able to articulate a set of features that discriminate the online social systems that we are interested in—the ones with "unawareness problems" we mentioned—from other online social systems. As mentioned above, we propose to take a twofold approach for this task: an empirical, bottom-up line that starts from paradigmatic examples and a top-down line that provides an abstract characterisation. We already took a first step along this second line with the WIT framework proposal that we summarise here.[4]

We start from the observation that HOSS are systems where one needs to *govern* the interaction of agents that are situated in a physical or artificial world by means of technological artefacts. The key notion is "governance" because in order to avoid hidden agency and other unawareness problems we need to control on one hand the frontier between the system itself and the rest of the world and, on the other, the activity of complex individuals that are at the root of HOSS. In order to elucidate how such governance is achieved we proposed the following tripartite view of HOSS (Fig. 1):

View 1: An *institutional* system, $\mathcal{I}$, that prescribes the system behaviour.

View 2: The *technological artefacts*, $\mathcal{T}$, that implement a system that enables users to accomplish collective actions in the real world ($\mathcal{W}$), according to the rules set out in $\mathcal{I}$.

View 3: The system as an organisation that exists in the *world*, $\mathcal{W}$, as the agents (both human and software) see it and with the events and facts that are relevant to it.

In other words, $\mathcal{W}$ may be understood as the "organisation" that is supported by an "online system" $\mathcal{T}$ that implements the "institutional conventions" $\mathcal{I}$.

---

[4] See [14] for a more leisurely discussion of the WIT proposal.

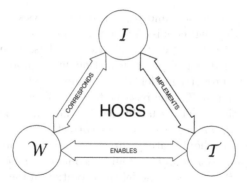

Fig. 1. The WIT trinity: the ideal system, $\mathcal{I}$; the technological artefacts that implement it, $\mathcal{T}$, and the actual world where the system is used, $\mathcal{W}$.

Notice that we are referring to one single system but it is useful to regard it from these three perspectives because each has its own concerns. Notice also, these three perspectives need to be *cohesive* or "coherent" in a very particular way: at any given time t, there is a *state of the system* s_t that is exactly the same for all agents that are in the system, and when an agent interacts with the system (in $\mathcal{W}$), that state of the system changes into a new state s'_t, which is again common to all agents, if and when the agent's action is processed by the system (in $\mathcal{T}$) according to the specifications of the system (in $\mathcal{I}$).

In order to make this cohesion operational, we define three binary relations between the views. As sketched in Fig. 1, the institutional world *corresponds* with the real world by some sort of a "counts-as" relationship [18]—and a mapping between entities in $\mathcal{W}$ and entities in $\mathcal{I}$—by which *relevant* (brute) facts and (brute) actions in $\mathcal{W}$ correspond to institutional facts and actions in $\mathcal{I}$ (and brute facts or actions have effects only when they satisfy the institutional conventions and the other way around). Secondly, $\mathcal{I}$ specifies the behaviour of the system and is *implemented* in $\mathcal{T}$. Finally, $\mathcal{T}$ *enables* the system in $\mathcal{W}$ by controlling all inputs that produce changes of the state and all outputs that reveal those changes.

4.1 A WIT Understanding of Conscientious Design

Conscientious design adds meaning to the WIT description by throwing light upon certain requirements that the three binary relations should satisfy. Thus, in the first phase of the cycle, the main concern is to make the design value-aware from the very beginning, in line with the recommendations of value-sensitive-design. That is, analyse systematically the *thoroughness, mindfulness* and *responsibility* qualifications of the system, so those ethical, social and utilitarian values that are significant for the stakeholders are made explicit. This examination would then pursue a proper operationalisation of the intended values so that they may be properly translated into institutional conventions. Note that it is in this phase where mindfulness and responsibility analysis of requirements are more present, while thoroughness is the focus of the next stage.

As suggested in [14], the operationalisation of those values together with the usual software engineering elements (functionalities, protocols, data requirements, etc.) should be properly modelled (in $\mathcal{I}$) and then turned into a specification that is implemented in $\mathcal{T}$. The passage from the elicitation of requirements to the modelling of the system is facilitated by the availability of *metamodels* [1] that provide the *affordances* to represent correctly those requirements. Ideally, such representation should satisfy three criteria: they should be *expressive*, they should be formally *sound* and it should become *executable*. The metamodel should also provide *affordances* to model the evolution of the system. Note that when relying on a "metamodel", its expressiveness will bias the way conscientiousness is reflected in the eventual specification.

The running system requires components for validation of the functionalities of the system, for monitoring performance and the devices to control transfer of information into and out of the system. These validation and monitoring devices should be tuned to the conscientious design decisions and therefore reveal how appropriate is the implementation of the system with respect to conscientious values and where risks or potential failures may appear.

4.2   WIT in Context

WIT is a useful simplification that needs to be placed within a wider setting. In this paper we will only point out three caveats that should be kept in mind:[5]

Caveat 1: *Cohesiveness* between $\mathcal{W}$, $\mathcal{I}$ and $\mathcal{T}$ is an ideal property that is not easy to achieve in practice.

Caveat 2: It should be obvious that HOSS are *not static* objects. Usually, each HOSS has a life-cycle where the process of evolution is not simple.

Caveat 3: HOSS are not developed in *isolation*. They exist within a larger social space where several other socio-technical systems exist and in many cases are linked to the one under design.

These caveats apply to the description of any HOSS but they have significant methodological implications for conscientious design. We hinted at some of those implications in different sections of this paper but a proper discussion is beyond the scope of the paper.

5   How to Achieve Conscientious Compliance

The abstract WIT and conscientious design ideas take rather concrete forms when building new HOSS.

---

[5] See [4] for some elaboration of 2 and 3.

5.1 An Example of Conscientious Design, the *uHelp app*

Picture a community of *monoparental* families that decide to provide mutual support in everyday activities: baby-sitting, picking up children from school, go shopping, substitute at work during an emergency, lending each other things like strollers or blenders. One may conceive an *app* that facilitates such coordination. But—sensitive to conscientious design—one wants to make sure that coordination is in accordance with the values of the community. In this case, for example, *solidarity*: everyone helps each other for free; *reciprocity*: no free riding; *involvement*: old people may want to help; *safety*: no one without proper credentials should be able to pick up a child; *privacy* (no revelation of personal data, of behaviour of members of the network); *trust*: you demand more trustworthiness in some tasks than others and trust is a binary relation that changes with experience.

You program the *app* so that it reflects those values faithfully and effectively. Moreover, you want the community to be aware of the degree of compliance/usefulness of the network, and that the community may change the specification to improve it or adapt to new preferences or values. Also you want the *app* to be unobtrusive, reliable, practical (light-weight, easy to download, easy to support, easy to update), and not contain hidden agency.

Abstracting away from the actual specification, the main conscientious-compliance features that the *app* should have are:

1. *From a practical perspective:* (i) Useful for the relevant coordination tasks, (ii) Faithful and responsive to the community's goals, preferences and values, (iii) Have the community in control of evolution (iv) No hidden agency.
2. *From an institutional perspective:* (i) shared ontology, (ii) common interaction model and interaction conventions (the *smartphone app*), (iii) govern a core coordination process: values, norms, governance (iv) controlled evolution: participatory, reliable, effective, (v) no unwanted behaviour.
3. *From a technical perspective:* (i) proper monitoring (key performing indicators, historical logs), (ii) automated updating (iii) robust and resilient *app*. (iv) Safe against intrusions and "zero information transfer" (only the intended information is admitted into the system and only intended information is revealed).

This type of application and the conscientious-design perspective have been under development in the IIIA for some time [15], and there is a working prototype, *uHelp*, that implements these ideas in a *smartphone app* and has already undergone field tests with actual users [12].

Where in WIT is conscientiousness

This example also serves to illustrate how conscientious design considerations may be reflected in the WIT cycle (Fig. 2):

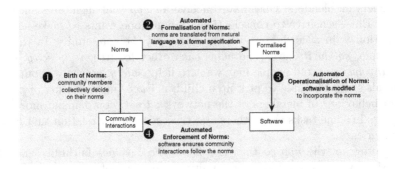

Fig. 2. Life-cycle of norms in the *uHelp app* from [15]

For specification: The *UHelp app* exists as a smartphone-based social network in W. It involves two realms: The first one consists of the physical components of the system, which includes smartphones, addresses, schools, ID cards, blenders and strollers, as well as the organisation of parents that own the application and the group of technicians that support is everyday use and maintenance. The other is the activities that are coordinated with the *app* (picking children up, help with shopping) and the activities that are needed to use the *app* (running a server, uploading the *app* in *iTunes*). Thus in order to describe (in $\mathcal{I}$) how it should work, WIT would need an *expressive description language* that should include coordination conventions, values, norms, and so on. In other words, a description language that can handle *mindful* and *responsible* values. On the other hand, the specification should be such that users are comfortable with the conventions that govern the system and its evolution; and in this respect, the system needs to be *thorough*.

For formalisation: Description needs to be made precise: How are values associated with norms? Does the system support norm changes with some formal mechanism? Is simulation the appropriate tool for validation and monitoring? In our case, *UHelp* is intended to have a development *workbench* that uses electronic institutions coordination and governance *affordances* (an EI-like metamodel [6]) that is being extended to handle values. Furthermore, the *UHelp* workbench shall contain also an argumentation environment for arguing about normative changes (to empower stakeholders) and a simulation module to test and anticipate (responsibly) potential changes of the system.

For implementation: One would like to rely on technological artefacts that make a *thorough* implementation of the specification of the system. Those artefacts may include devices like model checking, agent-mediated argumentation, agent-based modelling and simulation. In particular, the *uHelp* workbench shall be coupled with a platform that deals with the implementation of the functionalities of the value-based social network and also with the implementation and maintenance of the *app* itself.

What does it mean to be *conscientious* in the *uHelp app*?

This is a sketch of an answer for a *uHelp*-like HOSS.

Thorough: For specification purposes, a metamodel that *affords* proper representation, sound formalisation, correct implementation of: (i) Coordination and governance (activities, communication, social structure, data models, procedural norms, enforcement, etc.) (ii) Values, (ontology, norms, inference) (iii) Monitoring (KPI, use logs) (iii) Evolution (automated or participatory updating, validation).

Mindful: Proper elicitation and operationalisation of *values*, preferences and goals, sensible selection of functionalities; lucid assessment of performance; explicit *stakeholders entitlements and responsibilities*; sensible attention to *usability and culturally sensitive* issues; due attention to *privacy*. What *agency* is afforded by the system?

Responsible: (i) Clear and explicit commitments about *information transfer* in the system, uses of performance data, and about *management* of the system. (ii) Clear requirements and commitments of system *updating*: what may users do; what type of guarantees and requirements are part of the evolution process. (iii) Proper description of coordination behaviour (requirements and outcomes for intended behaviour of automated activities and support functionalities). (iv) Explicit description about *ownership* of the system, about relationship with *third-party software* and about *commercial* and other commitments with *third parties*.

5.2   Three Roads to Application

Rather than Quixotic fighting of *Facebook* windmills and trying to make existing HOSS conscientious-compliant we identify three lines of attack: (i) Conscientiousness by design, like the *uHelp* example; (ii) methods and devices to test the extent to which an existing HOSS is conscientious-compliant. This includes means to determine analytically whether a given HOSS has problems like hidden agency, insufficient user empowerment, inadequate social empathy; and (iii) *plug-ins* that may provide some conscientious-compliant features to existing HOSS.

6   Towards a New Research Programme

In order to support conscientious design, we propose a research programme (based on [14]) around the following five topics (see Fig. 3):

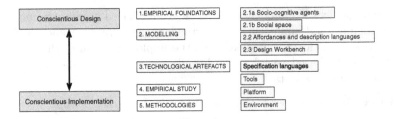

Fig. 3. The main challenges in the development of a framework for conscientious design of hybrid online social systems.

1. Empirical foundations: Conscientious design intends to build systems that support expected values and avoid unwanted features and outcomes. As we have been arguing in previous sections, we find that a systematic examination of actual socio-technical systems and of the values and unwanted outcomes involved need to be at the root of formal, technological and methodological developments in conscientious design. The outcomes should be, on one hand, a proper characterisation of HOSS and, on the other, a proper operationalisation of problematic manifestations in HOSS and the preventive and remedial features based on design conscientiousness.

2. Modelling: Conscientious design means: (i) that the creation of each HOSS be founded on a precise description of what the system is intended to be; (ii) that such description be faithfully implemented; and (iii) that the implementation actually works the way it is intended to work. In fact, it would be ideal if one could state with confidence the actual properties—scalability, accuracy, no unwanted side-effects, etc.—that the working HOSS has, because either we design the system with those properties in mind or because we are able to predicate them of an existing HOSS or an existing HOSS supplemented with *ad-hoc* plug-ins.

We propose to split the problem of conscientious modelling in three main parts: (2.1) Separate the design of a HOSS in two distinct concerns (the design of socio-cognitive agents and the design of a social space); (2.2) develop high-level description languages; and (2.3) develop a "design workbench" that provides concrete modelling components that translated the description of a HOSS into a specification.

2.1(a) Socio-cognitive agents. First it is important to provide a conceptual analysis of the types of agents that may participate in a HOSS. The significant challenge is to create agent models that exhibit true socio-cognitive capabilities Next to it is the challenge of developing the technological means to implement them; hence the definition of agent architectures using a formal and precise set of agent specification languages with the corresponding deployment and testing tools.

2.1(b) The social space. In addition one has to provide a sufficiently rich understanding of the social spaces which are constituted in HOSS. What are the relationships, what are the norms, how can it evolve, and a clarity about how this space is related to the external world. Any model would also need to consider how several HOSS may co-exist in a shared social space. Features that need to be included are openness, regulation, governance, local contexts of interaction, organisational and institutional structures.

2.2. Affordances and description languages. We need to identify the *affordances* that are needed, both, to achieve conscientious design in general, and also to support a *thorough* implementation of particular HOSS (as illustrated in Sect. 5). In other words, what are the concepts, analogies and expressions that a social scientist, an urban planner, a game designer or a sociologist may find more suitable to model agents and the social space of a HOSS. In practice, a description language for modelling agents should afford the means for the agent to be aware of the state of the system, of its own state, and to hold expectations of what actions it and other participants can take at a given state. For modelling the social space, the language should be able to express those elements that *afford* participants the means to have a shared ontology, a common interaction model and communication standards –so that actions may be attempted and their effects perceived—coupled with some form of governance.

2.3. Design workbench. It would include the concrete versions of the *affordances*. That is, the "vocabulary" that the description languages will use in order to model an actual system. So, for instance, if the system will involve norms, then the workbench would have norms expressed with a particular structure together with concomitant para-normative components like normative inference, nor-enforcement mechanisms, etc. In the *uHelp* example, we need functional norms that have the shape of "permissions" and they are represented as production rules.

3. Technological artefacts: The challenge is to build technological artefacts that facilitate and ensure the conscientious deployment of HOSS. One way of addressing this is to have an artefact for each modular component of the design workbench the components that are needed to assemble those modules as suggested in [13].

We have argued in favour of understanding the relationship between modelling and artefacts in terms of *meta-models* and *platforms* (see Subsect. 4.1 above, and Sect. 5 in [14]). A meta-model is a cohesive class of constructs (languages, operations, data structures) that are combined or instantiated to model a particular system (in $\mathcal{I}$). A platform is a collection of technological artefacts that implements (in $\mathcal{T}$) the systems that are modelled using the meta-model. Ideally, there is a specification language that serves to make the model precise and produces code that runs correctly on the platform. There are some frameworks that provide in some degree this coupling of meta-model and implementation [1].

One way to achieve formal soundness is to start with a meta-model with clear formal properties and develop a platform that implements faithfully those properties. Another is to start with an existing platform—*BrainKeeper, Amazon Turk, Ushahidi*—provide its formal counterpart and use it to analyse applications of the platform. In practice, the choice of metamodel and platform is a back and forth process [14].

4. Empirical study of HOSS: Complementing Topic 1, we find two further reasons to study working HOSS. One is to document compliance and failure of conscientious principles and recommendations, the other is to use the information that arises from their use as source data for socio-cognitive research.

5. Methodologies for conscientious design and deployment: The challenge is to develop a precise conceptual framework to describe conscientious features and methodological guidelines that prescribe how to recognise and achieve the intended properties and behaviour in conscientious HOSS. We need to explore key values like fairness, trustworthiness, social empathy in principled terms (see [10,17]) so that we can speak properly of achieving engineering tasks like requirement elicitation or tooling conscientiously.

7   Peroration in Four Claims

First: The era of online social systems that on the surface seem to satisfy augmented social needs is *here to stay*. However, the rise of such systems has been so dramatic that *we simply do not know* what the effects will be either psychologically, sociologically, culturally or politically.

Second: Some online social systems that involve human and artificial agency (HOSS) exhibit behaviours like hidden agency, inadequate stakeholder empowerment and lack of social empathy that may be problematic and deserve to be prevented or contended with in a sound manner.

Third: The challenge we face is to develop precise notions and the associated methodological guidelines and tools to design HOSS systems in a *conscientious* way that is *thorough, mindful* and *responsible*.

Fourth: This paper is a *call to arms* for such an initiative. Those of us working in the theory, design and implementation of agent-based systems, work in a field where there is an unharvested opportunity to apply our methods and tools in ways which could have impact far beyond that we might have imagined. It may mean a changing of the focus of our community and having to break away from our comfort zones describing idealised scenarios for agents, and in doing so we would need to be extremely humble about what we might achieve. But we should try, as the potential for sustained lasting impact for social and cultural good is potentially large.

The responsibility is substantial but the opportunity is ours.

Acknowledgements. The authors wish to acknowledge the support of SINTELNET (FET Open Coordinated Action FP7-ICT-2009-C Project No. 286370). This research was partially supported by project MILESS (MINECO TIN2013-45039-P).

References

1. Aldewereld, H., Boissier, O., Dignum, V., Noriega, P., Padget, J.: Social Coordination Frameworks for Social Technical Systems. Law, Governance and Technology Series, vol. 30. Springer, Cham (2016). doi:10.1007/978-3-319-33570-4

2. Brey, P.: Values in technology and disclosive computer ethics. In: Floridi, L. (ed.) The Cambridge Handbook of Information and Computer Ethics, pp. 41–58. Cambridge University Press, Cambridge (2010)

3. Castelfranchi, C.: InMind and OutMind; societal order cognition and self-organization: the role of MAS. Invited Talk for the IFAAMAS "Influential Paper Award", AAMAS 2013, Saint Paul, MN, US. http://www.slideshare.net/sleeplessgreenideas/castelfranchi-aamas13-v2?ref=httpMay2013

4. Christiaanse, R., Ghose, A., Noriega, P., Singh, M.P.: Characterizing artificial socio-cognitive technical systems. In: Herzig, A., Lorini, E. (eds.) Proceedings of the European Conference on Social Intelligence (ECSI 2014), Barcelona, Spain. CEUR Workshop Proceedings, vol. 1283, pp. 336–346. CEUR-WS.org, 3–5 November 2014

5. Collingridge, D.: The Social Control of Technology. St. Martin's Press, London (1980)

6. d'Inverno, M., Luck, M., Noriega, P., Rodriguez-Aguilar, J.A., Sierra, C.: Communicating open systems. Artif. Intell. **186**, 38–94 (2012)

7. Floridi, L. (ed.): The Onlife Manifesto: Being Human in a Hyperconnected Era. Springer, Cham (2015). doi:10.1007/978-3-319-04093-6

8. Friedman, B. (ed.): Human Values and the Design of Computer Technology. Cambridge University Press, Cambridge (1997)

9. Galliers, J.R.: The positive role of conflicts in cooperative multi-agent systems. In: Demazeau, Y., Mueller, J.-P. (eds.) Decentralized AI: Proceedings of the First European Workshop on Modelling Autonomous Agents in a Multi-agent World. Elsevier (1990)

10. Jones, A.J.I., Artikis, A., Pitt, J.: The design of intelligent socio-technical systems. Artif. Intell. Rev. **39**(1), 5–20 (2013)

11. Knobel, C.P., Bowker, G.C.: Values in design. Commun. ACM **54**(7), 26–28 (2011)

12. Koster, A., Madrenas, J., Osman, N., Schorlemmer, M., Sabater-Mir, J., Sierra, C., de Jonge, D., Fabregues, A., Puyol-Gruart, J., García, P.: u-Help: supporting helpful communities with information technology. In: Proceedings of the First International Conference on Agreement Technologies (AT 2012), Dubrovnik, Croatia, vol. 918, pp. 378–392, 15 October 2012

13. Noriega, P., Chopra, A.K., Fornara, N., Cardoso, H.L., Singh, M.P.: Regulated MAS: social perspective. In: Andrighetto, G., Governatori, G., Noriega, P., van der Torre, L.W.N. (eds.) Normative Multi-Agent Systems. Dagstuhl Follow-Ups, vol. 4, pp. 93–133. Schloss Dagstuhl-Leibniz-Zentrum fuer Informatik, Dagstuhl (2013)

14. Noriega, P., Padget, J., Verhagen, H., d'Inverno, M.: Towards a framework for socio-cognitive technical systems. In: Ghose, A., Oren, N., Telang, P., Thangarajah, J. (eds.) COIN 2014. LNCS, vol. 9372, pp. 164–181. Springer, Cham (2015). doi:10.1007/978-3-319-25420-3_11

15. Osman, N., Sierra, C.: A roadmap for self-evolving communities. In: Herzig, A., Lorini, E. (eds.) Proceedings of the European Conference on Social Intelligence (ECSI 2014), Barcelona, Spain. CEUR Workshop Proceedings, vol. 1283, pp. 305–316. CEUR-WS.org, 3–5 November 2014

16. Phillips, W.: LOLing at tragedy: Facebook trolls, memorial pages and resistance to grief online. First Monday **16**(12) (2011). http://dx.doi.org/10.5210/fm.v16i12.3168
17. Pitt, J., Busquets, D., Macbeth, S.: Distributive justice for self-organised common-pool resource management. ACM Trans. Auton. Adapt. Syst. **9**(3), 14 (2014)
18. Searle, J.R.: What is an institution? J. Inst. Econ. **1**(01), 1–22 (2005)
19. Simon, H.A.: The Sciences of the Artificial, 3rd edn. MIT Press, Cambridge (1996)
20. Singh, M.P.: Norms as a basis for governing sociotechnical systems. ACM Trans. Intell. Syst. Technol. (TIST) **5**(1), 21:1–21:23 (2014)
21. Trist, E.: The evolution of socio-technical systems. Occasional Paper, Ontario Ministry of Labour, 2 (1981)

Teams

Communication and Shared Mental Models for Teams Performing Interdependent Tasks

Ronal Singh[(✉)], Liz Sonenberg, and Tim Miller

University of Melbourne, Melbourne, Australia
ronals@student.unimelb.edu.au, {l.sonenberg,tmiller}@unimelb.edu.au

Abstract. Research shows that performance of human teams improves when members have a shared understanding of their task; that is, when teams develop and use a shared mental model (SMM). An SMM can contain different types of information or components and this paper investigates the influence on team performance of sharing different components. We consider two components of an SMM: intentions (e.g. goals) and world knowledge (e.g. beliefs) and investigate which component(s) contribute most to team performance across different forms of interdependent tasks. We performed experiments using a Blocks World for Team (BW4T) testbed for artificial agent teams and our results show that with high levels of interdependence in tasks, communicating intentions contributes most to team performance, while for low levels of interdependence, communicating world knowledge contributes more. Additionally, as is the case with human teams, higher sharedness correlated with improved team performance for the artificial agent teams. These insights can assist in the design of communication protocols that improves team performance when team members are engaged in interdependent tasks and help design artificial agents that can communicate effectively when working with humans as team mates.

Keywords: Task interdependence · Shared mental models · Joint action

1 Introduction

Agents perform tasks that range from independent tasks that does not require interactions with others to highly *interdependent tasks* requiring close and continuous interactions [14]. When faced with interdependent tasks, effective coordination and collaboration of team members become crucial. One of the key foundations of effective coordination and collaboration is having *shared mental models (SMM)*. Shared mental model has been defined as [1]: "knowledge structures held by members of a team that enable them to form accurate explanations

This paper was first published as *Singh R., Sonenberg L., Miller T.: Communication and Shared Mental Models for Teams Performing Interdependent Tasks. In: Osman N., Sierra C. (eds) AAMAS 2016 Workshops. LNCS(LNAI), vol. 10002, pp. 163–179. Springer International Publishing AG (2016).* doi:10.1007/978-3-319-46882-2_10.

S. Cranefield et al. (Eds.): COIN 2016 Workshops, LNAI 10315, pp. 81–97, 2017.
DOI: 10.1007/978-3-319-46882-2_10

and expectations for the task, and, in turn, coordinate their actions and adapt their behaviour to demands of the task and other team members".

More than a decade of research has correlated SMMs with improved team performance in human teams [12]. The basic assumption is that SMMs allow team members to anticipate the needs and actions of other members, thereby increasing team performance. Recent studies in human-agent and artificial agent teams have also found similar correlations [3,5]. SMMs can be broadly classified as either task work model or team work model. Task work concerns the task or job that the team is to perform, while team work concerns what has to be done in order to complete a task as a team [9]. SMMs can also be viewed as having different components [5,9], such as world knowledge and intentions. World knowledge includes knowledge of the current state of the environment and the team while intentions represent what the agents intend to do [4].

Four types of task interdependence have been identified for human activities: pooled, sequential, reciprocal, and team [14,15]. In sequential task interdependence, tasks are performed in a sequential order. For example, in a relay race each runner has to wait for the previous team member to pass on the baton. In reciprocal task interdependence, participants take their turn in completing part of the task. A key property associated with reciprocal task interdependence is interleaved execution: for example, surgical teams often work reciprocally. In team task interdependence, participants execute their individual tasks concurrently and may include *joint actions*. By "action", we mean the atomic actions that make up a task. In joint action, multiple participants execute a particular action concurrently, for example when two people lift a heavy object together. In pooled task interdependence, the participants can successfully execute tasks without any interaction with each other. Due to the simple nature of these tasks, we do not study such tasks in this paper. The four types of task interdependence forms a hierarchy of pooled-sequential-reciprocal-team, with this hierarchy representing increasing levels of dependence between team members as well as increasing needs for coordination [14].

While *sharedness* has been linked with better team performance, central to the notion of SMM is how much and what to share. There has been recent work investigating this question in multi-agent systems research, such as [5,11,17]. However, as far as the authors are aware, with the exception of Li et al. [10], studies in the related work only consider sequentially-interdependent tasks, rather than more tightly linked team and reciprocal tasks. A recent report [16] highlights the need for studies considering other types of interdependence, notably *intensive* task interdependence – a type that we characterise as a *joint action*.

The subject of this paper is the communication content, specifically *what* to share when team members engage in interdependent tasks. We investigate the influence of the two components of the SMM (world knowledge and intentions) on the team performance across different forms of interdependent tasks. We used search and rescue like scenarios for a team of artificial agents for the experiments. The scenarios were generated using a Blocks World for Teams (BW4T) testbed [8]. In BW4T, which is an extension of the classical blocks world domain, the teams' joint task is to find and deliver coloured blocks in a particular order. Using the testbed, we designed and executed two sets of experiments. The first set studies the influence of sharing the two components – world knowledge and intentions – on the team performance for each form of task interdependence. The second set introduces joint actions within sequential and reciprocal tasks and studies the influence of sharing the two components on team performance. Introduction of joint actions allows for a shift from sequential or reciprocal to team task interdependence where members execute individual actions concurrently.

The outline of the paper is as follows. Section 2 introduces SMM, along with related work. Section 3 describes the task and the testbed and provides the details of the artificial agents that we implemented. Section 4 details the experimental setup while Sect. 5 discusses the results. Sections 6 and 7 conclude the paper with a discussion.

2   Background and Related Work

Mental models are simplified representations used by individuals to explain and predict their surroundings [13]. These models comprise content and structure or relationships between the content. In addition, individuals can simultaneously hold multiple mental models. In a team setting, when team members interact, their mental models converge resulting in shared mental models.

To extend the concepts of SMM that has been well studied for human teams [12] to human-agent teams, Jonker et al. [9] proposed mental model ontologies. They view a team as a system. A team performs team activities and has physical components, e.g. team members. A team member is an agent with a mind comprising many mental models: all but one of which represent the mental models of others in the team. Based on this conceptualisation, they proposed a measure that could be used to assess the similarity or the overlap of agents' mental models. We discuss this measure in the next section.

2.1   Measuring SMM

While several methods exist for measuring SMMs for human teams [2], one for teams comprising artificial agents is Jonker et al. [9]. Harbers et al. [5] extended Jonker et al's similarity measure so that it could be applied to teams of agents and performed experiments to show that their similarity measure can be used to predict team performance. We discuss the extended version of the measure next. In the following discussions, similarity refers to the overlap of the mental model contents of the agents. We consider the SMM to be made of two components – world knowledge and intentions.

Figure 1 shows an example of SMM. Assume Bot 1 and Bot 2 are two agents engaged in a joint task. Each has its mental model. While engaged in their task, the agents may communicate their beliefs and goals, making their own beliefs and goals known to others. For example, notice that each agent has it's own

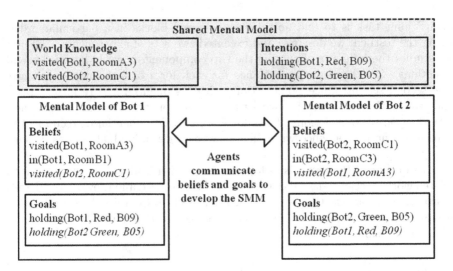

Fig. 1. Example SMM. The beliefs and goals of other agents are shown in italics. An agent has certain beliefs and goals that it is not required to communicate, e.g. *in (agent, room)*, and these may not part of the SMM.

as well as others' beliefs and goals, which are shown in italics. The SMM is a theoretical construct that can be used to represent the overlapping content of the mental models of the two agents. In the example, the SMM is composed of the components - world knowledge (beliefs) and intentions (goals).

Jonker et al. [9] and Harbers et al. [5] proposed a compositional measure of sharedness. We reproduce their definitions here with some simplifications. They view SMMs as having components, which can include sub-components. For example, Fig. 1 shows an SMM with two components. Examples of sub-components can be found in Sect. 3.3. The (sub)components can be queried by posing questions that all team members should be able to answer. The answers are used to compute the model agreements, which is a measure of the similarity of the answers provided by each agent for each question. Formally, let M be the set of all mental models, Q be the set of all questions, and $ans(m, q)$ be the answer of model $m \in M$ with respect to question $q \in Q$. The agreement between models M for questions Q is:

$$Ag(M, Q) = \frac{1}{|Q|} \sum_{q \in Q} \frac{|\cap_{m \in M} ans(m, q)|}{|\cup_{m \in M} ans(m, q)|} \tag{1}$$

If $|\cup_{m \in M} ans(m, q)| = 0$ then the agreement for question q is 0. Given a set of agents A, a set of mental models M_A (a model for each agent), and questions Q, we say that the model m is shared *to the extent* θ, denoted by $Sh(M, A, Q, \theta)$, with respect Q, iff $Ag(M_A \cup \{m\}, Q) >= \theta$. The compositional measure CS is:

$$CS(M, A, Q) = max\{\theta \mid Sh(M, A, Q, \theta)\}, \text{ if M is not composed}$$
$$CS(M, A, Q) = c(\{CS(m, A, Q) \mid m \in M\}), \text{ if M is composed} \tag{2}$$

Where m is a component of M and c is composition function, for example: $\sum_{m \in M} w_m CS(m, A, Q)$. Each component and sub-component can be weighted to model the relevance of each (sub)component. The weight of each (sub)component is $w_m \in [0, 1]$ and CS can be normalised to $[0, 1]$ by setting $\sum_{m \in M} w_m = 1$.

2.2 SMM and Task Interdependence

Interdependence is the central organising principle of *Coactive Design Method*, from Johnson et al. [7], which is a method aimed at designing systems in which humans and agents collaborate as teammates. They define interdependence as relationships between members of a team, and argue that these relationships determine what information is relevant for the team to complete (interdependent) tasks, and in that sense, the interdependent relationships define the *common ground* that is necessary. A number of studies have considered some of the different forms of task interdependence [5, 10, 17], and some have also measured sharedness [5, 9]. Generally, higher sharedness of mental models produces better team performance. For example, Harbers et al. [5] found higher sharedness correlated with better team performance. In their work, SMM were composed of world knowledge and intentions, which is how we view SMM in this work. Similarly, task interdependence has naturally been part of these studies. However, almost all involve sequentially interdependent tasks. The exception is Li et al. [10], who introduced joint action in sequentially interdependent tasks and Wei et al. [17], who studied tasks that were not very strongly sequential. They did this by creating subtasks that multiple agents could complete simultaneously. None of these have explicitly employed reciprocally interdependent tasks.

Mixed results have been reported for studies involving sequentially interdependent tasks in terms of which type of information or component contributes more to team performance, that is task completion times. Harbers et al. [5] reported that when agents communicated their intentions with others, the team performance improved more than if they shared world knowledge. However, Wei et al. [17] reported that beliefs contributed more to team performance than goals. While [17] did not measure sharedness, they view the agents mental models to comprise of two components, goals (intentions) and beliefs (world knowledge). We perform further experiments involving sequentially interdependent tasks and may help explain the difference between the two studies.

In a separate study, Li et al. [10] introduced joint action in sequentially interdependent tasks. They studied search and retrieval tasks using the BW4T testbed. In one setup, agents collaborated on a task in which some blocks were heavier, and required two agents to collect. The agents exchanged goals, beliefs, and both. Their experiments revealed that with joint actions, exchanging goals improved team performance, measured as completion time, more than sharing beliefs only. When agents shared their goals that fulfil the current team sub-goal with others, the other team members could start on a new task. This allowed the team to finish the team task more quickly.

These works show that sequentially interdependent tasks have been investigated, but other forms of task interdependence have not. This work aims to fill that gap.

3   Scenario: Blocks World for Teams

We used a BW4T testbed [8] for our experiments. As explained next, we modified the testbed to be able to setup tasks with joint actions.

Basic BW4T: In BW4T, teams find and deliver coloured blocks in a particular order. The environment has a set of rooms, each containing coloured blocks, and a drop zone. The agents search the rooms, find the required blocks and drop these in the drop zone. Agents have a map of area but do not know the location of the required blocks. Agents have to go to each room to perceive the blocks that are present in it. Agents cannot see each other but can communicate with others. A simplified map is shown in Fig. 2. Each room has one door. The teams' joint task, i.e. the sequence of colours, is displayed at the bottom left. A black triangle appears on top of a colour if the colour is dropped off. The room above the joint task is the drop zone. The agents are represented by either black squares or the colour the agent is holding, and their names are displayed in red. The basic version is well suited to perform experiments for sequential and reciprocal tasks. However, it does not explicitly support joint actions.

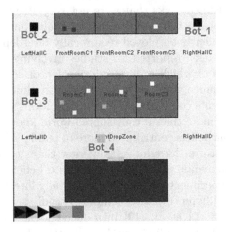

Fig. 2. Sample BW4T environment.

Modified BW4T: To design joint tasks that would be a fair representation of the different forms of task interdependence, we modified the testbed. In the original version, only one agent could be in a room at any one time. To implement joint actions, we follow Li et al. [10] and introduce "heavy blocks", which required two agents to carry to the drop zone. This means in our version, two agents can carry the same block simultaneous, and therefore can be in the same room at the same time. Secondly, for team task interdependence, the blocks could be delivered in any order, that is, we removed the sequential delivery requirement.

3.1 Task Design

We designed tasks to be able to test the effects of communication content on the team performance for each type of the task interdependence as well as later include joint action within other forms of task interdependence and test the effect of communication content on the team performance for each combination. Variations of two basic joint tasks (Fig. 3) has been used to realise the different forms of task interdependence.

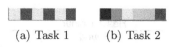

(a) Task 1   (b) Task 2

Fig. 3. Basic joint tasks used to simulate different types of task interdependence (Color figure online).

Team Task: In team tasks, agents execute their actions concurrently. The joint task had some *heavy* blocks. The heavy blocks required one agent to help the other lift it, and afterwards the first agent delivers it to the drop zone. The act of lifting the heavy block *together* is the joint action. Additionally, the agents could lift any colour. Consider the task shown in Fig. 3a. In this task, agents can lift both colours. The red blocks are heavy blocks. In order to remove the underlining sequential interdependence from this task, the agents could deliver the blocks in any order, for example, the second (red) block can be delivered before the first (yellow) block. Green, pink and red are heavy blocks in Task 2.

Reciprocal Task: In a reciprocal task, each agent takes it's turn in completing part of the task. In this task, the agents deliver a sequence of alternating colour sets in the order the colours appear in the task. Furthermore, each agent can lift colours from only one of the two distinct colour sets. Consider the task shown in Fig. 3a. For this task, one agent would be delivering yellow blocks while the other red ones. The blocks must be delivered in the order they appear. This means that agent delivering the red block now depends on the agent delivering the yellow blocks and vice-versa, making them reciprocally interdependent.

Sequential Task: In sequential task, the first three colours are delivered by one agent while the remaining three by another agent. The blocks must be delivered in the specified order, but the second agent is free to search for its coloured blocks while the first agent is delivering.

3.2 Agent Teams and Agent Behaviours

We had two team compositions; (1) 2-agent team and (2) 4-agent team. The 4-agent team was a 2×2-agent team, i.e. 2 sub-teams of 2 agents each.

This composition was required for certain tasks, such as reciprocal tasks in which we needed to have at least one agent for each of the two colour sets.

Agents were programmed in GOAL [6]. The BW4T testbed provides interfaces that enable GOAL agents to interact with it. Using these interfaces, the agents can perceive specific details of the environment, such as the blocks present in rooms, and can perform actions, such as picking up a block. The abstract decision cycle of an agent is shown in Fig. 4. The basic steps each agent takes are: (1) decide the colour to search for; (2) choose a room; (3) go to and search room; (4) if required block is found and is not heavy, pick it up; (5) if required block is found and is heavy, ask for help and wait. When help arrives, pick up the block; (6) deliver the block to the drop zone; (7) if help is requested, go to the particular room and help lift the heavy block.

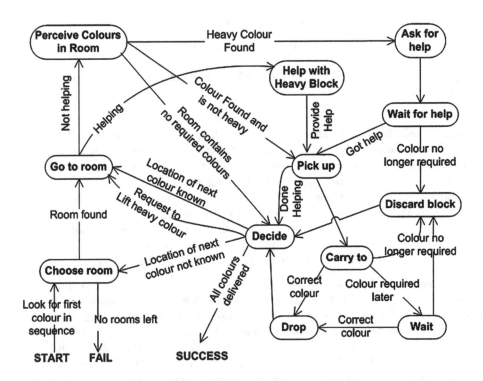

Fig. 4. Abstract decision cycle of an agent.

Initially, agents start searching for the first undelivered colour. However, agents use a two-block look-ahead protocol to determine which colour to deliver. If an agent knows the location of the first undelivered colour and has the intention of collecting it, remaining agents search for the second undelivered colour. If the one or more of the remaining agents know the location of the next required colour, they go to that room. However, only one will be able to collect the block. When the first colour is picked up, one agent collects the second colour while others start searching for the third colour. The aim of this is to ensure that sufficient time is dedicated to search. When required to lift a heavy block, an agent only asks for help when it is physically present at the heavy block. Other (helper) agents could potentially infer that help will be required soon and go to the location of the heavy block before the agent actually asks for help because the agent may tell others that it has the goal of going to the (heavy) block. However, our agents do not perform this level of reasoning and only go to help when asked. Furthermore, if one agent asks for help, all agents that are waiting to drop a block at the drop zone or those that are currently searching for their block will go to help. If the agent knows that the colour that it is searching for, has the intention of holding or is holding is no longer required, then it will discard the colour and go on to deciding what it will do next. Rooms are chosen randomly and the agents avoid visiting a room more than once unless the room contains multiple required blocks.

While the basic behaviours of agents are almost the same across the different forms of task interdependence, there are differences in the way agents reason about which colour to search for:

(1) Sequential and reciprocal tasks: Agents choose the first undelivered colour. If another agent has the goal of holding this colour, the agent chooses the next undelivered colour.

(2) Team Task: Blocks can be delivered in any order. Therefore, agents do not reason about when the block has to be delivered. Instead agents have to determine whether the block is heavy and ask for help.

While certain aspects of agent behaviours are different because of task interdependence, there are differences because of what the agents share with each other. Therefore, while the basic decision cycle shown in Fig. 4 is used by all agents, there are some variations in their implementation. The implementation has been guided by what the agents actually do with the information they receive and has been described later in Sect. 3.4. Therefore, if only one component is exchanged, the agent performs reasoning described for that component only.

3.3   Communication and SMM

Agents exchange messages that are indicative of the world knowledge and the intentions. To develop the shared mental model, agents communicate as soon as they have the required information. Agents exchange six sub-components, three each of goals and world knowledge. These sub-components were selected based on prior research work [5,10] and preliminary experiments revealed that each sub-component had the potential to improve team performance. The sub-components are communicated as messages, which are discussed next. The keyword *imp* stands for imperative and indicates what the agent intends to do.

The messages indicative of intentions are:

(1) imp(in(Sender, Room)): Sender intends to visit Room.
(2) imp(holding(Sender, Colour, Block)): Sender intends to collect Block of Colour.
(3) delivered(Sender, Colour, Block): Sender has delivered Block of Colour - implies agent has dropped current goal and may have a new goal.

The messages indicative of world knowledge are:

(1) blockLoc(Sender, Block, Colour, Room): Sender has perceived Block of required Colour in Room.
(2) pickedUp(Sender, Colour, Block): Sender has picked up Block of Colour.
(3) visited(Sender, Room): Sender has visited Room. This message is sent irrespective of whether room contains required blocks.

3.4 Using Shared Mental Models

Agents employ the following policies to SMM to choose their activities such that it prevents potential conflicts with the activities of others. The following outlines how the agents use the components of the shared mental model. We chose a straightforward use of each intention and world knowledge, which was sufficient to test the effect of the component on the team's performance and avoids side-effects that would have been introduced because of using more complex mechanisms. The intentions are used as follows:

(1) An agent will not adopt a goal to go to a particular room if another agent has the goal of going to that room. For reciprocal task, this logic applies when both agents are delivering blocks from the same colour set, that is in a 4-agent team and not in a 2-agent team.
(2) An agent will not adopt a goal to hold a block that has been delivered.
(3) An agent will not adopt a goal to hold a block/colour that another agent has the goal of holding — *unless* the block is heavy (both agents need to lift it together). For reciprocal tasks, this logic is applicable in a 4-agent team.

World knowledge is used as follows:

(1) An agent will not search for a colour if this been found by another agent.
(2) An agent will search for the next colour if the currently required colour has been picked up.
(3) An agent will not search a room that another agent has already searched.

Agents employ the above policies to SMM to reduce interference and duplication of effort. However, the agents have their own decision processes and may make decisions simultaneously. This may result in instances where the agents may adopt similar goals, for example to look for the same colour. Like Wei et al. [17], we simply implement a "first-come first-served" policy instead of implementing detailed negotiation mechanisms to assist agents resolve these issues.

4   Experiment Design

We ran a series of simulation experiments, measuring the following:

(1) Completion Time: Time it takes the team to complete the task. We used this measure as a proxy for team performance.
(2) Number of messages: We measured the total number of messages exchanged by the agents. We also counted the number of messages per component. These measures are indicative of the communication cost.
(3) Sharedness: We measured the sharedness of the agents' mental models. This is a compositional measure (see Sect. 2.1) and was calculated at the time any block was delivered to the drop zone. When one agent drops off a correct colour in drop zone, all agents log their belief and goal bases. These logs are then analysed to find the overlapping content, which is used to compute the sharedness values. The two components had a weight of 0.5 and each of the three sub-components had a weight of 0.33. In experiments where only one component was measured, the weight of the component was set to 1, and only questions related to that component were asked.

In case of sub-teams, we also measured the number of messages and sharedness of the agents with each sub-team.

Independent Variable. The independent variable is the component of the SMM. This variable has three values (see Sect. 3.3): (*1*) World Knowledge (WK); (*2*) Intentions (INT); and (*3*) World Knowledge and Intentions (ALL).

Table 1. Experimental setups (S1 – S6) for each type of task interdependence.

	Set 1				Set 2	
Team size	2 agents		4 agents		4 agents	
Map	1	2	1	2	1	2
Setup	S1	S2	S3	S4	S5	S6

Setup. We used two different maps, one for each task outlined in Sect. 3.1. Variations of each task gave us three different task interdependence types. We refer to Task 1 (Fig. 3a) as Map 1 and Task 2 as Map 2. The setups are as shown in Table 1. We had two sets. In set 1, we had four setups (S1-S4) (both maps combined with two team compositions) for each of the three types of task interdependence giving us 12 combinations.

Set 2 has two setups, S5 and S6, representing reciprocal and sequential tasks with joint actions respectively. Here the sub-teams were reciprocally or sequentially interdependent and were required to lift heavy blocks. We tested the effect of the SMM components on completion times by employing three communication strategies: (*1*) ALL-ALL: where agents exchanged the two components with every other agent. (*2*) WK-Within: where agents shared world knowledge within each sub-team but shared intentions with all agents. (*3*) INT-Within: where agents shared intentions within each sub-team but the world knowledge with all agents. For these two setups, we only used a 4-agent team because a 2-agent team would not have enabled us to fully test the effects of the two components. For example, we needed to have at least 2 agents in each sub-team to be able to test the effect of sharing a component within the sub-team. Combining S5 and S6 with the two types of task interdependence (sequential and reciprocal) gave us further 4 combinations, and a total of 16 combinations.

Combining each of the 12 combinations from Set 1 with the three components of the SMM (ALL, INT, WK) and the 4 combinations from Set 2 with the three communication strategies (ALL-ALL, WK-Within, INT-Within) resulted in 48 combinations in total. Each combination was run 30 times resulting in 1440 runs. Each map had 25 blocks pre-allocated to rooms and further 10 blocks were randomly generated giving a total of 35 blocks for each run. Each map had 9 rooms, 1 drop zone and 6 blocks in the joint task. Statistical significance tests were conducted using Wilcoxon rank-sum (WRS) and Kruskal-Wallis (KW) tests.

5   Results

This study was aimed at identifying the components that contributed most to team performance across different forms of task interdependence. Recall that going from sequential to team tasks represents increasing levels of dependence between agents as well as coordination requirements. For simplicity, we collapse the results of the two tasks (shown in Fig. 3) and report the averages.

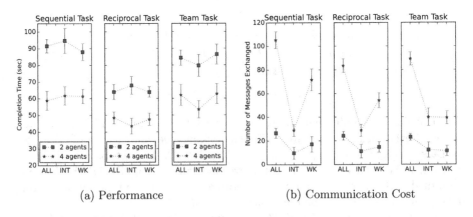

(a) Performance   (b) Communication Cost

Fig. 5. Performance and communication cost for different forms of task interdependence. The communication cost is expressed as the average number of messages exchanged by all team members. Error bars represent on standard deviation.

5.1   SMM Components and Team Performance

Figure 5a shows the average task completion times for the 2-agent and 4-agent teams performing different tasks. These results are for experiments resulting from setups S1-S4. Recall that a 4-agent team comprises 2 sub-teams of 2 agents each. For team tasks, the intentions contributed more to team performance than world knowledge. This finding is significant at 5% for all except two combinations and consistent for both team compositions. In the team task, some blocks were heavy and the agents could pick any colour. In such scenarios, knowing the intentions of team members allows agents to avoid duplicating their activities, therefore reducing interference. These results are in line with Li et al. [10], who reported that with joint actions, exchanging goals results in improved completion times.

However, for sequential and reciprocal tasks, different trends have been observed between 2-agent and 4-agent teams. For sequential tasks and 2-agent team, the world knowledge contributed significantly more ($p < 0.05$) than intentions in terms of task completion times. In this task setting, the first agent delivered first three blocks while the remaining three by the other agent. Because agents had separate sub-tasks, exchanging world knowledge helped the other agent find it's required blocks faster. However, for reciprocal tasks, this difference was less pronounced. We discuss this more later.

In 4-agent teams performing sequential tasks, no significant difference in terms of completion times were noted between the two components. However, it is worth noting that moving from 2-agent to 4-agent team, the importance of intentions increases. A similar trend occurs for reciprocal and team tasks. In these team settings, the agents within each sub-team could choose conflicting goals, for example, choosing the same block to deliver. By exchanging intentions, agents within sub-teams avoided duplicating their activities, therefore improving the completion times.

To make these trends clearer, we computed *component influence* (CI) for each task. CI is computed based on the difference between the completion times achieved when communicating both components and any one of the two components. To normalise the difference between completion times across different experiments, we used the *tanh* function. The CI for component c is:

$$CI_c = tanh(CompletionTime_{all} - CompletionTime_c)$$

The resulting values were normalised to between 0 and 1 using $CI_{normalised} = (CI - min(CI))/(max(CI) - min(CI))$. Figure 6 for 2-agent teams show that with increasing dependence between agents, that is, going from sequential to team interdependence, the importance of intentions increases while the importance of world knowledge decreases. For 4-agent team, the intentions were almost always more important than world knowledge.

SMM and Joint Actions. Results of experiments relating to setups S5 and S6 indicated that the difference between completion times of WK-Within and INT-Within is significant (p-value = 0.009) in favour of INT-Within. This indicates that sharing intentions within sub-teams and world knowledge with everyone

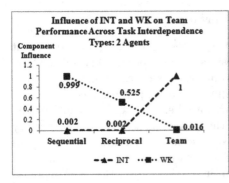 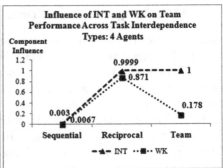

Fig. 6. The two graphs (2 agents and 4 agents) show that intentions become more important more as the level of interdependence increases and as the number of agents in each sub-team increases.

achieves the best team performance. This is consistent with our earlier findings that intentions and team tasks are positively correlated. Also, world knowledge and sequential and reciprocal tasks are positively correlated.

5.2 Communication Performance

Figure 5b shows the communication cost (average number of messages exchanged). The number of intentions exchanged was significantly lower ($p < 0.05$) than world knowledge for about two-thirds of the combinations. This indicates that agents generally have more information to communicate about the world than their intentions. There was no correlation between the number of messages and team performance. More communication resulted in worst performance in some cases, particularly for larger teams. This is due to the two-block look-ahead policy. When agents exchange information about possible blocks, in larger teams this often results is agents trying to collect the same block/colour and this increases the completion time. When agents only exchange intentions, all agents are required to find the blocks themselves, and so search randomly, thus reducing the number of unnecessary runs for the same block/colour. While it is clear that a mechanism could be designed to improve this by using a different look-ahead policy, we believe our policy is reasonable. Importantly though, this result shows that simply throwing more information towards agents can result in worse performance if significant thought is not given to how that information is used.

5.3 Analysis of Sharedness

We computed the sharedness in relation to each component at the time a block was delivered to the dropzone. Generally, higher sharedness correlates with improved completion times. For simplicity we show the data for team task and

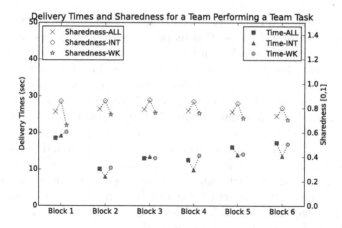

Fig. 7. Sharedness and delivery times for a 2-agent team engaged in a team task.

note that the results for sequential and reciprocal tasks are similar. For example, Fig. 7 shows the sharedness at the time each correct block is dropped off for team tasks. The plotted delivery times are the time differences between block deliveries. For team tasks, exchanging intentions achieved the best completion times and the sharedness was highest for this component. Notice that in Fig. 7, sharedness of intentions is highest across all six blocks and the delivery times when teams exchange intentions are fastest across most of the six blocks.

Sharedness and Sub Teams. We measured the sharedness of members within each sub-team for tasks solved by 4-agent teams. Sharing intentions resulted in the best completion times and the sharedness of intentions was highest for reciprocal and team tasks. For sequential tasks, we noted a significant increase in the importance of intentions compared to 2-agent team. This supports the finding that higher sharedness results in better completion times. The other consistent finding is that in situations where we may have members of sub-teams potentially duplicating their efforts, sharing intentions with each other helps avoid such conflicting actions and therefore, improves the completion times.

6   Discussion

We intended to identify the components contributing most to team performance across the different forms of task interdependence. Our results show that as the interdependence increases, the importance of intentions to team performance also increases. These results are in line with [5,10] who found that when team members exchanged intentions, the team performance improves. In [5], teams were engaged in sequential tasks and their team composition was similar to our 4-agent team while in [10], the authors introduced joint actions in sequentially interdependent tasks.

While our results are in line with the above works, we have observed that when team members can perform their sub-tasks independently, e.g. in 2-agent teams, exchanging world knowledge contributes more to team performance for sequential and reciprocal tasks. This makes sense intuitively: if other members provide potentially useful information, such as location of blocks that one is required to deliver, the team performance improves. This is a form of *soft interdependence* [7] where one team/member 'helps' another voluntarily. In case of 4-agent teams, we found that intentions contributed more to team performance across all forms of task interdependence. This indicates that team composition plays a role in which component is important to team performance.

Our findings that are partially consistent with [17] who found that for sequential tasks, beliefs contributed more to team performance. While this is consistent with the results of our 2-agent team, we noted a marked increase in the importance of intentions when 4-agent team was concerned. These differences may hinge on other factors, such as how effectively the agents use the information that it receives. This is an area of future work.

Finally, our findings are consistent with others (e.g. [5]) in terms the role SMM plays in improving team performance. Across all tasks and both team compositions, higher sharedness of SMM resulted in improved team performance.

7   Conclusions and Future Work

The four types of task interdependence form a hierarchy, from pooled to team, representing increasing levels of dependence between team members as well as increasing needs for coordination. We found that with increasing levels of interdependence, the importance of intentions increases as well. Team composition also plays a role in which component contributes more to team performance. In team compositions, where agents can perform their tasks independently, e.g. in sequential and reciprocal tasks, world knowledge contributed more to team performance. When multiple team members may be engaged in a single sub-task, the potential of interference increases and so does the importance of knowing the intentions of others.

A factor to investigate further is the reasoning capability of the agents; that is, how the agents reason with information that they receive from others. We also have not explicitly analysed the behavioural changes in the agents when agents switch from one task interdependence type to another, making this another opportunity for future investigation.

References

1. Cannon-Bowers, J.A., Salas, E., Converse, S.: Shared mental models in expert team decision making. In: Castellan, J., John, N. (eds.) Individual and Group Decision Making: Current Issues, pp. 221–246. Lawrence Erlbaum., Hillsdale, NJ (1993)
2. DeChurch, L.A., Mesmer-Magnus, J.R.: Measuring shared team mental models: A meta-analysis. Group Dyn. Theor. Res. Pract. **14**(1), 1 (2010)
3. Fan, X., Yen, J.: Modeling cognitive loads for evolving shared mental models in human-agent collaboration. IEEE Trans. Syst. Man Cybern. **41**(2), 354–367 (2011)

4. Harbers, M., Jonker, C.M., Van Riemsdijk, M.B.: Context-sensitive sharedness criteria for teamwork. In: Proceedings of AAMAS 2014, pp. 1507–1508. ACM (2014)
5. Harbers, M., Riemsdijk, M.V., Jonker, C.: Measuring sharedness of mental models and its relation to team performance. In: Proceedings of 14th Workshop on COIN, pp. 106–120. Verlag (2012)
6. Hindriks, K.: Programming rational agents in GOAL. In: Seghrouchni, A.E.F., Dix, J., Dastani, M., Bordini, R.H. (eds.) Multi-Agent Programming, pp. 119–157. Springer, US (2009)
7. Johnson, M., Bradshaw, J., Feltovich, P., Jonker, C., Riemsdijk, M.B.V.: Coactive design : Designing support for interdependence in joint activity. J. Hum. Robot Interact. 3(1), 43–69 (2014)
8. Johnson, M., Jonker, C., Riemsdijk, B., Feltovich, P.J., Bradshaw, J.M.: Joint activity testbed: blocks world for teams (BW4T). In: Aldewereld, H., Dignum, V., Picard, G. (eds.) ESAW 2009. LNCS, vol. 5881, pp. 254–256. Springer, Heidelberg (2009). doi:10.1007/978-3-642-10203-5_26
9. Jonker, C.M., Riemsdijk, M.B., Vermeulen, B.: Shared mental models. In: Vos, M., Fornara, N., Pitt, J.V., Vouros, G. (eds.) COIN -2010. LNCS (LNAI), vol. 6541, pp. 132–151. Springer, Heidelberg (2011). doi:10.1007/978-3-642-21268-0_8
10. Li, S., Sun, W., Miller, T.: Communication in human-agent teams for tasks with joint action. In: Dignum, V., Noriega, P., Sensoy, M., Sichman, J.S.S. (eds.) COIN 2015. LNCS (LNAI), vol. 9628, pp. 224–241. Springer, Cham (2016). doi:10.1007/978-3-319-42691-4_13
11. Manner, M.D., Gini, M.: Improving agent team performance through helper agents. In: Dignum, F., Brom, C., Hindriks, K., Beer, M., Richards, D. (eds.) CAVE 2012. LNCS (LNAI), vol. 7764, pp. 89–105. Springer, Heidelberg (2013). doi:10.1007/978-3-642-36444-0_6
12. Mohammed, S., Ferzandi, L., Hamilton, K.: Metaphor no more: A 15-year review of the team mental model construct. J. Manag. 36(4), 876–910 (2010)
13. Rouse, W.B., Morris, N.M.: On looking into the black box: Prospects and limits in the search for mental models. Psychol. Bullet. 100(3), 349 (1986)
14. Saavedra, R., Earley, P.C., Van Dyne, L.: Complex interdependence in task-performing groups. J. Appl. Psychol. 78(1), 61–72 (1993)
15. Singh, R., Miller, T., Sonenberg, L.: A preliminary analysis of interdependence in multiagent systems. In: Dam, H.K., Pitt, J., Xu, Y., Governatori, G., Ito, T. (eds.) PRIMA 2014. LNCS (LNAI), vol. 8861, pp. 381–389. Springer, Cham (2014). doi:10.1007/978-3-319-13191-7_31
16. Smith-Jentsch, K.A.: On shifting from autonomous to interdependent work. Technical report, NASA, Houston, Texas (2015)
17. Wei, C., Hindriks, K., Jonker, C.M.: The role of communication in coordination protocols for cooperative robot teams. In: Proceedings of International Conference on Agents and Artificial Intelligence, pp. 28–39 (2014)

An Empirical Approach for Relating Environmental Patterns with Agent Team Compositions

Mariana Ramos Franco[1(✉)], Gustavo A.L. Campos[2],
and Jaime Simão Sichman[1]

[1] Laboratório de Técnicas Inteligentes, Escola Politécnica,
Universidade de São Paulo, São Paulo, Brazil
ramos.franco@gmail.com, jaime.sichman@poli.usp.br
[2] Mestrado Acadêmico em Ciência da Computação,
Universidade Estadual do Ceará, Fortaleza, Brazil
gustavo@larces.uece.br

Abstract. The design of a rational organization composed of a team of agents is a challenging problem in domains such as collective robotics, cyber warfare, war games and military missions. In these domains, the team is designed to confront an opponent team with technical and numerical equivalence, and aiming to conquer areas where there are scarce resources of high economic value, that are distributed in locations within a territory whose topology is unknown. In these scenarios, it is hard for the agents to do the right thing. In addition to being competitive, the task environment is unknown, partially observable and dynamic. The challenge is how to design a rational team whose members are not ideal rational agents. This work argues that one approach is to implement a suitable organizational specification that fits the task environment, according to some previously defined environmental patterns that include both domain-specific and topological characteristics. In this work, we present an experimental evaluation of these patterns' influence on the performance of teams of agents evolving on the Agents on Mars scenario, a well-known agent programming testbed. The results of the evaluation show that organizational specifications that exploit this information perform better than others that don't.

Keywords: Organizations · Team formation · Engineering Multi-Agent systems

1 Introduction

The design of rational agents is a nontrivial task, especially in hard task environments. The hardest case corresponds to a multi-agent, unknown, partially observable, non-deterministic, sequential, continuous and dynamic environment [1]. The designer must be satisfied with a non-ideal rational agent to evolve in these domains. In a multi-agent domain, the challenge that arises is how to design the organization of the multi-agent system; more specifically, in competitive environments, the problem to solve is how to design a rational team of agents, each of them not ideally rational [2, 3].

© Springer International Publishing AG 2017
S. Cranefield et al. (Eds.): COIN 2016 Workshops, LNAI 10315, pp. 98–115, 2017.
DOI: 10.1007/978-3-319-66595-5_6

In our context, a MAS organization is "… a supra-agent pattern of emergent or predefined cooperation of the agents in the system, that could be defined by the designer or by the agents themselves, to achieve a purpose." [2]. The notion of team identifies an organizational paradigm where a group of agents must work together to achieve a common goal in a task environment. Each agent assumes a role and commits himself to attain some goals that are necessary to achieve the team's overall objective. The team maintains an explicit representation of its organization, called Organizational Specification (OS) [3].

A team of agents must be composed of some specialist agents to be able to operate in hard environments, such as exploring unknown places as foreign planets in a type of war where the ground squads realize campaigns for the installation of forces in resource-rich areas. The number of individual agents of each capability in a hetero-geneous team is its composition. In the organizational context, each agent assumes a role in the team and the team of agents can be divided into two or more groups of agents. The team adequate structure and composition, i.e., the number of groups in the team and the specialist agents in each group, are not known a priori in these hard environments, and will produce poor performance for the team if they were not done properly.

This work is a contribution for the sub problem of designing the teams' organizational structure, what is called in organization theory as the "synthesis problem", namely: "which structures are best suited to solve optimally certain types of problems?" [4], or "given a certain set of conditions to be satisfied, how to find the network which is best?" [5]. The problem considers that the designer knows in which kind of environment the team should evolve and his task is to determine a suitable organizational structure that fits the task environment.

We consider that a suitable team's organizational structure must fit the task environment in each domain. We focus on the relation between some environmental patterns in the task environment and the number of groups/squads of agents in the team structure, specially to assess the influence of this relation in the performance of a team designed to confront an opponent team with technical and numerical equivalence, and aiming to conquer areas where there are scarce resources of high economic value (clusters), that are distributed in locations within a territory whose topology is unknown.

We consider that the same approach can be applied in other domains in which the environment can be represented by a weighted graph, where the vertexes denote resources and possible locations for the agents, and the edges indicate the possibility of crossing from one vertex to another with a cost for the agent. In our work, a cluster is a "valuable area" represented by any connected subgraph in which the resource values in the vertices are greater than an inferior limit value of resource by vertex, and the sum of all values in the vertices is greater than an inferior limit value of resource by cluster. The notion of environmental pattern is defined based on some clusters' spatial attributes, whose values can be perceived by the teams when they explore the environment.

The main contribution of this paper is a methodological one – viz. an empirical approach for relating features of task environments to successful agent structural organization. In the context of the team composition, we consider that the designer has worked previously on the team's OS; his task is to refine the initial structural specification, determining which roles the agents can play in the groups, and how many groups and their cardinality are necessary to maximize the team's performance evaluation measure in an environment with previously known environment patterns.

The agents' team performance evaluation is domain-dependent. In our case, it is based on the *Agents on Mars* scenario, a testbed provided by the Multi-Agent Programming Contest [6]. The results of our evaluation show that organizational specifications that exploit this information perform better than others that don't. For example, the number of clusters leads, in some cases, to situations where it may be better for the whole team to occupy a single cluster, while in other cases it may be better to divide the team into smaller squads to try to gain control over multiple clusters in the environment.

2   Evaluation of the Organizational Design

Previous research in the field of organization theory has already focused on the evaluation of the quantitative effect of the organizational design on the SMA's performance.

Horling and Lesser [7] focused on the comparison of organizational paradigms. They present a survey of the major organizational paradigms used in multi-agent systems. These include teams and others human organizational patterns. They provided the descriptions of these patterns, their advantages and disadvantages, and examples of use. They argue that their work allows the designers to recognize a large set of structural possibilities, to realize comparative evaluation of organizational structures and then to select an appropriate organizational design for a domain and environment.

van der Broekwork et al. [8] proposed an approach for the analysis and the formal modeling of agent-based organizations. The approach addresses both the organization structure and its dynamics. The environment is considered as a special component of the organization model. It serves as a source of events for the organization. The environment is populated by agents, which under certain conditions may be allocated to organizational roles. By performing simulations and verification, the approach provides formal techniques and tools for different types of analysis of organization models.

Hodgson et al. [9] developed a framework that supports hierarchical modeling of teams of agents. A team (group) is a composite component that is characterized by several roles, which are enacted by agents and other teams. The framework focuses on the technical side of programming and implementation of SMA. The authors introduced a formal language for specifying the dynamics of individual roles and teams, providing different interesting types of analysis of the SMA dynamics.

Scerri et al. [10] have focused on studies about the properties and the performance of teams with hundreds of members. They developed a model of teamwork to address the limitations of others models applied to very large teams. The model organizes team members into sub teams that evolve dynamically, and into overlapping sub teams that work on sub goals of the overall team goal. They experimented these very large teams evolving in distinct domains, such as control of fire trucks responding to an urban disaster and simulated unmanned aerial vehicles in a battle space.

Grossi et al. [4, 11] argue that "organizational structures should be seen along at least three dimensions: power, coordination, and control". They provided a technical terminology for describing the notion of structural organization and its properties. The concepts are defined rigorously by means of concepts from graph theory. In addition to be useful for describing the organizational structure, they can be employed to provide a formal analysis of the effect of such structures on the activities in the SMA. Their formal tool can be useful to provide numerical analyses of the organizational structures, and for evaluating to what extent an organizational structure exhibits some characteristic properties such as robustness, flexibility and efficiency.

Machado et al. [12] developed a detailed discussion related to multi-agent patrolling and an empirical evaluation of possible patrolling solutions in domains such as computer networks and computer war games. The authors proposed different architectures of multi-agent systems, various evaluation criteria, applied in two experimental settings. They implemented a patrol simulator. The results show that some kinds of architecture can patrol an area, in certain circumstances, more adequately than others.

Furtado and Filho [13] described a simulator of crimes in an urban area. The user configures and allocates police forces in certain geographical regions and then interacts with the simulation, watching the crime behavior in the presence of preventive police. They described how studies involving simulations can help to determine whether a reorganization process is necessary and how it should be performed. The simulation results illustrate how to exploit opportunities for the system to be reorganized.

Although some of these detailed studies about structures had tried to answer the question of which structures are best suited to solve problems in environments that can change (or not) frequently, they do not address other properties that are intrinsic in hard task environments, as the case of a partially observable and unknown environment, neither any kind of analysis relating to patterns detected in this environment.

3 The Suitable Team Structure

The design of a rational agent team can be a very complex problem. The hardest case corresponds to an environment that is partially observable, nondeterministic, sequential, continuous, unknown and dynamic [1]. One of the main challenges associated with the design problem, involves the search for solutions for the synthesis problem, namely, "which structures are best suited to solve optimally certain types of problems?" [4]. In this context, the relation between the set of possible patterns of the environment and the set of possible organizational structures for a team is a necessary information for the designer of a rational team, i.e., that must be able to use this knowledge to revise the team formation, changing for a suitable structure when the team discovers the environment patterns or when these patterns change [14].

3.1 Environmental Patterns

We focus in this work on agent teams designed to confront opponent teams with technical and numerical equivalence, and aiming to conquer areas where there are scarce resources of high economic value, that are distributed in locations within a territory whose topology is unknown, but that can be discovered by the teams as the agents interact with their environment. The agent teams' territory can be a physical environment, as a battlefield in an unconventional war, where military groups are formed in order to realize campaigns to conquer certain areas in big cities, which were contained by traffickers and militias [15]. It can be a virtual battlefield in a war electronic game, multiplayer, online first-person shooter [16]. The battle can happen in the cyberspace as well, where usually anonymous cybernetic attacks occur, that are directed at political leaders, military systems, and any ordinary citizen, anywhere in the world [17].

These battlefields can be represented by a vertex-edge-labeled graph (weighted graph with two vertex functions). Formally, this vertex-edge-labeled graph $G = (V, E)$ consists of a set of vertices V and a set of edges E, which contains unordered pairs of distinct elements of V. Each vertex in the graph has a resource value and, optionally, an identifier. The resource value associated with a vertex and its identification are modeled respectively by a vertex value function vvf: $G(V) \rightarrow N$ and by a vertex labeling function vlf: $G(V) \rightarrow Idv$, where N is the set of natural numbers employed to value the resources in the vertices in V, and Idv is a subset of the natural numbers (e.g.: $\{1, \ldots, |V|\}$) employed to identify the $|V|$ vertices in V. Each edge in the graph indicates the possibility of crossing from one vertex to another. The cost of edge crossing for the agent is modeled by an edge value function evf: $G(E) \rightarrow R$, where R is the set of real numbers employed to value the costs in the edges in E.

The notion of environmental patterns in this work tries to capture the diversity of environments, i.e., how many "valuable areas", subgraphs representing the higher valued resources, appear in a graph G representing a battlefield. In our work, these "valuable areas" are called clusters. We consider that a cluster is any connected subgraph C of G in which the resource values in the vertices are greater than an inferior limit value of resource by vertex, and the sum of all values in the vertices is greater than an inferior limit value of resource by cluster.

To formally define the notion of cluster, let infVc denotes the inferior limit value of resource capacity by vertex in a cluster, and infCc the inferior limit value of resources capacity by cluster. We define the notion of cluster in the graph $G = (V, E)$ as any sub-graph $C = (V', E')$, such $V' \subseteq V$ and $E' \subseteq E$, that satisfies three conditions:

(1) $\forall v \in C(V'), vvf(v) \geq infVc$
(2) C is a connected sub-graph
(3) $\inf Cc \leq \sum_{v \in C(V')} vvf(v) \leq \sum_{v \in G(V)} vvf(v)$

The first condition ensures that the resource value associated with each vertex in a cluster C is greater than the inferior limit value of resource capacity by vertex. The second condition ensures that the clusters in the graph G can be a sub-graph C with only one (isolated) vertex with high value, or a sub-graph in which all vertices in C are not isolated. Finally, the third condition ensures that the sum of the resource values associated with all vertices in a cluster C is greater than the inferior limit value of resources capacity by cluster, that must be lesser than or equal the graph capacity, i.e., the sum of all values of resource capacity in the graph G.

Figure 1 illustrates the notion of a cluster $C = (V', E')$ in a graph $G = (V, E)$, when $|V| = 21$ vertices and $|E| = 27$ edges. The vertex identification was omitted in the figure. The vertices that are not graphically described by a circle in Fig. 1(a) represent the vertices v in V that satisfy the first condition to be a member of V′ when InfVc = 1, i.e., vvf(v) ≥ 1. The three selected sub-graphs in Fig. 1(b) represent those sub-graphs G′ in G that satisfies the first and the second condition to be a cluster C in G. The two selected sub-graphs in Fig. 1(c), C1 and C2, represent the sub-graphs G′ in G that are clusters, i.e., those that satisfy the three conditions when InfCc = 10, i.e., $\sum_{v \in C1(V1)} vvf(v) \geq 10$ and $\sum_{v \in C2(V2)} vvf(v) \geq 10$. When considering the distribution of values of vertices of a cluster C in G, two extreme cases are possible: highly diverse clusters with the maximum possible number of distinct values, and homogeneous clusters having vertices of the same value.

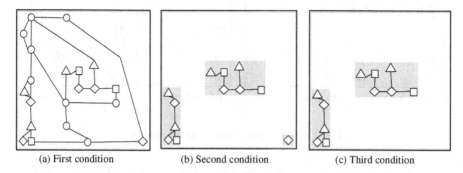

(a) First condition   (b) Second condition   (c) Third condition

Fig. 1. Clusters

The notion of environmental pattern associated with a vertex-edge-labeled graph G is defined as a tuple EP(G) = <S, N, H, D>, considering four attributes associated with the distribution of all clusters in G, such that: S (size) represents the mean number of vertices of the clusters in G; N (number) represents the quantity of clusters in G; H (homogeneity) is a boolean value which indicates if clusters in G have the same value; and D (dispersion) represents the approximate mean distance in number of vertices between the clusters in G. So, we have at least eight extreme case associated with these four attributes. The vertices in the clusters in Fig. 1(c) have different resource values, so that the value of: a circle is one, a square is two, a triangle value is three and a lozenge is four. Therefore, the environmental pattern associated with the graph in the figure is: S = 5, N = 2, H = 0 e D = 7. Figure 2 shows graphs with different cluster patterns, setting the parameters in the cluster conditions as infVc = 1 and infCc = 10.

The larger vertices in black color identify the vertices and edges that satisfy the three cluster's conditions. Figure 2(a)–(b) illustrate different sizes for the clusters. Figure 2(c)–(d) illustrates different number of clusters, three clusters in SC3 and five clusters in SC4. The graphs in Fig. 2(e)–(f) have different homogeneity values, i.e., the vertices in the clusters in SC5 have approximately the same value and the vertices in SC6 have not. Finally, different dispersion values are illustrated in Fig. 2(g)–(h), i.e., where the six clusters in SC7 are more dispersed on the graph and the six clusters in SC8 are more close to each other.

Our work considers that the attainment of a goal by a team involves a relation between its goal, its organizational specification and its external environment. The

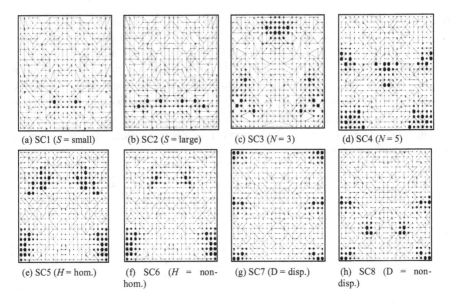

| (a) SC1 (S = small) | (b) SC2 (S = large) | (c) SC3 (N = 3) | (d) SC4 (N = 5) |

| (e) SC5 (H = hom.) | (f) SC6 (H = non-hom.) | (g) SC7 (D = disp.) | (h) SC8 (D = non-disp.) |

Fig. 2. Environments with different patterns

success of a team depends on their internal construction and on where it is placed to function. If the team's organizational specification is suitable for its external environment, or vice versa, the team will reach the desired objective. Moreover, from the point of view of the structural specification, in a great number of cases, the attainment of the team's goal depends on a few features in the external environment, and is independent of its details. We focus on the relation between the environmental patterns in the task environment and the number of groups/squads of agents in the team structure, especially to assess the influence of this relation in the performance of a team designed to confront an opponent team with technical and numerical equivalence.

3.2   Teams' Structural Organization

A team is a human organizational pattern that can be characterized by a set of cooperative agents, which have agreed to work together attempting to maximize their utility [18]. The designer must solve two related problems to design an agent team: the design of individual cooperative heterogeneous agents and the design of a rational team organization for these agents. The design of each kind of agent requires the formalization of the function that maps each sequence of perceptions into an action, that is necessary to realize tasks like to find and to conquer the best clusters, to defend these clusters, to attack the agents in the adversary team and to help the agents in the same team.

In relation to the agent organization, the designer must formally describe the team's organizational specification OS. In this work, this notion is based on the MOISE organizational modeling language [19, 20]. It decomposes the organizational specification OS = <SS, FS, DS> in three dimensions. The Structural Specification (SS) defines the roles, relationships between roles, and the team's groups. The Functional Specification (FS) defines the global goals and how these are decomposed into subgoals and missions. The deontic specification (DS) relates these two dimensions, identifying subsets of missions and goals in FS that are permitted and/or required for each role in SS.

The MOISE Structural Specification SS is built in three levels. Let Agents represents the set of N agents in the team, and Roles the set of M roles that can be played by any agent $A_i \in$ Agents. Let $AgR_j = \{A_i \,|A_i \in$ Agents plays a role $R_j \in$ Roles$\}$. At the individual level, the SS defines the set of behaviors that an agent $Ai \in AgRj$ is responsible for when he adopts the role R_j. At the social level, the SS defines three kinds of links between roles: authority, communication and acquaintance. An authority link $link(A_i, A'_i, aut)$ implies the existence of a communication link $link(A_i, A'_i, com)$, the latter implies the existence of an acquaintance link $link(A_i, A'_i, acq)$. For example, in the case where the link type is acquaintance, an agent source $A_i \in AgR_j$, playing a source role R_j, has a representation of the agent destination $A'_i \in AgR'_j$, playing a destination role R'_j. At the collective level, the SS defines the aggregations of roles in groups.

A group is created from a group specification indicating the subset of roles that should be played in the group and their respectively min-max cardinality (how many agents can play those roles), its set of subgroups and their respectively min-max cardinality and the sets of intra-group and inter-group links [20]. Figure 3(a) illustrates the MOISE structural specification of a team T composed of groups of agents Gr (min $= 1$; max $= 8$), that can play two roles C (min $= 1$; max $= 8$) and S (min $= 0$; max $= 7$), and one group of one agent that can play one role L (min $= 1$; max $= 1$).

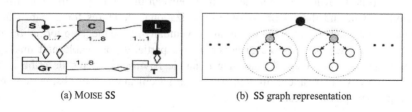

(a) MOISE SS   (b) SS graph representation

Fig. 3. An agent team's organizational structure

Hence, a MOISE structural specification SS can be viewed as a vertex-labeled graph $G = (V, E)$, whose vertexes V are playing role agents and whose edges E represent authority, communication and acquaintance links. Figure 3(b) illustrates the previous SS graph representation. The graph in Fig. 3(b) is one of the valid representations of the team organizational structures that can be generated from the MOISE SS in Fig. 3(a), where the structure of each sub-group Gr is represented by a tree, generated by the authority inter-group link between role L (agent in the black vertex) and role C (agents in the grey vertices), and the communication intra-group link between roles C and role S (agents in white vertices). Section 4.2 presents a concrete example to clarify some key points provided in this section in an abstract way.

3.3 The Environmental Patterns and the Teams' Structural Organizations

From the point of view of team composition, a team of agents able to operate in a hard environment, rather than being a homogeneous team, must be composed of specialist agents. In the organizational context, In the organizational context, each agent assumes a role in the team and the team of agents can be divided into two or more groups of agents. The adequate number of individual agents of each capability in each group and the number of groups in a heterogeneous team are not known a priori in the scenarios approached in our work. Discovering the optimal composition and structure are relevant features in the team design as it may avoid poor performance.

Our work is a contribution for the sub problem of designing the team' organizational structure, that is, which structures of specialist agents are best suited to solve optimally certain types of problems. We consider that the designer has worked previously on the team's organizational specification OS = <SS, FS, DS>, specifying which roles the agents can play in the groups and their links (SS), the team's current goals in its missions, the max-min number of agents that can commit with them (FS), and the agents that can or should commit to the goals and missions (DS). Given these previous information, the team composition task is to find a graph $Go = (Vo, Eo)$ that represents a suitable organizational structure in an environment represented by the graph $Ge = (Ve, Ee)$ with a known pattern $EP(Ge) = <S, N, H, D>$.

More specifically, to find Go the designer must solve two related choice problems: (a) to choose the number of groups of specialist agents and (b) to choose the cardinality of each group, such as the team structural specification SS is not violated and aimed to maximize the team's performance evaluation measure in the environment Ge. We believe that the knowledge about the relation between the set of possible patterns for the environment and the set of possible organizational structures for a team can be learned by some agents in the organization to eventually revise the team formation; this may be done when patterns are discovered in a partially observable and unknown environment, or when they change in a dynamic environment. We describe in the sequence how we experiment different structural specifications with distinct environmental patterns possibilities.

4 Experimental Evaluation

Our experimental approach consists of proposing different organizational specifications that are suitable for different environmental patterns (EPs), and can be adapted to generate knowledge about the agent teams' performance.

4.1 Evaluation Scenario

The application domain used in this work is the Agents on Mars scenario, developed in the Multi-Agent Programming Contest [6]. The task environment consists of a battlefield in an unconventional war, in which artificial agents have special sensors and actuators to explore and to conquer rich areas in natural resources, which are in unknown places. Although it seems a specific type of war application, where the ground squads realize campaigns for the installation of forces in the rich resource areas, the chosen specific scenario has the major components that occur in campaigns in a diversity of application domains.

The scenario environment shown in Fig. 4 is represented by a graph where the vertices denote water wells and possible locations for the agents, and the edges indicate the possibility of crossing from one vertex to another with an energy cost. A zone is a sub-graph covered by a team per a coloring algorithm based on the notion of domain [6]. Agents from different teams can be in a single vertex. The team with the highest number of agents dominates the vertex, which receives the dominant team color. An uncolored vertex inherits the color from its neighborhoods dominant team. If the graph contains a sub-graph with a colored border, all the nodes that are within this boundary receive the same color.

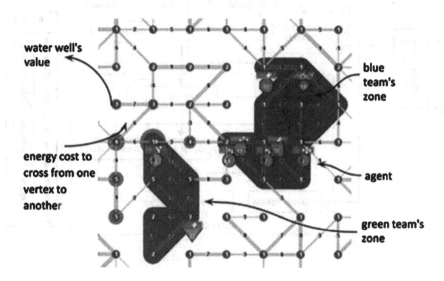

Fig. 4. Agents on Mars Scenario

At the beginning of the simulation, the map is unknown to the agents. Each team consists of 28 players that can be of five different types: explorers, sentinels, saboteurs, inspectors and repairers. These types define the characteristics of each agent such as life level, maximum energy, strength, and visibility. The roles also limit the possible actions that the agent can perform in the environment. For instance, explorers can discover water wells and help to explore the map, while sentinels have long-distance sensors and thus can observe larger areas, saboteurs can attack and disable enemies, inspectors can spy opponents, and repairers can repair damaged agents.

A team receives a cash reward whenever it reaches a major milestone. This reward can be used to empower the agents, increasing their maximum energy or strength. Different milestones can be reached during a competition, such as dominating areas with fixed values, having performed a successful number of attacks or well-succeeded defenses. If not used, the reward is added to the team's total score. The goal of each team is to maximize its score, defined as the sum of the values obtained by the occupied zones with the earned (and not yet spent) rewards in each step of the simulation.

4.2   Agent Teams

In our work [27], we decided to design BDI agents and to give emphasis on the functioning of the teams' organizations in graphs with different EPs. Each agent is composed of plans, a belief base and its own world model, that consists of a graph. It captures every detail received from the environment, such as explored vertices and edges, opponents' position, disabled teammates, etc. Figure 5 illustrates the block diagram adopted in the design of all agents in our team.

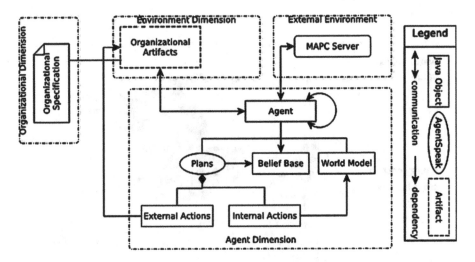

Fig. 5. Agents' Architecture

The world model consists of a graph representing the scenario environment. It captures every detail received from the environment (MAPC contest server). At each step, the agent's world model is updated with the percepts received from the MAPC server, and with the information received from the other agents. Some of the percepts received from the MAPC server are also stored in the agent's belief base, such as the agent's type, energy, position and team's rewards, thus allowing the agent to have a direct access to this information without access its world model. The agent decides which plan will be executed considering its beliefs and the local view of the world. In addition to the agents' types defined by the Scenario, we defined additional different roles in our system. Table 1 describes the mission related to each role.

Each of these roles has a mission associated with it, and can be played by one or more agents. The coordinator is a kind of agent internal to our system, which does not communicate with the MAPC server. Whenever the world model is updated, he computes which are the best zones in the graph and send this information to the other

Table 1. Types and missions of agents

Type	Mission
Explorer	Explores the whole graph by probing every vertex and surveying all edges on its path
Soldier	Tries to occupy one of the best zones indicated by the coordinator agent
Guardian	Defends the squad by attacking any opponent that is close to the team's zone
Medic	Repairs the agents in the squad
Soldier exp.	Explores the team's zone by probing the vertices whose values are unknown
Saboteur	Attacks any close opponent
Sentinel	Sabotages the opponent by moving inside its zone
Repairer	Repairs the saboteur and the sentinel
Coordinator	Builds its local view of the world through the percepts broadcasted by the other agents

agents. Although he determines the best areas of the map, each agent decides for himself which empty vertex he will occupy to form a zone or increase it. The coordinator is also responsible for creating the organizational specification, in the beginning of a competition, and for distributing the groups, roles and missions among the other agents. Figure 6 shows a diagram to illustrate one possible team's SS.

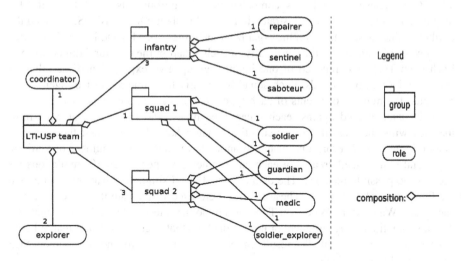

Fig. 6. Team structural specification

This team is composed of three infantry group, one coordinator, two explorers and the other sixteen agents divided into four squads. Each squad had nearly the same number of agents, and respected the number of agents of each type when assigning the roles. The team was developed using a platform for MAS programming called JaCaMo [21], which supports all levels of abstractions – agent, environment, and organization – that are required for developing sophisticated MAS, by combining three separate technologies: Jason for programming autonomous agents [22], CArtAgO for programming environment artifacts [23, 24], and MOISE for programming multi-agent organizations [25].

Jason is a Java-based interpreter for an extended version of the AgentSpeak programming language, for programming BDI agents. CArtAgO is a framework for environment programming based on the A&A meta-model [24]. In CArtAgO, the environment can be designed as a dynamic set of computational entities called artifacts, organized into workspaces, possibly distributed among various nodes of a network [21]. Each artifact represents a resource or a tool that agents can instantiate, share, use, and perceive at runtime. We made use of the organizational artifacts provided in Moise.

4.3   Description of the Experiments

The goal of our experiments was to evaluate the impact of the environmental patterns over teams' performance, by modifying the environmental pattern EP(G) = <S, N, H, D> in the Agent on Mars map, and measuring the performance of two adversary teams composed by the same BDI agents, but with two different organizational specifications OS = (SS, FS, DS). For each team, the performance measure adds the values of its conquered clusters with the earned rewards, as the team reaches a major milestone. The experiments tried to perceive the impact of the EP over teams' performance.

The experiments [26] consisted of seven teams: TG1, TG2, TG3, TG4, TG6, TG8 and TG10. These seven teams competed in 14 environments with different EPs, including the eight scenarios illustrated in Fig. 1. In relation to teams' OS, we fixed the attribute values associated with the organizational dimensions FS and DS, and modified the number of squads and the cardinality of each squad in the structural dimension SS. Each team TGN is composed of one infantry group, two explorers and the other 23 agents divided into n squads. Each squad had nearly the same number of agents, and respected the number of agents of each type when assigning the roles.

Each team played against each other three times, and the team that wins most matches wins the overall tournament. Each match had 750 steps and the map was randomly generated. From one match to another we changed the number of vertices, edges and high-valued areas. For each environment, we performed 10 simulations for each of the possible matches. The data collected in all simulation was the winner and the final score of each team. These metrics were used to indicate the performance of each team. We used the Wilcoxon T test as a hypothesis test to define for each match if the 10 simulations were sufficient or not to conclude that a team was better than other in a determined environment. The results of the Wilcoxon T test for the environment SC3 (Fig. 1) is shown in Table 2.

Table 2. Results of the Wilcoxon T test for SC3

	TG1	TG2	TG3	TG4	TG6	TG8	TG10
TG1		0,0059	0,0195	0,0020	0,0039	0,0371	0,0137
TG2	0,0059		0,6953	0,0488	0,0273	0,7695	0,6250
TG3	0,0195	0,6953		0,1602	0,0371	0,3750	0,0371
TG4	0,0020	0,0488	0,1602		0,1602	0,0840	0,0273
TG6	0,0039	0,0273	0,0371	0,1602		0,1602	0,2324
TG8	0,0371	0,7695	0,3750	0,0840	0,1602		0,6250
TG10	0,0137	0,6250	0,0371	0,0273	0,2324	0,6250	

The Wilcoxon T test is a non-parametric test for dependent samples that can indicate with some stated confidence level if a particular population tends to have larger values than other. Based on the results of the Wilcoxon T test, it's possible to represent the partial order of a certain number of teams given their performance in a specific environment by a partial order graph. Figure 7 illustrates the partial order graph obtained by drawing an edge from team A to team B whenever a significant difference ($p - value < 0.05$) exists between the performances of two teams.

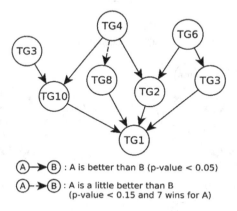

(A)→(B) : A is better than B (p-value < 0.05)

(A)-→(B) : A is a little better than B
(p-value < 0.15 and 7 wins for A)

Fig. 7. Example of a partial order graph

The direction of the edge will be from the team with better performance to the team with lower performance, and we omit the edges that can be extrapolated through a transitive closure, that is, those edges for which there is already a path connecting two teams. The dashed edges represent the matches for which the Wilcoxon T test came close to detect a significant difference between two teams ($p - value < 0.15$ and at least 7 wins for one team). Finally, it's possible that the same team appears twice or more times in graph as shown in Fig. 5, in which TG3 appears twice. This is necessary so that we can represent that TG3 achieved a better performance than TG10, but the same was not observed for TG6 and TG10. This analysis was performed on all environments and the results obtained are presented in the following subsections.

4.4 Obtained Results

Here, a cluster is any subgraph of the maps formed by vertices with value greater than 1 (infVc), in which the sum of all vertices is greater than 10 (infCc). In relation to clusters' size (S), in general, a team with a number of squads equal to the number of zones (a zone is a sub-graph covered by a team according to a coloring algorithm based on the notion of domain [6]) in the cluster does better. In the environment SC2 it's possible to divide the cluster in 6 zones to be occupied by the squads and, as shown in Fig. 8(a), TG6 is better than almost all the other teams, because: (i) a smaller number of squads is not effective in securing and defending bigger clusters, and (ii) a larger number ends up by causing some squads to disperse out of the cluster, making it difficult to conquer it.

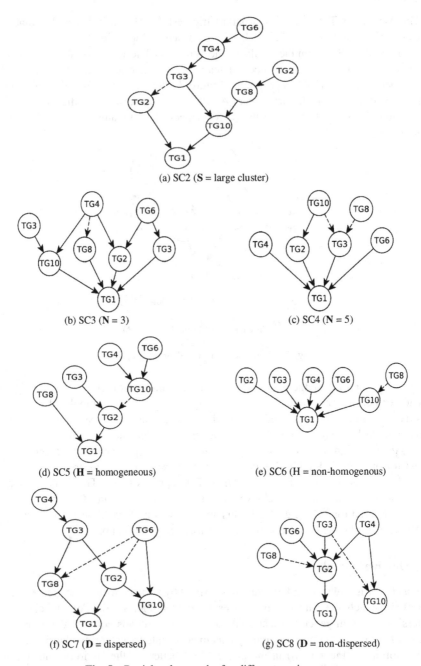

(a) SC2 (**S** = large cluster)

(b) SC3 (**N** = 3)

(c) SC4 (**N** = 5)

(d) SC5 (**H** = homogeneous)

(e) SC6 (**H** = non-homogenous)

(f) SC7 (**D** = dispersed)

(g) SC8 (**D** = non-dispersed)

Fig. 8. Partial order graphs for different environments

Regarding the number of clusters (N), the team must have a number of squads equal or closer to the number of clusters on the map. If the number is smaller, the team will not cover all good areas, which can then be easily occupied by the opponent. If the number of squads is greater than the number of clusters, some agents will be placed in areas of small values, weakening the squads' attack and defense. In Fig. 8(b) it is possible to see that for the environment SC3 with 3 clusters, TG3 performs better than TG10, while TG10 outperforms TG3 for SC4, which has 5 clusters.

Regarding the homogeneity (H), the experiments showed that finding and occupying the clusters with the highest values is critical in non-homogeneous environments. In these cases, it is better to balance among the teams (Fig. 8(c)) since the winner ends up being defined by the team that occupies the bigger clusters. This is good for teams with small number of squads, because there is a chance that they occupy the clusters with highest values, while the opponent with a larger number of squads ends up by spreading its agents in smaller and not valuable clusters.

Regarding the clusters' dispersion (D), the results showed that less dispersed clusters help teams with a larger number of squads to form larger areas than they could if the clusters (and the agents) were dispersed (Fig. 8(d)). Moreover, with the proximity of the clusters, the squads tend to be closer of each other, making it easier to attack the opponent. For example, TG3 and TG4 can dominate large areas in SC7, which often comprise two neighbor clusters, while TG8 occupies smaller areas and does not attack efficiently the opponents. However, in SC8, with the proximity of the clusters, TG8's squads tend to be closer, making it easier to attack the opponent, and thus helping TG8 to occupy sometimes areas that cover more than one cluster at the same time.

5 Conclusions and Further Work

Our evaluation tried to assess the impact of environmental patterns in the performance of a team of agents, designed to confront an "equivalent" opponent team, aiming to conquer areas with scarce resources of high economic value, in unknown locations in the environment. In our work, these areas were denoted as clusters and were employed to generate the notion of environmental pattern, which was essential to operationalize the evaluation.

We performed the evaluation considering the impact of the environmental patterns in a valued graph map over the performance of teams with the same functional and deontic specifications, but with a different structural specification, due the different numbers of squads and the cardinality of each squad in the team. Although our results are preliminary ones, we believe that they provide at least two contributions that can be exploited in the design of agents' teams when the task environment is hard, but that can be described in terms of environmental patterns.

The first contribution is related to the knowledge the designer can learn about these task environments, in order to assess whether a team will be able to selectively search for solutions in the map. The results of our evaluation provided some knowledge about the different organizational specifications that are suitable to different environmental patterns in the maps. In this sense, we hope to intensify this initial evaluation in two directions: (1) from the environment' side, to evolve scenarios that aggregate diversified environmental patterns, obtained from the combination of the different attribute values employed to represent patterns; and (2) from the team's side to extend the approach to other attribute values associated with the three dimensions employed to define organizational specifications.

The second contribution is related to the proper concretization of the notion of environmental pattern realized in the work. Considering this notion as a complementary representation of the state of the environment, and the consistent knowledge that can be provided by a more intensive evaluation of the impact of environmental patterns over the performance of teams, we believe that two possibilities are generated for the designer (or any artificial agent properly designed): (1) to predict the behavior of a team if he knows its goals, its organizational specification, and the current environmental patterns; (2) to define a suitable organizational specification for a team and the properties of its behavior if the agent knows the current environment pattern and team's goal. These are hypotheses that we hope to prove soon.

Acknowledgements. Jaime Simão Sichman is partially supported by CNPq, Brazil, grant agreement no. 303950/2013-7.

References

1. Russel, S., Norvig, P.: Artificial Intelligence: A Modern Approach, 3rd edn. Pearson Education, London (2010)
2. Boissier, O., Sichman, J.S.: Organization oriented programming. In: Tutorial Notes, 3rd. International Joint Conference on Autonomous Agents and Multiagent Systems (AAMAS 2004), New York (2004)
3. Coutinho, L., Sichman, J., Boissier, O.: Modeling dimensions for agent organizations. In: Dignum, V. (ed.) Handbook of Research on Multi-Agent Systems: Semantics and Dynamics of Organizational Models. IGI Global, Hershey (2009)
4. Grossi, D., Dignum, F., Dignum, V., Dastani, M., Royakkers, L.: Structural aspects of the evaluation of agent organizations. In: Noriega, P., Vázquez-Salceda, J., Boella, G., Boissier, O., Dignum, V., Fornara, N., Matson, E. (eds.) COIN -2006. LNCS, vol. 4386, pp. 3–18. Springer, Heidelberg (2007). doi:10.1007/978-3-540-74459-7_1
5. Harary, F.: Status and contrastatus. Sociometry **22**, 23–43 (1959)
6. Behrens, T., Köster, M., Schlesinger, F., Dix, J., Hübner, J.F.: The multi-agent programming contest 2011: a résumé. In: Dennis, L., Boissier, O., Bordini, R.H. (eds.) ProMAS 2011. LNCS, vol. 7217, pp. 155–172. Springer, Heidelberg (2012). doi:10.1007/978-3-642-31915-0_9
7. Horling, B., Lesser, V.: A Survey of Multi-Agent Organizational Paradigms. Computer Science Technical Report 04-45. University of Massachusetts (2004)
8. Broek, E.L., Jonker, C.M., Sharpanskykh, A., Treur, J., Yolum, P: Formal modeling and analysis of organizations. In: Boissier, O., Padget, J., Dignum, V., Lindemann, G., Matson, E., Ossowski, S., Sichman, J.S., Vázquez-Salceda, J. (eds.) AAMAS 2005. LNCS, vol. 3913, pp. 18–34. Springer, Heidelberg (2006). doi:10.1007/11775331_2
9. Hodgson, A., Roennquist, R., Busetta, P., Howden, N.: Team Oriented Programming with Simple Team. In: Proceedings of SimTecT 2000, Sydney, Australia, pp. 115–122 (2000)
10. Scerri, P., Xu, Y., Liao, E., Lai, J., Sycara, K.: Scaling teamwork to very large teams. In: Proceedings of the Third International Joint Conference on Autonomous Agents and Multiagent Systems (AAMAS 2004). ACM Press, New York (2004)

11. Grossi, D., Dignum, F., Dastani, M., Royakkers, L.: Foundations of organizational structures in multiagent systems. In: Proceedings Fourth International Joint Conference on Autonomous Agents and Multiagent Systems (AAMAS 2005), pp. 690–697. ACM Press, Utrecht (2005)

12. Machado, A., Ramalho, G., Zucker, J.-D., Drogoul, A.: Multi-agent patrolling: an empirical analysis of alternative architectures. In: Simão Sichman, J., Bousquet, F., Davidsson, P. (eds.) MABS 2002. LNCS, vol. 2581, pp. 155–170. Springer, Heidelberg (2003). doi:10. 1007/3-540-36483-8_11

13. Furtado, V., Filho, E.J.: A multi-agent simulator for teaching police allocation. In: Proceedings of the 17th conference on Innovative applications of artificial intelligence (IAAI 2005) - Volume 3, pp. 1521–1528 (2005)

14. Lu, H: Team formation in agent-based computer games. In: Pisan, Y. (ed.) Proceedings of the 2nd Australasian Conference on Interactive Entertainment, IE 2005, Sydney, Australia, pp. 121–124. ACM Press (2005)

15. Melo, A., Belchior, M., Furtado, V.: Analyzing police patrol routes by simulating the physical reorganization of agents. In: Sichman, J.S., Antunes, L. (eds.) MABS 2005. LNCS, vol. 3891, pp. 99–114. Springer, Heidelberg (2006). doi:10.1007/11734680_8

16. The Gamasutra Quantum Leap Awards: First-Person Shooters, GamaSutra. http://www. gamasutra.com/view/feature/1832/the_gamasutra_quantum_leap_awards_.php. Accessed 8 Feb 2016

17. Czosseck, C., Geers, K. (eds.): The Virtual Battlefield: Perspectives on Cyber Warfare. Cryptology and Information Security Series, vol. 3. IOS Press, Amsterdam (2009)

18. Carley, K., Gasser, L.: Computational organization theory. In: Weiss, G. (ed.) Multiagent Systems, pp. 299–330. MIT Press, Cambridge (1999)

19. Hübner, J.F., Sichman, J.S., Boissier, O.: A model for the structural, functional, and deontic specification of organizations in multiagent systems. In: Bittencourt, G., Ramalho, G.L. (eds.) SBIA 2002. LNCS, vol. 2507, pp. 118–128. Springer, Heidelberg (2002). doi:10. 1007/3-540-36127-8_12

20. Hübner, J., Sichman, J., Boissier, O.: Developing organised multiagent systems using the MOISE + model: programming issues at the system and agent levels. Int. J. Agent-Oriented Softw. Eng. 1–27 (2007)

21. Boissier, O., Bordini, R.H., Hübner, J., Ricci, A., Santi, A.: Multi-agent oriented programming with JaCaMo. Sci. Comput. Program. 78(6), 747–761 (2011)

22. Bordini, R.H., Hübner, J., Wooldridge, M.: Programming Multi-agent Systems in AgentSpeak using Jason. Wiley-Blackwell, Chichester (2007)

23. Ricci, A., Piunti, M., Viroli, M.: Environment programming in multi-agent systems: an artifact-based perspective. Auton. Agents Multi-Agent Syst. 23(2), 158–192 (2010)

24. Omicini, A., Ricci, A., Viroli, M.: Artifacts in the A&A meta-model for multi-agent systems. Auton. Agents Multi-Agent Syst. 17(3), 432–456 (2008)

25. Hübner, J., Boissier, O., Kitio, R., Ricci, A.: Instrumenting multi-agent organisations with organisational artifacts and agents. Auton. Agents Multi-Agent Syst. 20(3), 369–400 (2009)

26. Franco, M.R.: Avaliação Organizacional de Times de Agentes para o Multi-Agent Programming Contest. Master's thesis. Escola Politécnica da Universidade de São Paulo (2014)

27. Franco, M.R., Sichman, J.S.: Improving the LTI-USP team: a new JaCaMo based MAS for the MAPC 2013. In: Cossentino, M., Fallah Seghrouchni, A., Winikoff, M. (eds.) EMAS 2013. LNCS, vol. 8245, pp. 339–348. Springer, Heidelberg (2013). doi:10.1007/978-3-642-45343-4_19

Rights and Values

Monitoring Opportunism in Multi-agent Systems

Jieting Luo[1]([✉]), John-Jules Meyer[1], and Max Knobbout[2]

[1] Utrecht University, Utrecht, The Netherlands
{J.Luo,J.J.C.Meyer}@uu.nl
[2] Delft University of Technology, Delft, The Netherlands
M.Knobbout@tudelft.nl

Abstract. Opportunism is a behavior that causes norm violation and promotes agents' own value. In the context of multi-agent systems, it is important to constrain such a selfish behavior through setting enforcement norms. Because opportunistic behavior cannot be observed directly, there has to be a monitoring mechanism that can detect the performance of opportunistic behavior in the system. This paper provides a logical framework based on the specification of actions to specify monitoring approaches for opportunism. We investigate how to evaluate agents' actions to be opportunistic with respect to different forms of norms when those actions cannot be observed directly, and study how to reduce the monitoring cost for opportunism.

1 Introduction

Consider a common scenario. A seller sells a cup to a buyer and it is known by the seller beforehand that the cup is actually broken. The buyer buys the cup without knowing it is broken. The behavior results in promoting the seller's value (having money) but demoting the buyer's value (having a good cup). Such a social behavior intentionally performed by the seller is first named opportunistic behavior (or opportunism) by economist Williamson [13]. It is a typical social behavior that is motivated by self-interest and takes advantage of knowledge asymmetry about the behavior to promote an agent's own value, regardless of the other agent's value [9]. In the context of multiagent systems, we want to constrain such a selfish behavior through setting enforcement norms, in the sense that opportunistic agents receive a corresponding sanction when they violate the norm. On the one hand, it is important to detect it, as it has undesirable results for the participating agents. On the other hand, since opportunism is always in the form of cheating, deception and betrayal, meaning that the system does not know what the agent performs or even the motivation behind it (for example, in a distributed system), opportunistic behavior cannot be observed directly. Therefore, there has to be a monitoring mechanism that can detect the performance of opportunistic behavior in the system.

The short paper version of this paper has appeared in the proceedings of ECAI 2016, The Hague.

© Springer International Publishing AG 2017
S. Cranefield et al. (Eds.): COIN 2016 Workshops, LNAI 10315, pp. 119–138, 2017.
DOI: 10.1007/978-3-319-66595-5_7

This paper provides a logical framework based on the specification of actions to monitor opportunism. In particular, since monitors cannot read agents' mental states, we define opportunism as a behavior that causes norm violation and promotes agents' own value. Based on this definition, we investigate how to evaluate agents' actions to be opportunistic with respect to different forms of norms when those actions cannot be observed directly, and explore how to reduce the monitoring cost for opportunism based on the monitoring approaches we proposed. We study formal properties of our monitoring approaches in order to determine whether they are effective in the sense that whenever an action is detected to be opportunistic, it was indeed opportunistic, and that whenever an action was opportunistic, it is indeed detected.

2   Framework

In this section we introduce the models and the logical language we use, and define the concept of norms by means of our language.

2.1   Monitoring Transition Systems

Monitors cannot observe the performance of opportunism directly. However, actions can be represented and identified through the information about the context where the action can be performed and the property change in the system, which is called *action specification* [11] or *action description* [7]. Usually an action can be specified through its precondition and its effect (postcondition): the precondition specifies the scenario where the action can be performed whereas the postcondition specifies the scenario resulting from performing the action. For example, the action, dropping a glass to the ground, can be specified as holding a glass as its precondition and the glass getting broken as its effect. In this paper, we assume that every action has a set of pairs of the form $\langle \psi_p^a, \psi_e^a \rangle$, where ψ_p^a is the precondition of action a and ψ_e^a is the effect of performing action a in the context of ψ_p^a, both of which are propositional formulas. Sometimes a particular action a can have different results depending on the context in which it is performed. Based on this idea, we argue that action a can be represented through a set of pairs $D(a) = \{\langle \psi_p^a, \psi_e^a \rangle, ...\}$, each element indicating its precondition and its corresponding effect. The absence of a preconditioon means that the performance of the action is not context-dependent.

In this paper, the models that we use are transition systems, which consist of agents Agt, states S, actions Act and transitions $\mathcal{R}$ between states by actions. When an action $a \in Act$ is performed in a certain state s, the system might progress to a different state s' in which different propositions might hold. We also extend the standard framework with an observable accessibility relation $\mathcal{M}$. Note that in this paper we don't talk about concurrent actions for simplifying our model, meaning that we assume there is only one action to execute in every state. Moreover, actions are deterministic; the same action performed in the same state will always result in the same new state. Formally,

Definition 2.1. *Let* $\Phi = \{p, q, ...\}$ *be a finite set of atomic proposi-tional variables. A monitoring transition system over* Φ *is a tuple* $\mathcal{T} = (Agt, S, Act, \pi, \mathcal{M}, \mathcal{R}, s_0)$ *where*

- *Agt is a finite set of agents;*
- *S is a finite set of states;*
- *Act is a finite set of actions;*
- $\pi : S \to \mathcal{P}(\Phi)$ *is a valuation function mapping a state to a set of propositions that are considered to hold in that state;*
- $\mathcal{M} \subseteq S \times S$ *is a reflexive, transitive and symmetric binary relation between states, that is, for all* $s \in S$ *we have* $s\mathcal{M}s$*; for all* $s, t, u \in S$ $s\mathcal{M}t$ *and* $t\mathcal{M}u$ *imply that* $s\mathcal{M}u$*; and for all* $s, t \in S$ $s\mathcal{M}t$ *implies* $t\mathcal{M}s$*;* $s\mathcal{M}s'$ *is interpreted as state* s' *is observably accessible from state* s*;*
- $\mathcal{R} \subseteq S \times Act \times S$ *is a relation between states with actions, which we refer to as the transition relation labelled with an action; since we have already introduced the notion of action specification, a state transition* $(s, a, s') \in \mathcal{R}$ *if there exists a pair* $\langle \psi_p^a, \psi_e^a \rangle \in D(a)$ *such that* ψ_p^a *is satisfied in state* s *and* ψ_e^a *is satisfied in state* s'*, and both* ψ_p^a *and* ψ_e^a *are evaluated in the conventional way of classical propositional logic; since actions are deterministic, sometimes we also denote state* s' *as* $s\langle a \rangle$ *for which it holds that* $(s, a, s\langle a \rangle) \in \mathcal{R}$*;*
- $s_0 \in S$ *denotes the initial state.*

Norms are regarded as a set of constraints on agents' behavior. More precisely, a norm defines whether a possible state transition by an action is considered to be illegal or not. The same as [1], we simply consider a norm as a subset of $\mathcal{R}$ that is decided by the designers of the system. Formally,

Definition 2.2 (Norm). *A norm* η *is defined as a subset of* $\mathcal{R}$*, i.e.* $\eta \subseteq \mathcal{R}$*. Intuitively, given a state transition* (s, a, s')*,* $(s, a, s') \in \eta$ *means that transition* (s, a, s') *is forbidden by norm* η*. We say* (s, a, s') *is an* η*-violation if and only if* $(s, a, s') \in \eta$*. Otherwise,* (s, a, s') *is an* η*-compliant.*

From the way that we define a norm, we can realize two extreme cases: if norm η is an empty set, all the possible state transitions are η-compliant; and it is also possible that a norm leads to states with no legal successor, which means that agents can only violate the norm.

2.2   Logical Setting

The logical language we use in this paper is propositional logic $\mathcal{L}_{prop}$ extended with action modality, denoted as $\mathcal{L}_{modal}$. The syntax of $\mathcal{L}_{modal}$ is defined by the following grammar:

$$\varphi ::= p \mid \neg\varphi \mid \varphi_1 \vee \varphi_2 \mid \langle a \rangle \varphi$$

where $p \in \Phi$ and $a \in Act$. The semantics of $\mathcal{L}_{modal}$ are given with respect to the satisfaction relation "$\vDash$". Given a monitoring transition system $\mathcal{T}$ and a state s in $\mathcal{T}$, a formula φ of the language can be evaluated in the following way:

- $T, s \vDash p$ iff $p \in \pi(s)$;
- $T, s \vDash \neg\varphi$ iff $T, s \nvDash \varphi$;
- $T, s \vDash \varphi_1 \vee \varphi_2$ iff $T, s \vDash \varphi_1$ or $T, s \vDash \varphi_2$;
- $T, s \vDash \langle a \rangle \varphi$ iff $\exists s'$ such that $(s, a, s') \in \mathcal{R}$ and $T, s' \vDash \varphi$;

Other classical logic connectives (e.g.,"$\wedge$", "$\rightarrow$") are assumed to be defined as abbreviations by using $\neg$ and $\vee$ in the conventional manner. We write $T \vDash \varphi$ if $T, s \vDash \varphi$ for all $s \in S$, and $\vDash \varphi$ if $T \vDash \varphi$ for all monitoring transition systems T.

Given the language $\mathcal{L}_{modal}$, a norm η can be defined in a more specific way such that it contains all the state transitions that are forbidden by norm η. Norms are described in various ways so that they can represent the forbidden behaviors explicitly. Below we define three forms of norms: $\eta(\varphi, \psi)$, $\eta(\varphi, a)$ and $\eta(\varphi, a, \psi)$, each following an example for better understanding. Notice that it is only a choice in this paper and more forms of norms can be described and constructed based on our logical framework.

- **Norm $\eta(\varphi, \psi)$.** Let φ and ψ be two propositional formulas and T be a monitoring transition system. A norm $\eta(\varphi, \psi)$ is defined as the set $\eta_T(\varphi, \psi) = \{(s, a, s') \in \mathcal{R} \mid T, s \vDash \varphi \wedge \langle a \rangle \psi\}$. In the rest of the paper, we will write $\eta(\varphi, \psi)$ for short. This is the most simple form of norms. The interpreted meaning of a norm $\eta(\varphi, \psi)$ is simply that it is forbidden to achieve ψ in the states satisfying φ (φ-state) by any actions. The forbidden actions are implicitly indicated in this type of norms. For example, it is forbidden to keep the light on when everybody is sleeping, no matter you turn on the flashlight or the lamp or lighten the candle.

- **Norm $\eta(\varphi, a)$.** Let φ be a propositional formula, a be an action, and T be a monitoring transition system. A norm (φ, a) is defined as the set $\eta_T(\varphi, a) = \{(s, a', s') \in \mathcal{R} \mid T, s \vDash \varphi \text{ and } a' = a\}$. In the rest of the paper, we will write $\eta(\varphi, a)$ for short. The interpreted meaning of a norm $\eta(\varphi, a)$ is that it is forbidden to perform action a in a φ-state. This is the most common form in which the action and the context where the action is forbidden are explicitly represented, regardless of the effect that the action brings about. For example, it is forbidden to smoke in a non-smoking area.

- **Norm $\eta(\varphi, a, \psi)$.** Let φ and ψ be two propositional formulas, a be an action, and T be a monitoring transition system. A norm (φ, a, ψ) is defined as the set $\eta_T(\varphi, a, \psi) = \{(s, a', s') \in \mathcal{R} \mid T, s \vDash \varphi \wedge \langle a' \rangle \psi \text{ and } a' = a\}$. In the rest of the paper, we will write $\eta(\varphi, a, \psi)$ for short. The interpreted meaning of a norm $\eta(\varphi, a, \psi)$ is that it is forbidden to perform action a in φ-state to achieve ψ. In this type of norms, the action, the context where the action is forbidden and the effect that the action will bring about are all represented explicitly. For example, in China it is forbidden to buy a house based on mortgage when you already own one.

Sometimes, propositional formula φ, which is indicated in three types of norms above, is called the precondition of an action for action prescription [7]. However, it should be distinguished from the precondition ψ_p we introduced in action pairs. φ is used to characterize the context where the action(s) is forbidden to perform by the system, whereas ψ_p is used to represent in which situation the action can be physically performed. Certainly there are relationships between φ and ψ_p, which will be investigated in our monitoring approach for opportunism.

3   Defining Opportunism

Before we propose our monitoring approach for opportunism, we should formally define opportunism from the perspective of the system so that the system knows what to detect for monitoring opportunism. In our previous paper [9] we emphasize opportunistic behavior is performed by intent rather than by accident. However, monitors cannot read agents' mental states, so for monitoring we assume that agents violate the norms always by intention from a pragmatic perspective. For example, we always assume that speeding is performed with intention. In this paper we remove all the references to the mental states from the formal definition of opportunism in our previous paper [9], assuming that the system can tell agents' value promotion/demotion causing by an action. In short, from the perspective of the system, opportunistic behavior performed by an agent in a context with norms can be simply defined as a behavior that causes norm violations and promotes his own value.

Opportunistic behavior results in promoting agents' own value, which can be interpreted as that opportunistic agents prefer the state that results from opportunistic behavior rather than the initial state. For having preferences over different states, we argue that agents always evaluate the truth value of specific propositions in those states based on their value systems. For instance, the seller tries to see whether he gets the money from selling a broken cup in order to have a preference on the states before and after the transaction. After the transaction, the seller's value gets promoted, because the proposition he verifies (whether he gets the money) based on his value system becomes true. Based on this interpretation, we first define a function *EvalRef*:

Definition 3.1 (Evaluation Reference). *Let V be a set of agents' value systems, S be a finite set of states, and Φ be a finite set of atomic propositions, EvalRef : $V \times S \times S \rightarrow \Phi$ is a function named Evaluation Reference that returns a proposition an agent refers to for specifying his preference over two states.*

This function means that the proposition is dependent on the value system and the two states. For simplicity, we assume that for value promotion the truth value of the proposition that agents refer to changes from false to true in the state transition. For example, assuming that proposition p represents the seller earns money, the seller promotes his value in the way of bringing about p through selling a broken cup. Based on this assumption, we define *Value Promotion*, which is another important element of opportunistic behavior. We only limit the specification to one case in terms of the truth value of p.

Definition 3.2 (Value Promotion). *Given two states s and s', and an agent's value system V, his value gets promoted from state s to s', denoted as $s <_V s'$, iff $s \vDash \neg p$ and $s' \vDash p$, where $p = EvalRef(V, s, s')$.*

As we already introduced the notion of value for defining opportunism, it is natural to extend our logical setting with value systems. We define a tuple of the form $V = (V_1, V_2, ..., V_{|Agt|})$ as agents' value systems. A multi-agent system is a combination of a monitoring transition system and value systems, one for each agent, representing the evaluation standards of the agents in the system. Formally, a multi-agent system, $\mathfrak{M}$, is a tuple:

$$\mathfrak{M} = (\mathcal{T}, V)$$

where $\mathcal{T}$ is a monitoring transition system and V is a set of value systems for the agents. Now the syntax of $\mathcal{L}_{modal}$ still follows the one we defined above, and the semantics with respect to the satisfaction relation become of the form $\mathfrak{M}, s \vDash \varphi$ but are still defined in the same way as above.

Now we are ready to formalize opportunism from the perspective of the system. Again, comparing to the definition of opportunism in our previous work, we remove all the references to mental states (knowledge, intention) because it is impossible for monitors to detect any mental states, but we assume that the system can reason about agents' value promotion/demotion by an action based on the corresponding value systems. Firstly, we extend our language to also include $Opportunism(\eta, a)$, and then we extend the satisfaction relation such that the following definition holds.

Definition 3.3 (Opportunism). *Given a multi-agent system $\mathfrak{M}$ and a norm η, an action a performed by agent i in state s being opportunistic behavior is defined as follows: $\mathfrak{M}, s \vDash Opportunism(\eta, a)$ iff state transition $(s, a, s\langle a \rangle) \in \eta$ and $s <_{V_i} s\langle a \rangle$.*

Intuitively, opportunism is a state transition which is an η-violation. Besides, the state transition also promotes the value of the agent who performs action a (agent i) by bringing about p, which is the proposition that the agent refers to for having preference over state s and $s\langle a \rangle$. Action a performed in state s, more essentially state transition $(s, a, s\langle a \rangle)$, is opportunistic behavior from the perspective of the system. We illustrate this definition through the following example.

Example 1 (Selling a Broken Cup). Consider the example of selling a broken cup in Fig. 1. A seller sells a cup to a buyer. It is known only by the seller beforehand that the cup is actually broken. The buyer buys the cup, but of course gets disappointed when he uses it. Here the state transition is denoted as $(s, sell(brokencup), s')$. Given a norm $\eta(\top, sell(brokencup))$ interpreted as it is forbidden to sell broken cups in any circumstance, the seller's behavior violates norm η. Moreover, based on the value system of the seller, his value gets promoted after he earns money from the transition ($EvalRef(V_s, s, s') = hasmoney(seller)$, $\mathfrak{M}, s \vDash \neg hasmoney(seller)$, $\mathfrak{M}, s' \vDash hasmoney(seller)$). Therefore, the seller performed opportunistic behavior to the buyer from the perspective of the system.

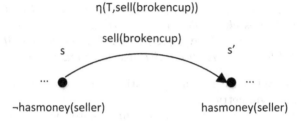

Fig. 1. Opportunistic behavior of selling a broken cup

4   Monitoring Opportunism

We propose monitoring approaches for opportunism in this section. A monitor is considered as an external observer that can evaluate a state transition with respect to a given norm. However, a monitor can only verify state properties instead of observing the performance of actions directly. Our approach to solve this problem is to check how things change in a given state transition and reason about the action taking place in between. Here we assume that our monitors are always correct, which means that the verification for state properties can always be done perfectly. One who doubts that this assumption is ideal can refer to [4] for the investigation about correctness of monitors, which is beyond the scope of this paper. In general, we consider monitoring as a matter of observing the system with an operator m such that $m(\varphi)$ is read as "φ is detected" for an arbitrary property φ.

We first define a state monitor m_{state}, which can evaluate the validity of a given property in a given state. We define state monitors in this paper in a similar way as we define knowledge in epistemic logic. This is because a monitor can be seen as an external observer that observes the behavior of the system objectively. Sentence "something is detected to be true" can be interpreted in the way "something is known to be true". We extend our logical language to also include $m_{state}(\varphi)$ and the satisfaction relation such that the following definition holds.

Definition 4.1 (State Monitors). *Given a propositional formula φ, a multi-agent system $\mathfrak{M}$, a state monitor m_{state} over φ is defined as follows: $\mathfrak{M}, s \vDash m_{state}(\varphi)$ iff for all s' sMs' implies $\mathfrak{M}, s' \vDash \varphi$. Sometimes we will write $m_{state}(\varphi)$ for short if clear from the context.*

Because state monitors are defined in a similar way to knowledge in epistemic logic, they correspondingly adopt the properties of knowledge.

Proposition 4.1 (Properties of State Monitors). *Given a multi-agent system $\mathfrak{M}$, and a state monitor m_{state} over φ, m_{state} is*

- *$\mathfrak{M} \vDash m_{state}(\varphi) \rightarrow \varphi$, meaning that what the state monitor detects is always considered to be true;*

- $\mathfrak{M} \vDash m_{state}(\varphi) \rightarrow m_{state}(m_{state}(\varphi))$, *meaning that the fact that something is detected to be true is always detected to be true;*
- $\mathfrak{M} \vDash \neg m_{state}(\varphi) \rightarrow m_{state}(\neg m_{state}(\varphi))$, *meaning that the fact that something is not detected to be true is always detected to be true;*

This proposition holds since our binary relation $\mathcal{R}$ is equivalence relation (reflexive, transitive and symmetric).

State monitors are the basic units in our monitoring mechanism. We can combine state monitors to check how things change in a given state transition and evaluate it with respect to a given set of norms. In Sect. 2, we introduced three forms of norms through which certain agents' behaviors are forbidden by the system. As we defined in Sect. 3, opportunistic behavior performed by an agent is a behavior that causes norm violations and promotes his own value, that is, opportunism is monitored with respect to a norm and a value system of an agent. Based on this definition, we design different monitoring opportunism approaches with respect to different forms of norms and discuss in which condition opportunism can be perfectly monitored. It is worth stressing that one important issue of this paper is to have an effective monitoring mechanism for opportunism in the sense that whenever an action is detected to be opportunistic, it was indeed opportunistic, and that whenever an action was opportunistic, it is indeed detected. Therefore, we will discuss this issue every time we propose a monitoring approach. We extend the language to also include $m_{opp}(\eta, a')$ and the satisfaction relation such that the following definition holds.

Definition 4.2 (Monitoring Opportunism with Norm $\eta(\varphi, \psi)$). *Given a multi-agent system $\mathfrak{M}$, a norm $\eta(\varphi, \psi)$ and an action a' performed by agent i in state s, whether action a' is opportunistic behavior can be monitored through a combination of state monitors as follows:*

$$\mathfrak{M}, s \vDash m_{opp}((\varphi, \psi), a') := m_{state}(\varphi) \wedge \langle a' \rangle m_{state}(\psi)$$

where

$$\mathfrak{M} \vDash \varphi \rightarrow \neg p, \quad \mathfrak{M} \vDash \psi \rightarrow p, \quad and \quad p = EvalRef(V_i, s, s\langle a' \rangle)$$

In order to detect whether action a' is opportunistic behavior in state s, we check if the state transition $(s, a', s\langle a' \rangle)$ is forbidden by norm $\eta(\varphi, \psi)$: because the interpreted meaning of norm $\eta(\varphi, \psi)$ is that it is forbidden to achieve ψ in φ-state by any actions, we check whether propositional formulas φ and ψ are successively satisfied in a state transition. Moreover, we assume the following implications in our model that φ implies $\neg p$ and ψ implies p, where proposition p is the proposition that agent i who performs action a' cares about based on his value system V_i. Since state s and $s\langle a' \rangle$ are not given and our monitors can only have partial information about the two states, we have a candidate set of states for state s and a candidate set of states for state $s\langle a' \rangle$ and any two corresponding states from them satisfy the resulting property of function $EvalRef$, which means that given the partial information the execution of action a' in state s

brings about p thus promoting agent i's value. The forbidden actions are not explicitly stated in the norm. Therefore, although the monitors cannot observe the performance of opportunistic behavior, it still can be perfectly detected with respect to norm $\eta(\varphi, \psi)$, which can be expressed by the following proposition:

Proposition 4.2. *Given a multi-agent system $\mathfrak{M}$, a norm $\eta(\varphi, \psi)$, and an action a' performed by agent i in state s, action a' is detected to be opportunistic with respect to $\eta(\varphi, \psi)$ in state s over $\mathcal{T}$ if and only if action a' was indeed opportunistic:*

$$\mathfrak{M}, s \vDash Opportunism((\varphi, \psi), a') \leftrightarrow m_{opp}((\varphi, \psi), a')$$

Proof. It trivially holds because the monitors detect exactly what the norm indicates and they are assumed to be correct.

Definition 4.3 (Monitoring Opportunism with Norm $\eta(\varphi, a)$). *Given a multi-agent system $\mathfrak{M}$, a norm $\eta(\varphi, a)$, and a pair $\langle \psi_p^a, \psi_e^a \rangle$ of action a ($\langle \psi_p^a, \psi_e^a \rangle \in D(a)$ and $\varphi \wedge \psi_p^a$ is satisfiable on $\mathfrak{M}$), whether action a' performed by agent i in state s is opportunistic behavior can be monitored through a combination of state monitors as follows:*

$$\mathfrak{M}, s \vDash m_{opp}((\varphi, a), \langle \psi_p^a, \psi_e^a \rangle, a') := m_{state}(\varphi \wedge \psi_p^a) \wedge \langle a' \rangle m_{state}(\psi_e^a)$$

where

$$\mathfrak{M} \vDash \varphi \wedge \psi_p^a \rightarrow \neg p, \ \mathfrak{M} \vDash \psi_e^a \rightarrow p, \ and \ p = EvalRef(V_i, s, s\langle a' \rangle)$$

In order to check whether action a' is opportunistic behavior (violates norm $\eta(\varphi, a)$ and promotes own value), we verify if action a' is performed in a φ-state. Besides, we check if action a' is the action that the norm explicitly states. Since the monitors cannot observe the performance of action a', we only can identify action a' to be possibly action a by checking if formulas ψ_p^a and ψ_e^a are successively satisfied in the state transition by action a', where ψ_p^a is action a's precondition and ψ_e^a is the corresponding effect. Similar to norm $\eta(\varphi, \psi)$, we assume that $\varphi \wedge \psi_p^a$ implies $\neg p$ and ψ_e^a implies p, where p is the proposition that agent i refers to based on his value system V_i. Again, with this approach we have a candidate set of states for state s and a candidate set of states for state $s\langle a' \rangle$ and any two corresponding states from them satisfy the resulting property of function $EvalRef$, which means that given the partial information the execution of action a' in state s brings about p thus promoting agent i's value.

Given a norm and an agent's value system, we can evaluate whether a state transition by an action is opportunistic behavior. However, since the monitors can only verify state properties instead of observing the performance of the action directly, we cannot guarantee that an action that is detected to be opportunistic was indeed opportunistic, which is given by the following proposition:

Proposition 4.3. *Given a multi-agent system $\mathfrak{M}$, a norm $\eta(\varphi, a)$, a pair $\langle \psi_p^a, \psi_e^a \rangle$ of action a ($\langle \psi_p^a, \psi_e^a \rangle \in D(a)$ and $\varphi \wedge \psi_p^a$ is satisfiable on $\mathfrak{M}$), an action*

a' performed by agent i in state s, action a' that is detected to be opportunistic was possibly opportunistic, which is characterized as

$$\mathfrak{M}, s \nvDash m_{opp}((\varphi, a), \langle \psi_p^a, \psi_e^a \rangle, a') \to Opportunism((\varphi, a), a')$$

Proof. This is because pair $\langle \psi_p^a, \psi_e^a \rangle$ might not be unique for action a within the actions that can be performed in φ-state. That is, we have a set of actions $Act' = \{a' \in Act \mid \mathfrak{M}, s \vDash m_{state}(\varphi \wedge \psi_p^a) \wedge \langle a' \rangle m_{state}(\psi_e^a)\}$, and action a indicated in norm η is one of them ($a \in Act'$).

Given this problem, we want to investigate in which case or with what requirement the action that is detected by the opportunism monitor is indeed opportunistic behavior. We first introduce a notion of *action adequacy*. An action $a \in Act$ is called adequate to achieve ψ at state $s \in S$ if and only if there exists a pair of $\langle \psi_p^a, \psi_e^a \rangle$ in $D(a)$ such that $\mathfrak{M}, s \vDash \psi_p^a$ and $\mathfrak{M}, s \vDash \langle a \rangle (\psi_e^a \to \psi)$ hold. $Ad(s, \psi)$ is a function that maps each state ($s \in S$) and a propositional formula ψ to a non-empty subset of actions, denoting the actions that are adequate to achieve ψ in state s, thus we have $Ad(s, \psi) \in \mathcal{P}(Act)$. And then we have the following proposition:

Proposition 4.4. *Given a multi-agent system $\mathfrak{M}$, a norm $\eta(\varphi, a)$, a pair $\langle \psi_p^a, \psi_e^a \rangle$ of action a ($\langle \psi_p^a, \psi_e^a \rangle \in D(a)$ and $\varphi \wedge \psi_p^a$ is satisfiable on $\mathfrak{M}$), an action a' performed by agent i in state s, the following statements are equivalent:*

1. $\mathfrak{M}, s \vDash m_{opp}((\varphi, a), \langle \psi_p^a, \psi_e^a \rangle, a') \leftrightarrow Opportunism((\varphi, a), a')$;
2. *there exists only one action $a \in \bigcup_{s \in S'} Ad(s, \top)$ that has pair $\langle \psi_p^a, \psi_e^a \rangle$, where* $S' = \{s \in S \mid \mathfrak{M}, s \vDash \varphi\}$.

Proof. From 1 to 2: Statement 1 implies that action a' that is detected to be opportunistic was indeed opportunistic. If it holds, then $a' = a$. Because we identify action a with pair $\langle \psi_p^a, \psi_e^a \rangle$, $a' = a$ implies that pair $\langle \psi_p^a, \psi_e^a \rangle$ is unique for action a within the set of actions $\bigcup_{s \in S'} Ad(s, \top)$. In other words, we cannot find one more action in $\bigcup_{s \in S'} Ad(s, \top)$ that also has a pair $\langle \psi_p^a, \psi_e^a \rangle$. From 2 to 1: If action pair $\langle \psi_p^a, \psi_e^a \rangle$ is unique for action a within $\bigcup_{s \in S'} Ad(s, \top)$, then once the pair is detected in the state transition we can deduce that $a' = a$. Hence, action a' is indeed opportunistic behavior. And from the proof of Proposition 4.3 we can see that action a is within the set of actions that are detected to be opportunistic, so if action a' was opportunistic behavior then it is indeed detected.

We can also derive a practical implication from this proposition: in order to better monitor opportunistic behavior, we should appropriately find an action pair $\langle \psi_p^a, \psi_e^a \rangle$ such that the possible actions in between can be strongly restricted and minimized. Assume that we use monitor $m_{opp}((\varphi, a), \langle \top, \top \rangle, a')$, the possibility that the opportunism monitor makes an error is extremely high, because every action that is available in φ-state will be detected to be opportunistic behavior.

Definition 4.4 (Monitoring Opportunism with Norm $\eta(\varphi, a, \psi)$). *Given a multi-agent system $\mathfrak{M}$, a norm $\eta(\varphi, a, \psi)$, and a pair $\langle \psi_p^a, \psi_e^a \rangle$ of action a $(\langle \psi_p^a, \psi_e^a \rangle \in D(a)$ and $\varphi \wedge \psi_p^a$ and $\psi \wedge \psi_e^a$ are satisfiable on $\mathfrak{M})$, whether action a' performed by agent i in state s is opportunistic behavior can be monitored through a combination of state monitors as follows:*

$$\mathfrak{M}, s \models m_{opp}((\varphi, a, \psi), \langle \psi_p^a, \psi_e^a \rangle, a') :=$$
$$m_{state}(\varphi) \wedge \langle a' \rangle m_{state}(\psi) \wedge m_{state}(\psi_p^a) \wedge \langle a' \rangle m_{state}(\psi_e^a)$$

where

$$\mathfrak{M} \models \varphi \wedge \psi_p^a \rightarrow \neg p, \;\; \mathfrak{M} \models \psi \wedge \psi_e^a \rightarrow p, \;\; and \;\; p = EvalRef(V_i, s, s\langle a' \rangle)$$

In order to check whether action a' is opportunistic behavior (violates norm $\eta(\varphi, a, \psi)$ and promotes own value), we verify if action a' is performed in a φ-state and secondly verify if action a' brings about ψ. Besides, as the forbidden action a is explicitly stated in norm η, we only can identify action a' to be possibly action a by checking if formulas ψ_p^a and ψ_e^a are successively satisfied in the state transition by action a', where ψ_p^a is action a's precondition and ψ_e^a is the corresponding effect. Similar to norm $\eta(\varphi, \psi)$ and $\eta(\varphi, a)$, we assume that $\varphi \wedge \psi_p^a$ implies $\neg p$ and $\psi \wedge \psi_e^a$ implies p, where p is the proposition that agent i refers to based on his value system V_i. Again, with the partial information our monitors have detected we have a candidate set of states for state s and a candidate set of states for state $s\langle a' \rangle$ and any two corresponding states from them satisfy the resulting property of function $EvalRef$, which means that given the partial information the execution of action a' in state s brings about p thus promoting agent i's value.

The same as we do with $\eta(\varphi, a)$, we cannot guarantee that an action that is detected to be opportunistic was indeed opportunistic, which is given by the following proposition:

Proposition 4.5. *Given a multi-agent system $\mathfrak{M}$, a norm $\eta(\varphi, a, \psi)$, a pair $\langle \psi_p^a, \psi_e^a \rangle$ of action a $(\langle \psi_p^a, \psi_e^a \rangle \in D(a)$ and $\varphi \wedge \psi_p^a$ and $\psi \wedge \psi_e^a$ are satisfiable on $\mathfrak{M})$, action a' that is detected to be opportunistic was possibly opportunistic, which is characterized as*

$$\mathfrak{M}, s \not\models m_{opp}((\varphi, a, \psi), \langle \psi_p^a, \psi_e^a \rangle, a') \rightarrow Opportunism((\varphi, a, \psi), a')$$

Proof. Similar to Proposition 4.3, it is because pair $\langle \psi_p^a, \psi_e^a \rangle$ might not be unique for action a within the actions that can be performed in φ-state to achieve ψ, and action a indicated in norm η is one of those actions.

Because in our framework the set of state transitions is finite, we can assume that all the possible state transitions are known beforehand. As all the state transitions in our framework are labelled with an action, we introduce a function called $Al(a)$, which maps each action to a non-empty subset of state transitions, denoting all the transitions labelled with action a. Thus we have $Al(a) \in \mathcal{P}(\mathcal{R})$. And then we have the following proposition:

Proposition 4.6. *Given a multi-agent system $\mathfrak{M}$, a value system set V, a norm $\eta(\varphi, a, \psi)$, a pair $\langle \psi_p^a, \psi_e^a \rangle$ of action a ($\langle \psi_p^a, \psi_e^a \rangle \in D(a)$ and $\varphi \wedge \psi_p^a$ and $\psi \wedge \psi_e^a$ are satisfiable on $\mathfrak{M}$), and an action a' performed by agent i in state s, the following statements are equivalent:*

1. $\mathfrak{M}, s \vDash m_{opp}((\varphi, a, \psi), \langle \psi_p^a, \psi_e^a \rangle, a') \leftrightarrow Opportunism((\varphi, a, \psi), a')$;
2. *there exists only one action $a \in \bigcup\limits_{s \in S'} Ad(s, \psi)$ that has a pair $\langle \psi_p^a, \psi_e^a \rangle$, where*

$$S' = \{s \in S \mid \mathfrak{M}, s \vDash \varphi\};$$

3. $\mathcal{R}' = \{(s, a', s') \in \mathcal{R} \mid \mathfrak{M}, s \vDash \varphi \wedge \psi_p^a \wedge \langle a' \rangle (\psi \wedge \psi_e^a)\} \subseteq Al(a)$.

Proof. The proof for from $1 \Rightarrow 2$ is the same as the proof of Proposition 4.4, so we are going to prove from $2 \Rightarrow 3$ and from $3 \Rightarrow 1$. We can consider ψ_p^a and ψ_e^a as two normal propositional formulas. From statement 2 it is clear that $\varphi \wedge \psi_p^a$ and $\psi \wedge \psi_e^a$ are successively satisfied in the state transition. From this we can divide the transitions into two classes: one for the transitions that $\varphi \wedge \psi_p^a$ and $\psi \wedge \psi_e^a$ are successively satisfied (denoted as $\mathcal{R}'$), and the other do not. Since pair $\langle \psi_p^a, \psi_e^a \rangle$ is unique to action a within $\mathcal{R}'$, all the transitions in $\mathcal{R}'$ are labelled with action a. Therefore, $\mathcal{R}'$ is a subset of $Al(a)$. From $2 \Rightarrow 3$ is concluded. From $3 \Rightarrow 1$, if all the transitions in $\mathcal{R}'$ are labelled with action a, then $a' = a$ and we can guarantee that action a' is indeed opportunistic behavior.

Example 1 (continued). We still use the example of selling a broken cup Fig. 2 to illustrate our monitoring approach. Here the state transition is denoted as (s, a', s') instead of $(s, sell(brokencup), s')$ because the monitor cannot observe the action directly. Given a norm $\eta(\top, sell(brokencup))$ and the seller's value system V_s, the system checks whether the seller performed opportunistic behavior. Firstly, the monitor doesn't need to check the context where action a' is performed because action $sell(brokencup)$ is forbidden in any context as norm η says. Secondly, the monitor tries to identify if action a' is indeed $sell(brokencup)$ as norm η indicates: assuming that $\langle hascup(seller) \wedge \neg hasmoney(seller), hascup(buyer) \wedge hasmoney(seller) \rangle$ is the pair we find for action $sell(brokencup)$, we check if both $\mathfrak{M}, s \vDash m_{state}(hascup(seller)) \wedge \neg hasmoney(seller)$ and $\mathfrak{M}, s' \vDash m_{state}(hascup(buyer) \wedge hasmoney(seller))$ hold. Moreover, the information we had for state s and s' implies that the seller's value gets promoted based on the value system V_s, as $EvalRef(V_s, s, s') = hasmoney(seller)$. If they all hold, action a' is detected to be opportunistic behavior. As the action pair we find is unique to action $sell(brokencup)$, action a' is indeed $sell(brokencup)$ thus being opportunistic.

However, if $\langle hascup(seller), hascup(buyer) \rangle$ is the pair that we find for action $sell(brokencup)$, then action a' is not necessarily $sell(brokencup)$ because possibly $a' = give(brokencup)$, meaning that $\langle hascup(seller), hascup(buyer) \rangle$ is not unique to action $sell(brokencup)$.

We proposed three approaches to monitor opportunistic behavior with respect to three different forms of norms. Based on the definitions of three approaches, the following validities hold: given an action a',

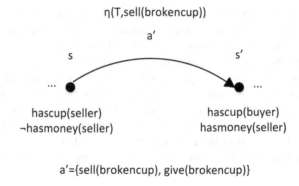

Fig. 2. Monitoring opportunism of selling a broken cup

$$\mathfrak{M} \models m_{opp}((\varphi, a, \psi), \langle \psi_p^a, \psi_e^a \rangle, a') \rightarrow m_{opp}((\varphi, \psi), a')$$
$$\mathfrak{M} \models m_{opp}((\varphi, a, \psi), \langle \psi_p^a, \psi_e^a \rangle, a') \rightarrow m_{opp}((\varphi, a), \langle \psi_p^a, \psi_e^a \rangle, a')$$

The interpreted meaning of the first validity is that, if action a' is detected to be opportunistic behavior with respect to norm $\eta(\varphi, a, \psi)$, then it will be also detected to be opportunistic behavior with respect to norm $\eta(\varphi, \psi)$. Similar with the second validity. This is simply because, the less information the norm gives, the more actions are forbidden to perform. The state transitions that violate norm $\eta(\varphi, a, \psi)$ is the subset of the state transitions that violate norm $\eta(\varphi, \psi)$ or $\eta(\varphi, a)$. This gives us an implication that the approach to monitor opportunistic behavior with respect to $\eta(\varphi, a, \psi)$ can be used to monitor the other two ones, because $\eta(\varphi, a)$ can be represented as $\eta(\varphi, a, \top)$ and $\eta(\varphi, \psi)$ can be represented as $\eta(\varphi, a, \psi)(\forall a \in Act)$. But there is monitoring cost involved. Apparently the approach with respect to $\eta(\varphi, a, \psi)$ is the most costly one because we need to check more things compared to the other two ones. We will study our monitoring mechanism with cost in the next section.

5   Monitoring Cost for Opportunism

We investigate monitoring cost for opportunism in this section. We first propose several ideas about how to reduce monitoring cost in general, and then combine them with our monitoring approaches for opportunism.

5.1   Monitoring Cost

For designing a monitoring mechanism, we not only think about whether it can perfectly detect agents' activities, but also consider if it is possible to decrease the cost involved in the monitoring process. In this section, we will study monitoring cost for opportunism based on the approaches we proposed in the previous section.

There is always cost involved when we monitor something, and the cost depends on what we want to check and how accurate the result we want to get. For example, checking DNA is more expensive than checking a finger print. Our basic idea in this paper is that a monitor is considered as an external observer to verify state properties, and that given a set of propositional formulas X as state properties, we verify the conjunction of formulas from X through combining state monitors. Therefore, we define monitoring cost through a function $c : \mathcal{L}_{prop} \to \mathbb{R}^+$. Intuitively, given a state property denoted by a propositional formula φ, function $c(\varphi)$ returns a positive real number representing the cost that it takes to verify φ. Such costs can be deduced from expert knowledge and are assumed to be given.

Definition 5.1 (Monitoring Cost). *Cost c over state properties $\mathcal{L}_{prop}$ is a function $c : \mathcal{L}_{prop} \to \mathbb{R}^+$ that maps a propositional formula to a positive real number. Given a set of propositional formulas X, we also define $c(X) := \sum_{\varphi \in X} c(\varphi)$ for having the cost of monitoring a set X.*

Given a set of propositional formulas X, the cost of monitoring X is the sum of the cost of verifying each element in X. However, if it holds for $\varphi, \varphi' \in X$ that $\varphi \neq \varphi'$, and $\varphi \to \varphi'$, then monitoring $X \backslash \{\varphi'\}$ is actually the same as monitoring X: when φ is detected to be true, φ' is also true; when φ is detected to be false, φ' is also false. But $c(X \backslash \{\varphi'\})$ is less than $c(X)$ if we logically assume that there is no inference cost[1]. This leads us to have the following definition *Largest Non-inferential Subset*:

Definition 5.2 (Largest Non-inferential Subset). *Given a monitoring transition system $\mathfrak{M}$ and a set of formulas X, let $X_{\mathfrak{M}}$ be the largest non-inferential subset such that for all $\varphi \in X_{\mathfrak{M}}$ there is no $\varphi' \in X_{\mathfrak{M}}$ with $\varphi \neq \varphi'$ such that $\mathfrak{M} \vDash \varphi \to \varphi'$.*

Proposition 5.1. *Given a monitoring transition system $\mathfrak{M}$, a set of formulas X and its largest non-inferential subset $X_{\mathfrak{M}}$, it holds that $c(X_{\mathfrak{M}}) \leq c(X)$.*

Proof. It holds obviously because $X_{\mathfrak{M}}$ is a subset of X.

Therefore, given a set of propositional formulas we want to verify, we always look for its largest non-inferential subset before checking anything in order to reduce the monitoring cost. Certainly, there are more properties among those formulas but we leave them for future study.

For reducing monitoring cost, it is also important to verify a set of propositional formulas $X = \{\varphi_1, ..., \varphi_n\}$ in a certain order instead of checking each formula $\varphi_i (1 \leq i \leq n)$ randomly. Besides, given the truth property of conjunction that a conjunction of propositions returns false if and only if there exists at least one false proposition, we can stop monitoring X once a proposition is

---

[1] Assuming that inference cost is lower than monitoring cost is logical, as we only need to compute the inference relation among formulas in the machine while monitoring usually requires setting up costly hardwares (such as cameras).

detected to be false because it has already made the conjunction false, regardless of the truth value of the rest of the propositions. Therefore, it is sensible to sort the propositions in X in ascending order by cost before checking anything, when the sorting cost is much lower than the monitoring cost. In order to introduce this idea, we first define the function of monitoring cost for a sequence and the notion of cost ordered sequence. In total, we have $n!$ sequences over X. A sequence over X is denoted as $\lambda(X)$ and the set of all the sequences over X is denoted as $L(X)$. The function of monitoring cost for a sequence and an ordered sequence by monitoring cost are defined as follows:

Definition 5.3 (Monitoring Cost for Sequences). *Given a set of propositional formulas $X = \{\varphi_1, ..., \varphi_n\}$ and a sequence $\lambda(X)$, the monitoring cost of checking $\lambda(X)$ is defined as follows:*

$$c(\lambda(X)) := \sum_{i=1}^{n} c(\varphi_i)d_i,$$

where

$$d_i = \begin{cases} 0 & \text{if } m(\varphi_{i-1}) = \text{ false or } d_{i-1} = 0 \ (i > 1); \\ 1 & \text{otherwise.} \end{cases}$$

With this function of monitoring cost for a sequence, the monitoring process will stop and no more monitoring cost will have after a false proposition is detected. Given a random sequence $\lambda(X)$ for monitoring, each proposition formula in X is likely to be true or false. We call each combination about the truth value of the formulas a scenario. Since there are $|X| = n$ propositions in X and each proposition can be detected to be true or false, there are in total 2^n scenarios about the truth value of the propositions in X. If the probability of each scenario to present is $p_i (i = 1, ..., 2^n)$, the expected value of the monitoring cost of $\lambda(X)$ can be expressed in the following way:

$$E(c(\lambda(X))) = p_1 \sum_{i=1}^{n} c(\lambda(X)[i]) + p_2 \sum_{i=1}^{n} c(\lambda(X)[i]) + ... + p_{2^n} c(\lambda(X)[1])$$

Formula $\sum_{i=1}^{n} c(\lambda(X)[i])$ represents the monitoring cost for the scenario where all the propositions are detected to be true, and formula $\sum_{i=1}^{n} c(\lambda(X)[i])$ represents the monitoring cost for the scenario where all the propositions are detected to be true except the last one,..., $c(\lambda(X)[1])$ represents the monitoring cost for one scenario where the first proposition is detected to be false. The expected value of the monitoring cost of $\lambda(X)$ is the finite sum of the probability of each scenario to present times the monitoring cost for the scenario.

Typically, when a priori probability for each formula $\varphi \in X$ being true is $1/2$, that is, the probability of each scenario to present is $1/2^n$, we can sort the propositions in X in ascending order by monitoring cost. In order to propose this idea, we first introduce the notion *Cost Ordered Sequence*.

Definition 5.4 (Cost Ordered Sequence). *Given a set of propositional formulas X, a cost ordered sequence X_c is a sequence over X ordered by the monitoring cost of each element in X such that $X_c \in L(X)$ and for $0 \leq i \leq j$ we have $c(X_c[i]) \leq c(X_c[j])$. In general, such a sequence is not unique because it is possible for two propositions to have the same monitoring cost; in this case we choose one arbitrarily.*

A cost ordered sequence X_c represents the monitoring order over X: we follow the order in X_c to check the elements in X one by one. In general, we can reduce the monitoring cost if we follow the cost ordered sequence, which is represented by the following proposition:

Proposition 5.2. *Given a set of propositional formulas X and a cost ordered sequence X_c over X, if a priori probability that each formula $\varphi \in X$ is true is $1/2$, the expected value of the monitoring cost of X_c is the lowest in that of any sequence over X, that is, $E(c(X_c)) \leq E(c(\lambda(X)))$, where $\lambda(X) \in L(X)$.*

Proof. Because a priori probability that each formula $\varphi \in X$ is true is $1/2$, the probability of each scenario to present is $1/2^n$. As we discussed above, since there are $|X| = n$ propositions in X and each proposition can be detected to be true or false, there are in total 2^n scenarios about the truth value of the propositions in X, and the monitoring cost for each scenario can be calculated according to Definition 5.3. Let us use $Scen(X)$ to denote the set of all the scenarios about the truth value of the propositions in X, and each scenario from $Scen(X)$ denoted as $\hat{\varphi}$, contains for each proposition $\varphi \in X$ either *true* or *false*. Therefore, the expected value of the monitoring cost of any $\lambda(X)$ is formalized as

$$E(c(\lambda(X))) = \frac{1}{2^n} \sum_{\hat{\varphi} \in Scen(X)} \sum_{i=1}^{n} c(\varphi_i)d_i$$

$$= \frac{1}{2^n} \left(\sum_{i=1}^{n} c(\lambda(X)[i]) + \sum_{j=1}^{n} \sum_{i=1}^{j} 2^{n-j} c(\lambda(X)[i]) \right)$$

$$= \frac{1}{2^n} \left(\sum_{i=1}^{n} c(\lambda(X)[i]) + \sum_{i=1}^{n} 2^{n-n} c(\lambda(X)[i]) + ... + 2^{n-1} c(\lambda(X)[1]) \right),$$

where $\sum_{i=1}^{n} c(\lambda(X)[i])$ represents the monitoring cost for the scenario where all the propositions are detected to be true, and $\sum_{i=1}^{n} 2^{n-n} c(\lambda(X)[i])$ represents the monitoring cost for the scenario where all the propositions are detected to be true except the last one, ..., and $2^{n-1} c(\lambda(X)[1])$ represents the monitoring cost for the scenarios where the first proposition is detected to be false. From this equation we can see that the monitoring cost of the propositions at the front of the sequence strongly influence the value of $E(c(\lambda(X)))$: the lower monitoring cost the propositions at the front have, the less value $E(c(\lambda(X)))$ returns. Thus, the expected value of the monitoring cost of X_c is the lowest in all the sequences over X.

5.2   Reducing Monitoring Cost for Opportunism

Until here we investigated monitoring cost for any finite set of formulas generally. We can apply the above ideas to monitoring opportunism. Recall that opportunism is monitored with respect to a norm and a value system. Given a norm $\eta(\varphi, a, \psi)$ and a value system V_i, we evaluate a state transition (s, a', s') by checking whether set $X_1 = \{\varphi, \psi_p^a, p\}$ hold in state s, and whether $X_2 = \{\varphi, \psi_e^a, p\}$ hold in state s', where $\langle \psi_p^a, \psi_e^a \rangle \in D(a)$ and $p = EvalRef(V_i, s, s')$. Note that we cannot combine set X_1 and X_2 into one set because we verify the formulas from the two sets in different states. The inferences reltion among the formulas give rise to the relation between different monitoring approaches.

Proposition 5.3. *Given a multi-agent system $\mathfrak{M}$, a norm $\eta(\varphi, a, \psi)$, a pair $\langle \psi_p^a, \psi_e^a \rangle$ of action a ($\langle \psi_p^a, \psi_e^a \rangle \in D(a)$ and $\varphi \wedge \psi_p^a$ and $\psi \wedge \psi_e^a$ are satisfiable on $\mathfrak{M}$), and an action a', if*

$$\mathfrak{M} \vDash (\varphi \rightarrow \psi_p^a) \wedge (\psi \rightarrow \psi_e^a),$$

then

$$\mathfrak{M} \vDash m_{opp}((\varphi, \psi), a') \rightarrow m_{opp}((\varphi, a, \psi), \langle \psi_p^a, \psi_e^a \rangle, a');$$

if

$$\mathfrak{M} \vDash \psi_e^a \rightarrow \psi,$$

then

$$\mathfrak{M} \vDash m_{opp}((\varphi, a), \langle \psi_p^a, \psi_e^a \rangle, a') \rightarrow m_{opp}((\varphi, a, \psi), \langle \psi_p^a, \psi_e^a \rangle, a').$$

Proof. If $\mathfrak{M} \vDash (\varphi \rightarrow \psi_p^a) \wedge (\psi \rightarrow \psi_e^a)$ holds, we have the largest non-inferential subset of X_1, $(X_1)_\mathfrak{M} = \{\varphi\}$, and the largest non-inferential subset of X_2, $(X_2)_\mathfrak{M} = \{\psi\}$, which means that we only need to verify φ in the initial state and ψ in the final state of any state transition. Thus, if action a' is detected to be opportunistic with norm $\eta(\varphi, \psi)$, it is also the case with norm $\eta(\varphi, a, \psi)$. We can prove the second statement similarly.

This proposition implies that when the above inference holds we can monitor opportunism with the approach $m_{opp}((\varphi, \psi), a')$ (or $m_{opp}((\varphi, a), \langle \psi_p^a, \psi_e^a \rangle, a')$) rather than $m_{opp}((\varphi, a, \psi), \langle \psi_p^a, \psi_e^a \rangle, a')$ for saving monitoring cost.

Together with our general ideas about monitoring cost, we propose the following steps to monitor opportunism: given a multi-agent system $\mathfrak{M}$, a norm $\eta(\varphi, (a), (\psi))$ in any form, a pair $\langle \psi_p^a, \psi_e^a \rangle$ and an action a' performed by agent i in state s, in order to check whether action a' is opportunistic behavior,

1. Check if there is any inference in $\mathfrak{M}$ among the formulas we need to verify in state s $X_1 = \{\varphi, \psi_p^a, p\}$ and $s\langle a' \rangle$ $X_2 = \{\varphi, \psi_e^a, p\}$, find out the largest non-inferential subsets $(X_1)_\mathfrak{M}$ and $(X_2)_\mathfrak{M}$, and choose the corresponding monitoring approach;

2. Sort all the formulas from $(X_1)_{\mathfrak{M}}$ and $(X_2)_{\mathfrak{M}}$ in a sequence ordered by monitoring cost $((X_1)_{\mathfrak{M}} \cup (X_2)_{\mathfrak{M}})_c$;
3. Verify all the formulas from $((X_1)_{\mathfrak{M}} \cup (X_2)_{\mathfrak{M}})_c$ one by one; when one formula is detected to be false, the monitoring process stops and action a' is detected not to be opportunistic behavior; otherwise, it is detected to be opportunistic behavior.

With the above steps, the monitoring cost for opportunism can be reduced statistically when the monitoring is performed for lots of times. For a single time of monitoring, we still cannot guarantee that the monitoring cost is reduced with the above steps, as possibly (only) the last formula in the sequence ordered by cost is detected to be false, for which the monitoring cost is the highest compared to any sequence ordered at random.

6   Related Work

Opportunism is a social and economic concept proposed by economist Williamson [13]. While scholars from social science have studied this typical social behavior from various perspectives [5,6], the investigation of opportunism in multi-agent system is still new. [9] proposes a formal definition of opportunism based on the situation calculus, which forms a theoretical foundation for any further study related to opportunism. Compared to the definition in [9], we remove all the references to mental states for proposing our monitoring approaches, but still captures norm violation and agents' own-value promotion that the system can recognize and reason about.

The specification of actions is a crucial element in our framework and monitoring mechanism. In general, it consists of the precondition of an action that specifies when the action can be carried out and the effect of an action that specifies the resulting state. A lot of logic formalisms are constructed based on this idea, such as Hoare logic [8] and the situation calculus [10]. In Hoare logic, the execution of a program is described through Hoare triple $\{P\}C\{Q\}$, where C is a program, P is the precondition and Q is the postcondition, which is quite close to our approach of action pair $\langle \psi_p^a, \psi_e^a \rangle$. In the situation calculus, the effect of action is specified through successor state axioms, which consist of positive consequences and negative consequences.

Our work is also related to norm violation monitoring. Norms have been used as a successful approach to regulate and organize agents' behaviors [12]. There are various ways of the specification of norms and norm violations such as [2]. Similar to [1], we only consider a norm as a subset of all possible system behaviors. About norm violation monitoring, [4] proposes a general monitoring mechanism for the situation where agents' behaviors cannot be perfectly monitored. It studies different types of monitors and provides a logical analysis of the relations between monitors and norms to be monitored. Our work is strongly inspired by them, but we focus on the situation where agents' actions cannot be observed directly but can be reasoned about through checking how things change, assuming state properties can be perfectly verified. In the sense of inference, our monitoring approaches are rather similar to Artikis' methods of complex event recognition in norm-governed multi-agent systems [3], which take as input streams of low-level events (sensor-based events), such as a change in temperature, and combine them to infer complex high-level events of interest, such as the start of a fire incident.

7   Conclusion

Opportunism is a behavior that causes norm violation and promotes agents' own value. In order to monitor its invisible performance in the system, we developed a logical framework based on the specification of actions. In particular, we investigated how to evaluate agents' actions to be opportunistic with respect to different forms of norms when those actions cannot be observed directly, and studied how to reduce the monitoring cost for opportunism. We proved formal properties aiming at having an effective and cost-saving monitoring mechanism for opportunism. Future work can be done on value: in our monitoring approaches it is assumed that we can reason whether an action promotes or demotes the value with a value system and how things change by the action, but a value system is still like a black box that we still don't know how the propositions we detect relate to a value system. Moreover, in our framework every state transition is labelled with an action and an agent. We can improve the effectiveness of our monitoring mechanism by attaching *capability* to agents. In this way, given an agent with its capability, some possible actions that were performed by the agent can be eliminated. About reducing monitoring cost, apart from inference more properties among formulas can be studied concerning about the relations among the formulas we detect for monitoring opportunism.

References

1. Agotnes, T., Van Der Hoek, W., Rodriguez-Aguilar, J.A., Sierra, C., Wooldridge, M.: On the logic of normative systems. In: Proceedings of the Twentieth International Joint Conference on Artificial Intelligence (IJCAI 2007), pp. 1181–1186 (2007)
2. Anderson, A.R.: A reduction of deontic logic to alethic modal logic. Mind **67**(265), 100–103 (1958)
3. Artikis, A., Sergot, M., Paliouras, G.: An event calculus for event recognition. IEEE Trans. Knowl. Data Eng. **27**(4), 895–908 (2015)
4. Bulling, N., Dastani, M., Knobbout, M.: Monitoring norm violations in multi-agent systems. In: Proceedings of the 2013 International Conference on Autonomous Agents and Multi-agent Systems, pp. 491–498 (2013)
5. Cabon-Dhersin, M.-L., Ramani, S.V.: Opportunism, trust and cooperation a game theoretic approach with heterogeneous agents. Rational. Soc. **19**(2), 203–228 (2007)
6. Chen, C.C., Peng, M.W., Saparito, P.A.: Individualism, collectivism, and opportunism: a cultural perspective on transaction cost economics. J. Manag. **28**(4), 567–583 (2002)

7. Fiadeiro, J., Maibaum, T.: Temporal reasoning over deontic specifications. J. Logic Comput. **1**(3), 357–395 (1991)
8. Hoare, C.A.R.: An axiomatic basis for computer programming. Commun. ACM **12**(10), 576–580 (1969)
9. Luo, J., Meyer, J.-J.: A formal account of opportunism based on the situation calculus. AI & SOCIETY, 1–16 (2016)
10. McCarthy, J.: Situations, actions, and causal laws. Technical report, DTIC Document (1963)
11. Reiter, R.: Knowledge in Action: Logical Foundations for Specifying and Implementing Dynamical Systems. MIT Press, Cambridge (2001)
12. Shoham, Y., Tennenholtz, M.: On the synthesis of useful social laws for artificial agent societies (preliminary report). In: AAAI, pp. 276–281 (1992)
13. Williamson, O.E.: Markets and hierarchies: analysis and antitrust implications: a study in the economics of internal organization (1975)

The Role of Values

Klara Pigmans[1]([⊠])[iD], Huib Aldewereld[2], Virginia Dignum[1][iD],
and Neelke Doorn[1][iD]

[1] Delft University of Technology, Delft, The Netherlands
k.a.m.pigmans@tudelft.nl
[2] Hogeschool Utrecht, Utrecht, The Netherlands

Abstract. Decision-making processes involving multiple stakeholders
can be rather cumbersome, turbulent and lengthy. The stance of some
stakeholders, upholding their individual interests, can slowdown or even
block such processes. Recent research suggests that a focus on the values of the stakeholders could benefit those decision-making processes.
However, the role of the values is not yet fully understood. To investigate the interaction between values, norms, and resulting actions in
decision-making processes, we introduce a conceptual model to explore
the relations between these concepts. The conceptual model presented in
this paper is a first step towards a framework to model decision-making
processes with the aim of understanding the role that values play in
decision-making processes.

1 Introduction

Decision-making processes with multiple stakeholders can be complex, depending on stakeholders' behaviour [16,18]. For example, in the Netherlands, the
decision about flooding the Hedwig polder has been a heated debate among the
stakeholders. The decision to flood the polder of 299 hectare located in South-
Western Netherlands, was taken already in 1977 to compensate for earlier lost
ecological landscape. This decision has been both contested and supported ever
since, by the different involved stakeholders, which include local residents, Dutch
and various Belgium parliaments, environmental groups, farmers, and the European Commission. This is a classic example of how the stance of the stakeholders
can slowdown or even block the decision-making process, and correspondingly
the related (plans for) development.

Another example is an urban flood management case that took place in the
South of the Netherlands [17], in which it took decades to come to a decision
that was accepted by all stakeholders. The different authorities involved had
conflicting interests, farmers had interests that differed greatly (large scale cattle
farming vs. organic, small scale), and relations between some of stakeholders
were so troubled, because of conflicting interests, that some of the stakeholders
refused to communicate directly to other stakeholders.

To understand the development of such decision-making processes and the
reason why some of them are turbulent or cumbersome, we need to explore

© Springer International Publishing AG 2017
S. Cranefield et al. (Eds.): COIN 2016 Workshops, LNAI 10315, pp. 139–148, 2017.
DOI: 10.1007/978-3-319-66595-5_8

the relation between the concepts involved in those processes. Research [9,14] suggests that values can play an important role in decision-making processes and that a value sensitive approach could therefore benefit such processes.

Moreover, at a closer look, it seems that it is not necessarily a value in itself that influences the process. On the contrary, values are generally so vaguely defined that stakeholders all acknowledge their importance in abstract terms. It is rather the conception [15] that stakeholders have of this value that can differ among the stakeholders and that influences their take on the process. For example, justice is a value that is generally considered to be important, yet, what justice entails is a topic of debate [10].

In this paper we present a conceptual model to explore the relation between values, value conceptions, norms and the corresponding actions. By doing so, we take a first step towards the means to model these concepts in a decision-making context, which is needed to understand the way these concepts interact and how they influence the decision-making processes. The goal of this research is to explore and show what role values take in decision-making processes and whether a focus on the values and value conceptions provides a better means to solve difficult cases, as suggested by the earlier research in [9,14].

With this conceptualisation, we take a first step to formalise the role of moral and social values. By exploring the assumption that a value sensitive approach can benefit complex decision-making processes, we aim in a later stage to support those processes with tools in which these insights are embedded.

The remainder of this paper is structured as follows. In the next section we discuss the ideas behind the concepts, based on literature. In Sect. 3 we describe and depict the collective and the individual structure of decision-making processes, and the conceptual model of the role of values in these processes. Section 4 discusses the context of this research by describing related work. In Sect. 5 our conclusions and ideas for future work are presented.

2   Background

Before we can come to a conceptual model of values in decision-making processes, we first need to understand what the relevant concepts are and why these are taken into account. Therefore we start with discussing the definitions of the concepts in this section.

2.1   Values

Values are defined in many different ways, e.g. as an enduring belief that a specific end-state is desirable over another [19], what a person or group considers important in life [11], or as guiding principles of what people consider important in life [2].

We assume that values can be considered to be more or less universal, like Schwartz and Rokeach state in their separate value surveys [2], but also like the values in decision-making as stated by [1]. Justice, freedom, benevolence, and security are values that are broadly considered important in different cultures, organisations, and societies. The interpretation of these values is a different story, as explained below in Sect. 2.2.

In addition, ample research has been done on value typologies. The surveys of [20] resulted in 10 key value types describing relations between values, including power, hedonism, benevolence and security. Earlier, [19] concentrated on the connection between values and behavior, distinguishing *terminal values* such as 'family security' and 'freedom', and *instrumental values* such as 'courage' and 'responsibility'. Since we are taking the decision-making process as our point of reference, the value hierarchy for management decisions [1] provides an interesting model as well. Bernthal distinguishes a business firm level, economic system level, society level, and an individual level. In multi-stakeholder decision-making processes in the public sector, these levels are very relevant: often stakeholders are involved that are entrepreneurs or companies with business level values, including profits, survival, growth. Then if resources are involved, economic system values apply, such as allocation of resources, production and distribution of goods and services. The governmental authorities are likely to have societal values: culture, civilization, order and justice. Last, individuals will have values such as freedom, opportunity, self-realisation, and human-dignity.

Our aim is to get a high level understanding of the concept 'value' in relation to norms, conceptions and actions. Further, we assume that values that stakeholders have do not change in the course of the process. Therefore, we consider values to be fixed, enduring guiding principles of what people think is important in life [2].

2.2   Context and Value Conceptions

Each agents operates in a certain context, which influences how the value is perceived. "Context is any information that can be used to characterise the situation of an entity" [5], including emotional history with the value and experience of the stakeholder in decision-making with respect to the value.

The context influences an agent's conception of a value. The difference between values and the conception of those values is –in slightly different wording–, described by [15] as *contested concepts* and *conceptions*. He describes contested concepts as unitary and vague concepts, e.g. liberty and social justice. In this research we consider such contested concepts as values.

The conceptions of these values are contested since they are an interpretation of what the value should look like in practice. And there are multiple conceptions possible for one single value, guiding principles can be explained in different ways, as addressed in Sect. 3.2.

2.3   Vision and Collective Decision-Making Process

Since this research focuses on values in decision-making processes in particular, we include the vision and the collective decision-making process in our conceptualisation. The vision is expressed by an authority in long term documents or in vision reports, and represents the institutional objective with respect to the value, as also discussed in [7] as part of the abstract level. In order to accomplish this vision a collective decision-making process has to take place. In this process, the vision and the norms of the agents are combined to come to a decision about which collective action to take.

2.4   Agents, Norms and Actions

We use definition of agents as indicated by [8]: "agents are autonomous entities with reasoning and communicative capabilities, and therefore suitable to (..) simulate and represent real-life entities displaying the same autonomy. The decision-making process has several stakeholders, which are represented as agents. An agent can represent an individual stakeholder or a stakeholders collective [12, p. 31], e.g. an organisation or farmers that unite their voice during the process.

We use the definition of norms as described by [3]: norms regulate the behaviour of agents by describing the actions they must (or must not) execute in specific situations.

An agent will take action to comply with the norm.

3   Conceptual Model of the Role of Values

In this section we describe how the concepts are related to each other. The conceptual model that we present in this section has both an individual structure, describing the concepts that are relevant for the individual agents, as well as a collective structure representing the collective concepts of the decision-making process. We first describe the two structures separately, after which we connect them into the conceptual model. All is explained using an example.

3.1   The Collective Structure

The collective concepts in multi-stakeholder decision-making processes represent the commonalities in the process. The collective structure in itself seems rather straight forward, as depicted in Fig. 1.

The collective decision-making process is initiated to realise the vision of authorities. This vision is derived from one or more values. The decision-making process leads to collective actions that will contribute to the realisation of the vision, and therefore the value.

A **value** is assumed to be a guiding principle that is acknowledged in general terms by the stakeholders. In this case we use *water safety* as the example of an underlying value. Since we assume that values are acknowledged by all stakeholders, they are part of the collective structure. We assume that values are defined in abstract terms which are not contested as such. For instance water safety could be described as being safe from floods, we assume stakeholders do not oppose this.

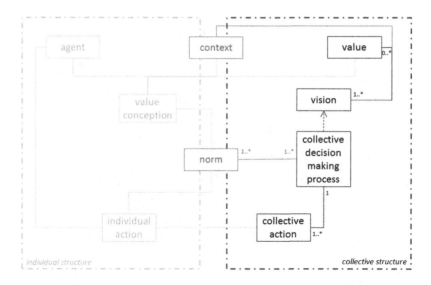

Fig. 1. Collective structure.

The **vision** expresses a 'collective objective', e.g. no floods should occur in the urban areas of the region. The vision is expressed in long term planning reports by the province and the municipality, including at least one value, such as *water safety*, but other values, such as *culture* could be expressed in the vision as well. For simplicity's sake, we only focus on one value here. There can be values that are not taken into account in the vision that actually do play are role during the process.

In Fig. 1, the **collective decision-making process** (CDMP) follows from the vision. The collective decision-making process does not take place at a single moment in time, but includes meetings, discussions, deliberations, one-to-one meetings, newsletters, informative events and compensation negotiations. In policy making, it often takes decades to get to the point where a decision is actually agreed upon. Without an expressed vision, there is no CDMP to translate this vision into actions. The vision is the motive for the process.

The **collective action** following from the CDMP is in the end enabled by all agents. In the water safety example, the action could be to adjust the flow of the river that causes floods in the urban areas in the region, to evacuate an area or build a dike. There can be more than one collective action following from the CDMP, but a collective action is always the outcome of an CDMP.

3.2   The Individual Structure

Because of the many inter-dependencies with the collective structure, the individual structure can not be depicted as a stand-alone separate structure, but we can still discuss the concepts themselves individually.

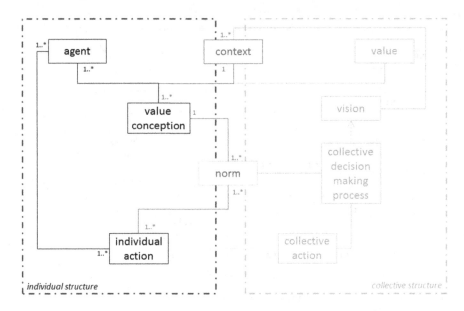

Fig. 2. The individual structure of decision-making processes.

A **value conception** is the conception of a value, so it has a direct relation to value, to the context that influences the value conception and the agent who has the value conception. A value can be related to multiple value conceptions, with the value water safety this could include risk prevention, flood defense, flood mitigation, flood preparation, and flood recovery. In addition, an agent can have multiple conceptions: one agent can perceive flood defense and flood recovery combined as water safety. A value conception directly influences one or more norms of an agent (Fig. 2).

The stakeholders that are involved are all represented as **agents**, for instance water authorities, municipality, inhabitants, agricultural entrepreneurs, property developers. One agent can have multiple value conceptions, and a value conception can be related to more than one agent.

One or more **individual actions** are taken by agents based on one or more norms they have. If the norm of an agent for risk prevention would be 'building on riverbanks is forbidden', an agent could decide to comply with the norm by taking the action to build in an area where building is permitted. Further, an agent can have multiple individual actions and, an individual action can be related to more than one agent if more than one agent performs this same action.

3.3   The Structures Combined in the Conceptual Model

The conceptual model of the role of values in multi-stakeholder decision-making processes is depicted in Fig. 3. The collective structure and the individual structure are related in multiple ways, including through context and norms, which are part of both structures.

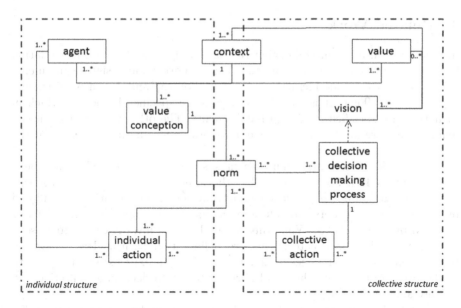

Fig. 3. Conceptual model of values, context, conceptions, norms, and actions in decision-making processes.

Value conceptions are influenced by the **context** of an agent. Based on e.g. historic encounters with other agents which may or may not have included conflicts, or an emotional history with the value, an agent has the intention to enable the joint decision, or an agent does not have this intention. The level of experience can determine how convincing an agent can be. One can imagine that an experienced project manager, or a long term resident of area at stake have more authority and experience than e.g. a young new resident. This context will influence the conception an agent has.

Norms are based on the value conception. Complying with the norms contributes to the value conception. As illustrated above, a norm for risk prevention could be 'building on riverbanks is forbidden'. A value conception can be related to one or more norms. Norms are related to one value conception. The agents' norms influence the collective decision-making process, since the norms prescribe what agents will comply with (or not) as an outcome of the process.

Moreover, the vision follows from the value and the context. The vision 'no floods in urban areas' comes from the value water safety in a context of water governance in a riverine region where stakeholders are likely to have a history with the value, and with decision-making in this respect.

Finally, the individual actions and the collective actions need to be aligned for the collective decision-making process to be successful. As earlier mentioned, the agents need to intent to enable a collective action, since unanimity is needed in order to perform the action. One or more individual actions need to enable one or more collective actions.

4   Related Work

In philosophical literature on engineering and design, e.g. [21], a direct relation between values and norms is indicated. Values, norms and design requirements are described as a value hierarchy, with values on top and design requirements at the bottom. There it is stated that values are specified by norms, which in their turn are specified by design requirements. The other way around, design requirements are in place for the sake of a norm, and a norm is in place for the sake of a value.

In the field of normative multi-agent systems, the use of values has been explored by [3,4,7]. First, [3] describes the interaction between system norms –norms that are imposed on the agents by a system–, actions that are regulated by those norms, and personal values of the agents that are being promoted or demoted by those actions. While this is useful for the investigation into reasons why agents follow or violate norms, we believe that such a clear separation between the norms and values does not exist. Therefore, we express the need to further explore the way values and norms interact to determine collective and individual action.

Second, [4] argues that a value can be seen as a preference that can be discussed and debated. They describe norms to constitute a link between values and behavior, where norms serve this value. Their framework explores a connection between values, norms, goals and actions. In this research we want to take this one step further by exploring the role of these concepts in decision-making processes.

Third, the OMNI framework [7] discusses norms, values, context and social structures thoroughly, where each concept is located in a three by three matrix with three different levels and three dimensions. Yet, values, agents, roles and actions are not discussed in terms of their direct relationship with each other, but rather in relation to the levels and the dimensions. To fully understand their role in decision-making processes we need to further explore these direct relations.

In addition, to represent multi-stakeholder decision-making, to better understand the complex social phenomena occurring, a modelling framework needs to be chosen that has sufficient modelling capabilities to represent all important aspects of the problem. For this, we will relate to the agent organization approach as described by [6] to model the interactions between stakeholders together with and within the organizational structures they are part of. Also, we will relate to the framework of [13] who model individuals and institutions as the key components to capture, analyse and understand the domain and its complexities. We aim to build up on their research, but with values and the conceptions of values as the major component to relate to the social structure, searching for common ground rather than differences in interests.

5   Conclusion and Future Work

Turbulent or cumbersome decision-making processes can slowdown or even block the plans for spatial development. Values are considered to play an important role in preventing or overcoming conflicts in such processes. In order to understand how values influence these processes, we discussed the relevant concepts and the relations between them. This resulted in a conceptual model with an individual structure and a collective structure. The individual structure of value conceptions, agents, and individual actions was then related to the collective structure, containing values, vision, collective decision-making process and collective action. Norms and context are concepts that are part of both structures. This conceptual model is the first step to explore and understand the concepts of decision-making processes.

So far, we did not take institutional aspects such as roles and rules into account. Further research is needed to expand the conceptual model with those aspects, including clear and detailed definitions on the attribute level. After expanding the conceptual model, the next step will be to formalise the concepts and relations, so that we can start modelling values in complex decision-making processes.

Acknowledgements. We would like to thank the reviewers for their suggestions to improve and sharpen the paper. This work is part of the Values4Water project, subsidised by the research programme *Responsible Innovation*, which is (partly) financed by the Netherlands Organisation for Scientific Research (NWO) under Grant Number 313-99-316. The work of Neelke Doorn is supported by NWO under Grant Number 016-144-071.

References

1. Bernthal, W.: Value perspectives in management decisions. J. Acad. Manag. **5**(3), 193–196 (1962)
2. Cheng, A., Fleischmann, K.: Developing a meta-inventory of human values. Proc. Am. Soc. Inf. Sci. Technol. **47**(1), 1–10 (2010)
3. da Silva Figueiredo, K., Silva, V.T.: An algorithm to identify conflicts between norms and values. In: Balke, T., Dignum, F., Riemsdijk, M.B., Chopra, A.K. (eds.) COIN 2013. LNCS, vol. 8386, pp. 259–274. Springer, Cham (2014). doi:10.1007/978-3-319-07314-9_14
4. Dechesne, F., Di Tosto, G., Dignum, V., Dignum, F.: No smoking here: values, norms and culture in multi-agent systems. Artif. Intell. Law **21**, 79–107 (2013)
5. Dey, A.: Understanding and using context. Pers. Ubiquit. Comput. **5**(1), 4–7 (2001)
6. Dignum, V., Padget, J.: Multiagent organizations. In: Weiss, G. (ed.) Multiagent Systems. MIT Press (2013)
7. Dignum, V., Vázquez-Salceda, J., Dignum, F.: OMNI: introducing social structure, norms and ontologies into agent organizations. In: Bordini, R.H., Dastani, M., Dix, J., Fallah Seghrouchni, A. (eds.) ProMAS 2004. LNCS, vol. 3346, pp. 181–198. Springer, Heidelberg (2005). doi:10.1007/978-3-540-32260-3_10
8. Dignum, V., Meyer, J.-J., Weigand, H., Dignum, F.: An organizational-oriented model for agent societies. In: Proceedings of the International Workshop on Regulated Agent-Based Social Systems: Theories and Applications (RASTA 2002), at AAMAS, Bologna, Italy (2002)
9. Doorn, N.: Governance experiments in water management: from interests to building blocks. Sci. Eng. Ethics **22**(3), 755–774 (2016)

10. Doorn, N.: Exploring responsibility rationales in research and development (r&d). Sci. Technol. Hum. Values **37**(3), 180–209 (2012)
11. Friedman, B., Kahn, P.H., Borning, A.: Chapter 4: Value sensitive design and information systems. In: The Handbook of Information and Computer Ethics, pp. 69–101. Wiley (2008)
12. Ghorbani, A.: Structuring socio-technical complexities: modelling agent systems using institutional analysis. Ph.D thesis, Delft University of Technology (2013)
13. Ghorbani, A., Bots, P., Dignum, V., Dijkema, G.: MAIA: a framework for developing agent-based social simulations. J. Artif. Societ. Soc. Simul. (JASSS) **16**(2), 1–19 (2013)
14. Glenna, L.: Value-laden technocratic management and environmental conflicts: the case of the New York City watershed controversy. Sci. Technol. Hum. Values **35**(1), 81–112 (2010)
15. Jacobs, M.: Sustainable development as a contested concept. In: Dobson, A. (ed.) Fairness and Futurity. Oxford University Press (1999)
16. Kolkman, M., Kok, M., van der Veen, A.: Mental model mapping as a new tool to analyse the use of information in decion-making in integrated water management. Phys. Chem. Earth **30**, 317–332 (2005)
17. Pigmans, K., Doorn, N., Aldewereld, H., Dignum, V.: Decision-making in water governance: from conflicting interests to shared values. In: Asveld, L., van Dam-Mieras, M.E.C., Swierstra, T., Lavrijssen, S.A.C.M., Linse, C.A., van den Hoven, M.J. (eds.) Responsible Innovation 3: A European Agenda? Springer (2017)
18. Reed, M.: Stakeholder participation for environmental management: a literature review. Biol. Conserv. **141**, 2417–2431 (2008)
19. Rokeach, M.: The Nature of Human Values. Free Press, New York (1973)
20. Schwartz, S.: Are there universal aspects in the structure and contents of human values? J. Soc. Issues **50**(4), 19–45 (1994)
21. Van de Poel, I.R.: Translating values into design requirements. In: Michelfelder, D.P., McCarthy, N., Goldberg, D.E. (eds.) Philosophy and Engineering: Reflections on Practice, Principles and Process. PET, vol. 15, pp. 253–266. Springer, Dordrecht (2013). doi:10.1007/978-94-007-7762-0_20

On the Minimal Recognition of Rights in Holonic Institutions

Jeremy Pitt[1], Jie Jiang[2(✉)], and Ada Diaconescu[3]

[1] Imperial College London, Exhibition Road, London SW7 2BT, UK
[2] University of Surrey, Guildford GU2 7XH, UK
jie.jiang@surrey.ac.uk
[3] Télécom ParisTech, IMT 46 Rue Barrault Paris, 75013 Paris, France

Abstract. In one aspect of her study of collective action, Ostrom proposed eight design principles for the supply of institutions for sustainable common-pool resource management. Computational logic has been used to formalise an executable specification of six of these principles for resource allocation in open multi-agent systems and networks. However, the eighth principle, *nested enterprises*, is structural rather than procedural, and the seventh principle, *minimal recognition of rights*, concerns a critical relationship between the components of that structure – not just the *right to self-organise*, but essentially *enough* (i.e. minimal) rights to self-organise. In previous work, the idea of holonic institutions has been proposed to satisfy the requirement of polycentric self-governance in complex systems of nested enterprises. This paper investigates the axiomatic specification of Ostrom's seventh principle as a constraint on the holonic structure and sketches a testbed prototype, as a prelude to a more systematic investigation into values, conflict resolution and the trade-off between rights and powers in holonic institutions.

Keywords: Electronic institutions · Holonic architectures · Self-organisation · Rights · Powers · Conflict resolution

1 Introduction

Based on extensive fieldwork, Ostrom showed [12] that it is possible for a community (of *appropriators*) to develop its own solution to a "tragedy of the commons" situation, i.e. a collective action situation featuring open access to a communal resource, in which appropriators are incentivised to act (rationally) to maximise their short-term utility, even if that results in (irrationally) the depletion of the resource in the long term. These solutions, which successfully sustained the resource over extended periods of time, were based on sets on conventional rules, with which the appropriators voluntarily agreed to comply and so constrain their own otherwise unrestricted actions. There was also a mutual agreement not to repudiate these rules: as conventional rather than physical rules they could be broken. Therefore the appropriators could not refuse to accept that the rules

S. Cranefield et al. (Eds.): COIN 2016 Workshops, LNAI 10315, pp. 149–169, 2017.
DOI: 10.1007/978-3-319-66595-5_9

should be monitored for compliance, that they should be enforced, or that proportional graduated sanctions should be imposed for transgression.

Ostrom called these sets of rules *self-governing institutions*, based on the idea that those affected by the rules should participate in their formation, selection and modification, hence self-governance. However, just positing an arbitrary set of rules was not in itself enough: sometimes there were such rules and the common-pool resource was *not* sustained. She observed that the self-governing institutions that successfully sustained the resource had eight features in common, otherwise one or more of the features were weak or missing altogether.

She then went one step further, which was to turn to the issue of *supply*. She argued that, faced with a collective action situation, it was not necessary to trust in "evolution" (in the sense that the appropriators would form, select and modify an institution which exhibited the necessary characteristics). Instead, since it is now known what the necessary characteristics are, it should be possible to *design* institutions with those characteristics from the beginning. To address this issue, Ostrom proposed eight *institutional design principles* for the supply of institutions for sustainable common-pool resource management [12].

Computational logic, specifically the Event Calculus [8], has been used to formalise an executable specification of the first six of these principles, related to boundary conditions, congruence, self-determination, monitoring, sanctions and conflict resolution (see Sect. 2.1). Simulations of resource allocation in open multi-agent systems showed that as more of these principles were axiomatised, the more likely it was that the agents could self-organise an "institution" that maintained participation and sustained the system [19]. Additionally, it was shown that by axiomatising a theory of distributive justice [20] in the context of an economy of scarcity, over time a fair allocation (as measured by the Gini index) could be achieved, despite the allocation at any one timepoint being unfair (given that at each timepoint, since some agents received zero allocation, there was no metric that would return a indicator that the allocation was fair) [13].

The six principles used in these experiments could all be given a procedural interpretation and hence an executable (declarative) specification. Furthermore, all of these simulations used either a single institution, or when there were multiple institutions, they were all independent and their internal operations did not interfere with each other. However, the eighth principle, *nested enterprises*, is structural rather than procedural, and is specifically concerned with the interaction and inter-dependence between multiple institutions and their relational arrangements. The seventh principle, *minimal recognition of rights*, concerns a critical relationship between the components of that structure – not just the *right to self-organise*, but essentially *enough* (i.e. minimal) rights to self-organise.

These last two principles are critical for issues of *scale*. This was a particular concern for Ostrom in her later work: e.g. whether or not global scale collective action problems (like climate change) demanded top-down solutions [11]. For Ostrom, the answer was at best ambiguous, but one factor was clear: that as systems scaled up and became more complicated, it was the weakness of the seventh principle and the lack of *polycentric* self-governance (multiple centres of decision-making) that was the root cause of systemic failure. By contrast, polycentric self-governance enabled meaningful and sustainable behaviours were observed to emerge from a seemingly chaotic complex system [10].

The idea of *holonic institutions* [3,18] has been proposed to satisfy the requirement of polycentric self-governance in complex systems of nested enterprises. This enables an investigation of the axiomatic specification of Ostrom's seventh principle, as a constraint on the holonic structure, pursued in this paper.

Accordingly, the paper is structured as follows. Section 2 reviews the background to this work, covering Ostrom's institutional design principles, their axiomatic specification in a dialect of the Event Calculus, and the relation to dynamic norm-governed multi-agent systems [1]. Section 3 reviews the idea of holonic institutions, which converges the benefits of institutions and conventional rules for regulating behaviour with the management of complexity, scale, diversity, stability and robustness afforded by holonics. Section 4 contains the critical contribution of the paper, with an attempt to characterise the "minimal recognition of rights" (to self-organise) in terms of an "empowerment" component and an "entitlement" component (cf. voting in [14]), and axiomatise these two components in terms of the Event Calculus. The outcome is that while the eighth principle is structural, its characterisation in terms of holonic institutions does enable an analysis and formalisation of the seventh principle within the same framework. Section 5 sketches a testbed prototype to investigate the seventh and eighth principles by means of simulations. Further and related work is considered in Sect. 6, and some concluding remarks are made in Sect. 7, specifically as the trade-off between rights and powers impacts the *values* manifested in, or by, holonic institutions.

2 Background

This section reviews some of the background to this work. We begin with a summary of Ostrom's institutional design principles in Sect. 2.1, continue with the axiomatisation of the principles in the Event Calculus in self-organisng electronic institutions in Sect. 2.2, and consider these as a special sub-class of dynamic norm-governed multi-agent systems in Sect. 2.3. This lays the foundations for the formal analysis of the "nested enterprise" and "minimal recognition of rights" design principles in respectively Sects. 3 and 4.

2.1 Ostrom's Institutional Design Principles

Ostrom's institutional design principles are, of course fully specified in [12] and have been well-documented in previous works (e.g. [19]). They are reproduced here for completeness (to make this paper self-contained) and for a point of clarification (see below). Therefore the design principles for a self-governing institution to *sustain* a common-pool resource, as originally specified in [12, p. 90], are listed in Table 1. Subsequent extensive fieldwork has corroborated these principles with only minor modifications [2], and that institutions for sustainable common-pool resource management do exhibit these eight features. Correspondingly, research has also revealed numerous examples where absence of one or more of the principles led to depletion of the resource.

Table 1. Ostrom's institutional design principles

P1	Clearly defined boundaries	P2	Congruence between rules and local conditions
P3	Collective-choice arrangements	P4	Monitoring
P5	Graduated sanctions	P6	Conflict-resolution mechanisms
P7	Minimal recognition of rights to organise	P8	Nested enterprises

Design principle P1 is concerned with ensuring clear distinctions between who is and is not a member of the institution, and which common-pool resources are, or are not, managed by the institution. The second principle P2 is about ensuring that appropriation rules are congruent with local environmental conditions (e.g. ration in times of shortage and free-hand in times of excess, and not the other way round) and to provision rules which themselves may incur costs (time, labour, money, etc.). The third principle P3 concerns self-determination, and ensuring that "most" appropriators who are affected by the rules participate in the decision-making processes controlling the selection and modification of the rules. Principle P4 requires that monitors, who audit appropriator behaviour, are themselves appropriators or are appointed by and accountable to them. Principle P5 states that non-compliant appropriators should be sanctioned according to a principle of proportionality (although see [17]), and Principle P6 specifies that conflict resolution mechanisms should be "rapid" and "low-cost".

As indicated above, Principle P8 is concerned with structure, specifically that all the activities covered by the first six principles, i.e. provision, appropriation, self-determination, monitoring, enforcement, conflict resolution and governance, are organised in multiple layers of nested enterprises. Principle P7 concerns a particular constraint on the relationships between layers.

Particularly interesting successes and failures in complex systems, where the eighth principle is required, have often been highlighted by the corresponding presence or absence of principle P7. One notable success story is the rice plantations in Bali, where crop planting is a careful trade-off between water scarcity and pest dispersion dynamics, and was carefully managed by a process of prayer and signalling which connected base-level farmers to entire regions through the a meso-level of water temples [9]. A notable failure documented by Ostrom [12, p. 175–177] is the example of fisheries in Canada, where a federal insistence of a "one size fits all" policy over-rode local arrangements that could take specific contextual, seasonal, historical and other environmental factors into account. This led to collapse of the local fishing stocks and industries.

In general, we are concerned with axiomatisation of all the principles for self-organising multi-agent systems, although it is the formalisation of Principle P7, in the context of a representation of structure in Principle P8 in terms of *holonic* institutions (see Sect. 3), that is the primary subject of investigation. For this, though, we first outline our overall approach to the axiomatisation.

2.2   Axiomatisation of the Principles

To address the problem of resource allocation in open multi-agent systems, where there is no centralised controller, institutional design principles P1-P6 were formally specified in computational logic, specifically using a dialect of the Event Calculus (EC) [8], which could then be operationalised as a logic program. As such, the logic program constitutes both a specification and executable code for algorithmic self-governance [19].

The EC is a logic formalism for representing and reasoning about actions or events and their effects. The EC is based on a many-sorted first-order predicate calculus. For the dialect used here (referred to as "the" Event Calculus), the underlying model of time is linear, so we use non-negative integer time-points (although this is not an EC restriction). We do not assume that time is discrete (the numbers need not correspond to a uniform duration) but we do impose a relative/partial ordering for events: for non-negative integers, $<$ is sufficient.

An *action description* in EC includes axioms that define: the action occurrences, with the use of happensAt predicates; the effects of actions, with the use of initiates and terminates predicates; and the values of the fluents, with the use of initially and holdsAt predicates. Table 2 summarises the main EC predicates. Variables, that start with an upper-case letter, are assumed to be universally quantified unless otherwise indicated. Predicates, function symbols and constants start with a lower-case letter.

Table 2. Main predicates of the Event Calculus (EC).

Predicate	Meaning
Act happensAt T	Action Act occurs at time T
initially $F = V$	The value of fluent F is V at time 0
$F = V$ holdsAt T	The value of fluent F is V at time T
Act initiates $F = V$ at T	The occurrence of action Act at time T initiates a period of time for which the value of fluent F is V
Act terminates $F = V$ at T	The occurrence of action Act at time T terminates a period of time for which the value of fluent F is V

Where F is a *fluent*, which is a property that is allowed to have different values at different points in time, the term $F = V$ denotes that fluent F has value V. Boolean fluents are a special case in which the possible values are *true* and *false*. Informally, $F = V$ holds at a particular time-point if $F = V$ has been *initiated* by an action at some earlier time-point, and not *terminated* by another action in the meantime. In our case, we are particularly interested in those fluents which specify the (institutionalised) powers (**pow**), permissions (**per**) and obligations (**obl**) of an agent, i.e. we want to know when **pow**$(Agent, Action) = true$, **per**$(Agent, Action) = true$, and **obl**$(Agent, Action) = true$.

Events initiate and terminate a period of time during which a fluent holds a value continuously. Events occur at specific times (when they *happen*). A set of events, each with a given time, is called a *narrative*.

The utility of the Event Calculus comes from being able to reason with narratives. Therefore the final part of an EC specification is the domain-independent "engine" which computes what fluents hold, i.e. have the value *true* in the case of boolean fluents, or what value a fluent takes, for each multi-valued fluent. This can be used to compute a "state" of the specification in terms of the fluents representing institutional facts. This state changes over time as events happen, and includes the roles, powers, permissions and obligations of agents, and the values assigned to each of the fluents (in particular, which method is used for access control, which method is used for winner determination, and so on).

For example, considering design principle P1, suppose an agent G is assigned to the role of *gatekeeper*, and so is empowered to admit an agent A as a *member* to the institution I, by an *assign* action, depending on the access control method.

$$assign(G, A, member, I) \quad \text{initiates} \quad role\_of(A, member, I) = true \quad \text{at} \quad T \quad \leftarrow$$
$$\mathbf{pow}(G, assign(G, A, member, I)) = true \quad \text{holdsAt} \quad T$$

$$\mathbf{pow}(G, assign(G, A, member, I)) = true \quad \text{holdsAt} \quad T \quad \leftarrow$$
$$applied(A, I) = true \quad \text{holdsAt} \quad T \quad \wedge$$
$$acMethod(I) = attribute \quad \text{holdsAt} \quad T \quad \wedge$$
$$role\_of(G, gatekeeper, I) = true \quad \text{holds} \quad T \quad \wedge$$
$$role\_conditions(member, A, I) = true \quad \text{holdsAt} \quad T$$

$$\mathbf{pow}(G, assign(G, A, member, I)) = true \quad \text{holdsAt} \quad T \quad \leftarrow$$
$$applied(A, I) = true \quad \text{holdsAt} \quad T \quad \wedge$$
$$acMethod(I) = discretionary \quad \text{holdsAt} \quad T \quad \wedge$$
$$role\_of(G, gatekeeper, I) = true \quad \text{holdsAt} \quad T$$

If the agent A has applied to join the institution (i.e. the gatekeeper cannot arbitrarily assign membership) and *acMethod* is *attribute*, then the agent G occupying the role of gatekeeper is empowered to assign the role *member* provided the applicant satisfies certain (external) role conditions. The conditions could include, for example, not exceeding a fixed number of non-compliant actions, a duration since the last non-compliant action, and so on. Similarly, if the *acMethod* is *discretionary*, then the *gatekeeper* is empowered to assign the role without conditions, according to its (internal) decision-making, which could yet make reference to external conditions.

Given a sequence of events, i.e. a narrative, it is then possible to animate (query) the specification to determine what powers, permissions and obligation hold at the start of the narrative, at the end, and at each time point in-between.

2.3   Dynamic Norm-Governed Multi-agent Systems

In our experience with formalising the principles, the first six are, or can be given, an operational, functional or procedural reading which is amenable to declarative specification in this form. However the eighth principle is structural and the seventh principle is concerned with specific relationships between layers in that structure.

For principle P7, the sub-text states that "the rights of appropriators to devise their own institutions are not challenged by external governmental authorities" [12, p. 90]. In some earlier works, which were dealing with only a single institution, the significance of this principle was underestimated (and when paraphrased in terms of autonomy, "whatever rules the members agree to govern their affairs, no external authority can overrule them", even somewhat inaccurately). The key issue is that the *right* to self-organisation should not be challenged by external authorities, but specific outcomes of the self-organisation can be.

For example, suppose an "inner" institution specified its system of graduated sanctions as "First offence: fine €5. Second offence: fine €10. Third offence: execution". An external authority, one with *power* over the inner institution, could well challenge and deny this on the grounds that executing people is not something considered acceptable; in fact, it is illegal and subject to sanction. The external authority should not be able to challenge or deny the *right* of the inner institution to self-organise its system of graduated sanctions, although it can deny specific configurations. This is the nuance that we need to capture in the formalisation of the seventh principle, for which the framework of dynamic norm-governed (multi-agent) systems [1] is required.

This framework allows agents to modify the rules or protocols of a norm-governed system at runtime. The framework defines three components: a specification of a norm-governed system, a protocol stack for defining how to change the specification, and a topological space for expressing the "distance" between one specification instance and another.

Firstly, the norm-governed specification expresses five aspects of social constraint: the physical capabilities; the institutionalised powers; the permissions, prohibitions and obligations of the agents; the sanctions and enforcement policies that deal with the performance of prohibited actions and non-compliance with obligations; and the designated roles of empowered agents.

Secondly, the protocol *stack* is used by the agents to modify the rules or protocols of a norm-governed system at runtime. This stack defines a set of object level protocols, and assumes that during the execution of an object protocol the participants could start a meta-protocol to (try to) modify the object-level protocol. The meta-protocol could initiate a meta-meta protocol to modify the meta-protocol, and so on. Finally "transition" protocols define the conditions in which an agent may initiate a meta-protocol, who occupies which role in the meta-protocol, and what elements (the *degrees of freedom*: DoF) of an object protocol can be modified as a result of the meta-protocol execution. Given a set of DoF, by assigning a value to each DoF, we get a *specification instance*.

Thirdly, a set of rules R implicitly defines a specification space $\mathcal{L}$, where each instance of the specification space is characterised by a different assignment of values to each parameter in each rule. The size of this space is given by

$$| \mathcal{L} | = (V_{1,1} \times V_{1,2} \times \ldots \times V_{1,P_1}) \times (V_{2,1} \times V_{2,2} \times \ldots \times V_{2,P_2}) \times \ldots \times$$
$$(V_{R,1} \times V_{R,2} \times \ldots \times V_{R,P_R})$$

where $V_{i,j}$ is the number of values that the jth parameter of rule i can take, P_i is the number of parameters of rule i, and R is the number of rules in the set.

This is the basis for defining a *specification space* as a 2-tuple, where one component is the set of all possible specification instances and the other component is a function d which defines a "distance" between any pair of elements in the set. It then possible to define rules which prohibit certain instances, or which limit the "distance" that movement between specification instances is "allowed", as illustrated in Fig. 1.

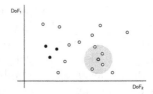

Fig. 1. An illustrative specification space with two DoF

In this figure, there are two DoF. Unfilled circles represent "allowable" specification instances, and filled circles are prohibited instances. The circle with the bold perimeter in the middle of the shaded area is the current specification instance, the rule specifying the "distance" that can be moved when changing instances limits the changes to the four instances included within the gray area. (Note that this distance is also a DoF, and therefore also changeable.)

3   Holonic Institutions

3.1   Holonic Systems

A *holonic system* (or *holarchy*) is composed of interrelated subsystems, each of which are in turn composed of sub-subsystems and so on, recursively, until reaching a lowest level of "elementary" subsystems. As emphasised by Koestler [7], each such intermediary sub-system must play a dual role and be both an autonomous whole controlling its parts; and a dependent part of a supra-system. This helps construct large systems with macro-goals from intermediary components able to achieve partial goals.

3.2   Holonic Institutions

Figure 2-a depicts a generic conceptual model (abstract architecture) of holonic institutions to help address the questions above. In short, each holonic institution features two complimentary regulatory components implementing their dual roles, for "inward" and "outward" regulation. *Inward regulation* includes the internal rules, governance and adaptation functions for achieving a goal. *Outward regulation* merges, via conflict resolution and negotiation, the institution's own common goal with the (supra-)institutions' common goals. This results in the compromise goal that the institution agrees to pursue. Each holonic institution is encapsulated within a *membrane* providing *membership-control* functions. At a high level of abstraction, this approach addresess the issue of the *composition* of institutions (Fig. 2-b). Institution adaptation relies on feedback from members and from the institution's evaluation of its goal achievement; it is propagated progressively from lower to upper holonic levels. Furthermore, this component-oriented design helps formalise, understand and analyse composite institutions, providing a key basis for addressing the challenge of institutional complexity.

A somewhat superficial use of holonic systems would be just to capture the hierarchical decomposition implicit in the simple expression of Ostrom's eighth principle as nested enterprises, concerning just the provision and appropriation systems. However, Ostrom's nested enterprises considers all forms of provision, appropriation, monitoring, enforcement, conflict resolution and other governance activities as different enterprises operating in multiple layers. Therefore, invoking the full "power" of holonic systems offers the possibility of considering the distinct enterprises as social (i.e. interacting) constructs in their own right, even if it is atomic level actors who are performing these actions, "as if" the enterprise did it for itself (cf. the notion of "counts as" in the Jones and Sergot account of institutionalised power [6]). This also enables the characterisation of the holon's dual role, both inward ("selfish", or dealing with an "inner realm"), and outward ("transcendental", or dealing with an "outer realm"), and lines of demarcation between the two, for example in terms of boundaries, jurisdictions and sovereignty (i.e. the authority to self-govern).

Therefore the characterisation of Ostrom's principle P8 in terms of holonic institutions is concerned with much more than hierarchical decomposition. It is more significantly concerned with capturing the requirements of polycentric governance [3, 18] and the management of multi-scale, multi-criteria optimization (or sub-optimization). Note that "sub" is used here in the sense that there will be conflicting goals, not all of which can be satisfied, and the checks, balances, compromises and effective conflict resolution mechanisms that enable meaningful and sustainable behaviours to emerge from complex systems need to be carefully considered. Principle P7 is a crucial element of this.

The above considerations provide a generic architectural overview on the manner in which *holonic institutions* can be constructed and maintained to address the aforementioned questions and achieve the advantages enabled by holonic principles. However, it also provides a handle on how to formalise the

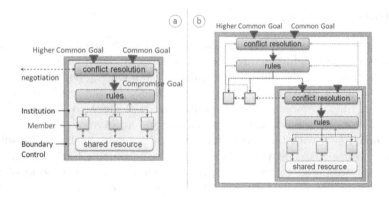

Fig. 2. (a) Institution *holon* with dual role: inward/selfish & outward/transcendental; (b) Supra-institution with several institutions/members

minimal recognition of rights, by characterising the requirements of the rulesets of the "inner" and "outer" (supra) institutions in Fig. 2-b.

4   The Minimal Right to Self-organise

In this section, we try to be precise about what the "minimal recognition of rights" entails for the structural relationship between an institutional holon and its supra-institutional holon(s); and similarly with its sub-institutional holons. We start by giving a characterisation of the right (to self-organise), before considering how this could be recognised as conditions on the rulesets of the inner and outer holonic institutions. Finally, we give some thought to the issue of "minimality".

4.1   Right = Empowerment + Entitlement

In previous work on voting [14], the notion of *enfranchisement* (the right to vote) was characterised by two components, an *empowerment* component and an *entitlement* component. The empowerment component required having the institutionalised power to establish conventional facts (i.e. a vote for or against), that no one could object to "appropriate" exercise of the power, and that removing the power would result in sanction. The entitlement aspect required unhindered access to the voting "machinery", an obligation that the vote would be counted correctly, and an obligation for the result to be declared correctly.

Analogously, the right to self-organise – or the recognition by the supra-level institution of the right of any of its sub-institutions to self-organise – can be characterised by an *empowerment* component and an *entitlement* component. For the empowerment component we have that:

- an institution should be empowered (have the power) to self-organise, i.e. its own institutionalised power should give control over, and responsibility for, representation, participation, and rule-selection etc. to its member entities;

- there should be no entity in the supra-level institution that is empowered to object to "appropriate" exercise of these institutionalised powers; and
- inappropriate exercise of such a power in the supra-level institution should be subject to sanction.

For the entitlement component we have that:

- the sub-institution should be represented in the deliberative assemblies of the supra-level institution;
- the supra-level institution should provide an appeals procedure for conflicts that cannot be resolved by the dispute resolution processes specified by the sub-institution; and
- the sub-institution should be entitled to access and operate the "machinery" of self-organisation.

We next develop a logical axiomatisation of each aspect of the two components.

4.2   The Empowerment Component

For an institutional holon to be empowered to self-organise, it simply requires operational-, collective- and constitutional-choice rules that implement the first six of Ostrom's principles. That is, there should be some protocol and associated institutionalised power(s) that determine: boundaries over representation and participation; selection and modification of collective choice arrangements; appointment and performance of monitors and monitoring; and the system of sanctions and appeals. These are, of course, precisely the rules specified in [19].

Preventing objection to "appropriate" exercise of these powers requires the following. First, we define a specification space $\mathcal{L}$ as described in Sect. 2.3. Then, let $\mathcal{R}$ be a set of rules. For each rule $R \in \mathcal{R}$ identify the set of *changeable components*, or degrees of freedom (DoF), and for each DoF, identify the set of values it can take. (For example, for the collective choice rule deciding which operational choice rule to decide a resource allocation, the DoF is the resource allocation method; and its values are ration, queue, priority, etc.) Then the specification space $\mathcal{L}$ is every permutation of values that can be assigned to each DoF in each rule, and a *specification instance* is one such assignment of values.

Given a set of entities (holons) $\mathcal{H}$, the state of an institution at time $(I_t \in \mathcal{H})$ is defined by:

$$I_t = \langle \mathcal{M}, L, \epsilon \rangle_t$$

where:

- $\mathcal{M}$ is the set of member holons, such that $\mathcal{M} \subseteq \mathcal{H}$
- L is a specification instance of $\mathcal{L}$
- ϵ is the local environment consisting of brute facts and institutional facts.

However, some of the instances might be prohibited by the supra-institution $I' \in \mathcal{H}$. Therefore, to represent the fact that no supra-institution can object to an "appropriate" exercise of the power to self-organise, in the rules of I' something of the following form is required:

$$\mathbf{pow}(H, object(H, L, I, I')) = true \quad \text{holdsAt} \quad T \quad \leftarrow$$
$$\quad role(H, I') = monitor \quad \text{holdsAt} \quad T$$
$$object(H, L, I, I')) \quad \text{initiates} \quad objected(L, I) = true \quad \text{at} \quad T \quad \leftarrow$$
$$\quad \mathbf{pow}(H, object(H, L, I, I')) = true \quad \text{holdsAt} \quad T \wedge$$
$$\quad specification\_instance(I) = L \quad \text{holdsAt} \quad T \quad \wedge$$
$$\quad prohibited(L) = true \quad \text{holdsAt} \quad T$$
$$object(H, L, I, I') \quad \text{initiates} \quad sanction(H, I') = 404 \quad \text{at} \quad T \quad \leftarrow$$
$$\quad role(H, I') = monitor \quad \text{holdsAt} \quad T \quad \wedge$$
$$\quad specification\_instance(I) = L \quad \text{holdsAt} \quad T \quad \wedge$$
$$\quad prohibited(L) = false \quad \text{holdsAt} \quad T$$

This axiom states that a holon H in supra-institution I' has the power to object to a specification instance used by member-institution I only if it occupies the necessary role in I' (*monitor*, say). However, exercising such power will only be effective when the specification instance L selected by I is prohibited in I'. Otherwise, a sanction will be initiated. This means that the right of I to self-organise into whatever specification instance it chooses is not challenged by any external authority, like I', although specific applications of that right can be challenged. Note here that "404" is an *error code* used in I' to denote particular misuses of institutionalised power, in this case objecting to a specification instance that is not prohibited. The consequence of this sanction may be a penalty: for example, it may be fined, removed from the role of *monitor*, or both.

Finally, let us suppose, firstly, that we take the approach of Robert's Rules of Order to self-organisation, i.e. that anything is allowed unless someone objects; and secondly, that there is a holon in I' that, by occupying the role of *head* is empowered to veto specification instances selected by I. However, while this holon may be empowered to veto specification instances, it may not be *permitted* to exercise that power, unless a holon that is empowered to object (by the above axiom) has done so. Using the veto without permission initiates a sanction.

$$\mathbf{pow}(H, veto(H, L, I, I')) = true \quad \text{holdsAt} \quad T \quad \leftarrow$$
$$\quad role(H, I') = head \quad \text{holdsAt} \quad T$$
$$\mathbf{per}(H, veto(H, L, I, I')) = true \quad \text{holdsAt} \quad T \quad \leftarrow$$
$$\quad role(H, I') = head \quad \text{holdsAt} \quad T \quad \wedge$$
$$\quad objected(L, I) = true \quad \text{holdsAt} \quad T$$
$$veto(H, L, I, I') \quad \text{initiates} \quad sanction(H, I') = 405 \quad \text{at} \quad T \quad \leftarrow$$
$$\quad role(H, I') = head \quad \text{holdsAt} \quad T \quad \wedge$$
$$\quad \mathbf{per}(H, veto(H, L, I, I')) = false \quad \text{holdsAt} \quad T$$

Similarly, "405" is an *error code* used in I' to denote the misuses of institutionalised power of vetoing a specification instance without permission.

The monitor and the head roles could be performed by the same agent. In this case, challenging a member-institution's usage of a particular specification instance could just be done with a veto, which is however not permitted unless the specification instance is prohibited by the supra-institution. But while separating out the power to monitor and the power to veto adds complexity it also adds flexibility, because it means that prohibited instances can still be tolerated if no-one objects.

4.3   The Entitlement Component

It may be supposed from the previous section that the empowerment component is a constraint on an institution's freedom to manoeuvre, because some arrangements of the rules (i.e. certain specification instances) are prohibited, and can be vetoed. In return for this loss, the right confers some entitlements, which are satisfied by certain obligations in the supra-level institution.

The first of these is that there is an entitlement to representation and participation in the deliberative assemblies of I'. This can be formalised using the same form of constitutional choice rules in I' that were present in I, based on axiomatising Ostrom's principles P1–P6. The extent to which this entitlement is satisfied can be evaluated using a framework for procedural justice [16].

Similarly, a process should be defined in I' which deals with the resolution of conflicts in I which cannot be handled by I itself (for example, the Court of Arbitration for Sport resolves legal disputes which the governing authorities of the sports themselves cannot resolve themselves, or considers appeals against the decisions of this authorities). Complex dispute resolution procedures can be defined in the Event Calculus [15].

Finally, the entitlement to access the "machinery" of self-organisation is an abstract concept that we will not develop further here. Suffice to say it (probably) involves a number of basic "freedoms", such as the freedom of assembly and freedom of speech; and material rather than illusional choice (as discussed above, and also avoiding any inevitability about self-organisation).

4.4   Minimal Recognition

Finally, we consider the implications of the *minimal* recognition of the right to self-organise. However, several case studies where the principle is not met have been studied in some detail [12, ch. 5], and although "minimal" could be taken to imply such kind of quantifiable threshhold or an identifiable set of baseline conditions, it is difficult to identify a precise specification.

Therefore, if we were to try to define this for ourselves, one way might be to use the specification space and the distance function defined between "allowable" specification instances. This suggests three possible minimality conditions.

Firstly, we could compute the outer institution tolerance as the ratio of allowable specification instances to the total number of specification instances. A higher number indicates that the outer institution is more tolerant of inner institution self-organisation than a lower number.

A second metric could be the inner institution total freedom to manoeuvre, as measured by the total distance that the specification instances are allowed to change. If there were n specification instances $l_1, \ldots, l_n$, this is computed by:

$$\Sigma_{i=1}^{n} \Sigma_{j=1}^{n} d(l_i, l_j)$$

Thirdly, a metric could be defined accruing to the average number of specification instances that can be accessed from any one specification instance. Suppose that τ is the upper limit on the distance that can be moved. Then the number of specification instances that can be reached from any given specification instance l_i is:

$$\mathbf{card}(\{l_j | d(l_i, l_j) < \tau\})$$

If we computed the average number of specification instances that could be reached from an arbitrary specification instance, then this would be an indicator of the extent of self-organisation available from any instance.

However, with all of these metrics, what constitutes a *minimal* tolerance is not clear, and would most likely be application specific. Even then, while a quantitative evaluation might be indicative, it seems that minimal is most likely to be a relative, qualitative, assessment. We return to this issue in Sect. 7.

5   Testbed Prototype

In this section, we present the design for a simulation testbed that is being developed to experiment with the axiomatisation of principles P7 and P8 specified in the previous section. We propose to build on the axiomatisation previously developed [19], to examine the effect on sustainability of a common-pool resource using self-organising electronic institutions with Ostrom's design principles activated, or not. The intention is to examine the balance between the right (of an inner holon) to self-organise and the power (of an outer holon) to constrain that self-organisation. Our experimental hypothesis is that when there is no right to self-organise the inner holon is unsustainable (as documented by Ostrom [12]), but when there is no power to constrain the inner holon becomes undemocratic or unmanageable (respectively, because of vested interests usurping power, or because sanction are reputable and cannot be enforced). However, we stress that this is work in progress, and simply a starting point for examining what is a complex and nuanced issue.

5.1   Classes

Figure 3 shows the relationship between the classes of the testbed prototype, in which the actions and fluents identified in the previous section are all properties or methods of a class. Note here that the class diagram is a continuation of the one presented in [19] and tries to specify the actions and relations that are essential for P7 and P8.

Similarly, there are mainly four types of roles that can be assigned to an agent in an institution holon, i.e., *member*, *gatekeeper*, *monitor* and *head*. The role *member* is indicated by the *member_of* relation between institution holons, i.e., an institution holon may contain a number of member-institutions. When an agent is assigned the role of member in an institution holon, it is granted the permission to appropriate resources from the common pool of that institution holon. Agents enacting the role *gatekeeper* are in charge of assigning memberships to eligible agents who apply to join the institution holon and excluding agents who exceed the violation allowance specified by the institution holon. Agents enacting the role *monitor* are responsible of monitoring the behaviour of the members in the institution holon and report misbehaviour when detected. Agents enacting the role *head* are in charge of allocating resources to requesting members and sanctioning corresponding agents when violations are reported.

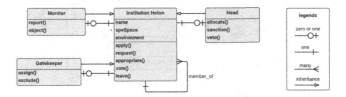

Fig. 3. Testbed class diagram

The difference here is the relationship between the members and their inhabited institutions: in the holonic setting, an institution (referred to as suprainstitution) contains a number of members each of which may itself be an institution (referred to as member-institution) that contains members in a recursive manner. It has to be noticed that the specification spaces of institutions at different levels have different governance scopes. A supra-institution's specification space contains rules that regulate the behaviour of its members, with some of these rules even regulating what kinds of rules the members may use to regulate their inner members. That is, some of the rules adopting by the member-institutions might be prohibited by the supra-institution, which is reflected by the *object* action of the monitor class and the *veto* action of the head class. For example, a supra-institution may require that all its member-institutions use the same access control method to recruit members and the same exclusion method to exclude members.

5.2 States

Figure 4 shows the state transition diagram of agents in holonic institutions. When an agent is a member of an institution, it has two possible states: active member or inactive member. To be an active member, an agent has to apply for a membership and then the gatekeeper will either reject the application or assign the agent the member role according to the access control method specified by the institution. When an active member appropriates more resources than it is allowed to, there are two possible results. One is that the violation is detected by the monitor and reported to the head of the institution, in which case the agent becomes inactive member. The other is that the violation is not detected and thus not reported to the head, in which case the agent remains being an active member in the institution.

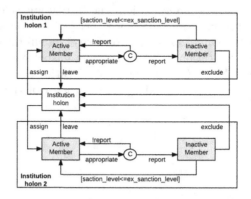

Fig. 4. Agent state diagram

From the state of being an inactive member, an agent may either be (1) released back to be an active member if its violation does not exceed the allowance specified by the institution, or (2) excluded by the head from the institution in which case the agent loses its membership in that institution. In the latter case, the agent becomes an independent entity by itself who can again apply to join another institution or remain being independent. The active member in an institution may also choose to leave the institution voluntarily and becomes an independent entity. For example, an active member may choose to leave an institution when it is not satisfied with the regulations imposed by the institution.

5.3   Algorithm

In this section, we focus on **P7** (minimal recognition of rights to self-organise) and **P8** (nested enterprises) and try to sketch the sequence of the testbed's possible actions and events, as shown in Algorithm 1. It has to be noticed that the algorithm is simply a starting point for building simulations to investigate the two principles.

$Principle1$ & $Principle8 \leftarrow true$;
$H^+ \leftarrow \{I | I \in \mathcal{H}, \exists I' \in \mathcal{H}, member\_of(I', I)\}$;
$H^- \leftarrow \{I | I \in \mathcal{H}, \exists I' \in \mathcal{H}, member\_of(I, I')\}$;
$\forall I \in H^+ : \exists c \in \mathcal{H}, member\_of(c, I)$. initially $role\_of(c, I) = head$;
$\forall I \in H^+ : \exists g \in \mathcal{H}, member\_of(g, I)$. initially $role\_of(g, I) = gatekeeper$;
$\forall I \in H^+ : \exists b \in \mathcal{H}, member\_of(b, I)$. initially $role\_of(b, I) = monitor$;
$\forall I \in H^-$. initially $\exists \bar{\mathcal{L}}_I \subset \mathcal{L}_I, \forall l_I \in \bar{\mathcal{L}}_I : prohibited(l_I)$;
$t \leftarrow 0$;
while $(t < t_{max})$ **do**
   foreach $I \in H^+$ **do**
      $\hat{H} \leftarrow \{I' | I' \in \mathcal{H}, member\_of(I', I)\}$;
      foreach $I' \in \hat{H}$ **do**
         if *Principle3* **then**
            /* sub-members vote for changing the specification
              instance   */
            $cfv(c', specification\_instance, I')$;
            $\forall I'' \in \mathcal{H}$:
            $member\_of(I'', I').vote(I'', X, specification\_instance, I')$;
            $declare(c', W, specification\_instance, I')$;
         else
            $declare(EXT, W, specification\_instance, I')$;
      end
      if *Principle7* **then**
         /* monitor of the supra-institution objects to
            specification instances   */
         $\forall I' \in O, O \subset \hat{H} : object(b, \_, I', I)$;
         /* head of the supra-institution vetos specification
            instances   */
         $\forall I' \in V, V \subset \hat{H} : veto(c, \_, I', I)$;
      else
         foreach $I' \in \hat{H}$ **do**
            $declare(c, \tilde{W}, specification\_instance, I')$;
         end
      end
   end
   $t \leftarrow t + 1$;
end

Algorithm 1. Algorithm for the holonic CPR testbed

Initially we set **P1** (clearly defined boundaries) and **P8** to be true and assign for each institution holon a head, a gatekeeper and a monitor, with time t being set to 0. The algorithm then cycles over t until a maximum amount of time steps t_{max} is reached.

In each time step, for each member-institution of an supra-institution, if **P3** (collective-choice arrangements) is active, the head calls for a vote (cfv) on changing the specification instance, and the change may concern various rules such as access control, resource allocation, and etc. All the agents in the member-institution may vote for the change and the head declares the winner specification instance W. Without P3, similarly as that in [19], the specification instance for the current cycle is declared by an external partner EXT who re-evaluates it periodically. It is possible that the newly selected specification instance is prohibited by the supra-institution, and thus may be *objected* by the monitor of the supra-institution. Moreover, the head of the supra-institution may *veto* the newly selected specification instance. In both cases, the right of the member-institution to self-organise into a particular specification instance is challenged by the supra-institution. If **P7** is active, only when the newly selected specification instance is prohibited by the supra-institution shall the monitor of the supra-institution object to the new specification instance; only when the new specification instance has been objected is the head of the supra-institution permitted to veto the new specification instance, otherwise the monitor and the head will be sanctioned. Without P7, the supra-institution, like a dictator, fully controls which specification instance the member-institutions should use.

6   Related and Further Work

The formal characterisation of rights has, of course, been the subject of study in legal, social and organisational theory, ethics and moral philosophy for some considerable time. However, we are not aware of any similar attempt to characterise the *right to self-organise* in computational logic, nor to situate it in the context of structured interacting entities like holonic institutions.

There are though related studies that can be of significant relevance. For example, one such is the concept of *duty*. Right and duty have been characterised as "correlatives" [21], in the sense that when one agent has a right against another, then that other owes a duty to the first. An enrichment of the analysis of "right = empowerment + entitlement" could entail an associated duty component which could become useful in characterising the minimality conditions.

One direction of further research is, of course, to complete the formal specification in the Event Calculus, define some metrics for minimal recognition, and build simulations using the testbed comparable to those previous experiments [13,19]. The experimental hypothesis is that those systems with layered institutions would sustain themselves (and their resources) for longer if the rulesets of inner and outer institutions contain provisions of the kind specified here.

A second direction of work is, in the context, to deepen the analysis of the sources of, the resolution of, conflicts between inner and outer institutions and between two or more inner institutions. A preliminary investigation of this issue can be found in [5], but it seems that there is a need to distinguish different types of conflict (within a holon, between peer holons, and between inner/outer holons) as different conflict resolution mechanisms may well be required.

However, while this research would confirm the principle as a necessary condition of sustainable common-pool resource management, it would be a somewhat blunt instrument. What would be really interesting to know is where the *balance* is in the trade-off between the rights of the inner institution to self-organise on the one hand, and the power of the outer institution to constrain that self-organisation. This is an investigation that is also being actively pursued, as we believe this will shed some light on this concept of *minimal* recognition, which remains far from clear at the moment. Note that this will probably also be an adaptive, context-sensitive balance. That said, we intend to use the testbed specified in Sect. 5 to implement simulations and quantitatively investigate such trade-off in different scenarios. One example would be the regulations of a supra-institution on how its member-institutions may recruit and exclude members, which relates to the first design principle of clearly defined boundaries.

7   Summary and Conclusions

There is an ongoing research programme into the formalisation of Ostrom's institutional design principles in computational logic, and specifically the Event Calculus. The aim of this research is to design self-organising electronic institutions to address the problem of sustainable resource allocation in open multi-agent systems. This has a potentially wide range of applications, for example in ad hoc, vehicular and sensor networks; in cloud and grid computing; in virtual organisations; and in infrastructure management using socio-technical systems.

This paper has particularly focused on the formalisation of the seventh principle, the minimal recognition of rights. Although this is clearly still work in progress, the primary contributions of this paper are:

- to characterise the *right to self-organise* in terms of empowerment and entitlement components, and to begin a formal specification in terms of the Event Calculus;
- to identify the *recognition* of that right (to self-organise) as conditions on the rulesets of "inner" and "outer" holonic institutions; and
- to consider the *minimal* recognition of that right, as conditions or metrics defined on a specification space.

However, perhaps the concept of "minimality" presents the greatest challenge, as it may be resistant to mere quantification with respect to the specification space. Our intuition though, is that the minimality is actually a function of *qualitative values* held by the members themselves: that it is not the total number of available specification instances, or the freedom to manoeuvre as specified by the total movable distance; or indeed any other objective metric. Instead, it is the value that the members themselves put on having certain specification instances available to them, and the freedom to self-organise between these specific instances, that is the critical element of minimality. But this is, of course, rather harder to identify, let alone measure; although a promising line of inquiry is offered by the study of *interactional justice*, whereby subjective individual opinions of fairness (or value) are aggregated into objective collective opinions.

Furthermore, it may not even be certain specification instances that are directly of value, but that these are the specification instances that indirectly create other social, moral or fungible values, with which the institution's members, either individually or collectively, are really concerned. In such circumstances, the link between the value and the minimal set of specification instances that support that value may not even be recognised by the agents themselves. This may have severe implications in trying to build socio-technical systems for self-organising digital communities, say, and indicates that aspects of value-sensitive design [4] and other initiatives that emphasise values derived from a study of social practices are critical in the future development of open multi-agent systems.

Acknowledgements. The authors would particularly like to thank Pompeu Casanovas for conversations which have significantly helped to clarify numerous issues in rights and powers, but any persistent misunderstandings are our own. We are also very grateful for the many helpful comments of the anonymous reviewers.

The first author has been partially supported by the UK EPSRC Grand Challenge project No. EP/I031650/1 *The Autonomic Power System*.

References

1. Artikis, A.: Dynamic specification of open agent systems. J. Logic Comput. **22**(6), 1301–1334 (2012)
2. Cox, M., Arnold, G., Villamayor Tomás, S.: A review of design principles for community-based natural resource management. Ecol. Soc. **15**(4), 38 (2010)
3. Diaconescu, A., Pitt, J.: Holonic institutions for multi-scale polycentric self-governance. In: Ghose, A., Oren, N., Telang, P., Thangarajah, J. (eds.) COIN 2014. LNCS (LNAI), vol. 9372, pp. 19–35. Springer, Cham (2015). doi:10.1007/978-3-319-25420-3_2
4. Friedman, B., Kahn, P., Borning, A.: Value sensitive design and information systems. In: Himma, K., Tavani, H. (eds.) The Handbook of Information and Computer Ethics, pp. 69–101. Wiley (2008)
5. Jiang, J., Pitt, J., Diaconescu, A.: Rule conflicts in holonic institutions. In: IEEE SASO Workshops (FoCAS), pp. 49–54 (2015)
6. Jones, A., Sergot, M.: A formal characterisation of institutionalised power. J. IGPL **4**(3), 427–443 (1996)
7. Koestler, A.: The Ghost in the Machine. Hutchinson Publisher, London (1967)
8. Kowalski, R., Sergot, M.: A logic-based calculus of events. New Gener. Comput. **4**, 67–95 (1986)
9. Lansing, J., Kremer, J.: Emergent properties of Balinese water temple network: coadaptation on a rugged fitness landscape. Am. Anthropol. **95**, 97–114 (1993)
10. Ostrom, E.: Beyond markets and states: polycentric governance of complex economic systems. In: Grandin, K. (ed.) Les Prix Nobel. The Nobel Prizes 2009, pp. 408–444. Nobel Foundation, Stockholm (2010)
11. Ostrom, E.: Thinking about climate change as a commons. In: 15th Annual Philip Gamble Memorial Lecture, pp. 1–34. UMass Amherst (2011)
12. Ostrom, E.: Governing the Commons: The Evolution of institutions for Collective Action. Cambridge University Press, Cambridge (1990)
13. Pitt, J., Busquets, D., Macbeth, S.: Distributive justice for self-organised common-pool resource management. ACM Trans. Auton. Adapt. Syst. **9**(3), 14:1–14:39 (2014)

14. Pitt, J., Kamara, L., Sergot, M., Artikis, A.: Voting in multi-agent systems. Comput. J. **49**(2), 156–170 (2006)
15. Pitt, J., Ramirez-Cano, D., Kamara, L., Neville, B.: Alternative dispute resolution in virtual organizations. In: Artikis, A., O'Hare, G.M.P., Stathis, K., Vouros, G. (eds.) ESAW 2007. LNCS (LNAI), vol. 4995, pp. 72–89. Springer, Heidelberg (2008). doi:10.1007/978-3-540-87654-0_3
16. Pitt, J., Busquets, D., Riveret, R.: Procedural justice and 'fitness for purpose' of self-organising electronic institutions. In: Boella, G., Elkind, E., Savarimuthu, B.T.R., Dignum, F., Purvis, M.K. (eds.) PRIMA 2013. LNCS, vol. 8291, pp. 260–275. Springer, Heidelberg (2013). doi:10.1007/978-3-642-44927-7_18
17. Pitt, J., Busquets, D., Riveret, R.: The pursuit of computational justice in open systems. AI Soc. **30**(3), 359–378 (2015)
18. Pitt, J., Diaconescu, A.: Structure and governance of communities for the digital society. In: Workshop on Self-Improving System Integration at IEEE International Conference on Autonomic Computing (ICAC), pp. 279–284 (2015)
19. Pitt, J., Schaumeier, J., Artikis, A.: Axiomatisation of socio-economic principles for self-organising institutions: concepts, experiments and challenges. ACM Trans. Auton. Adapt. Syst. **7**(4), 39:1–39:39 (2012)
20. Jasso, G., Törnblom, K.Y., Sabbagh, C.: Distributive justice. In: Sabbagh, C., Schmitt, M. (eds.) Handbook of Social Justice Theory and Research. LNCS (LNAI), pp. 201–218. Springer, New York (2016). doi:10.1007/978-1-4939-3216-0_11
21. Sergot, M.: A computational theory of normative positions. ACM Trans. Comput. Logic **2**(4), 581–622 (2001)

Author Index